Frommer's

Florence & Tuscany
day BY day®
5th Edition

by Donald Strachan &
Stephen Brewer

FrommerMedia LLC

Contents

Published by:

Frommer Media LLC

Copyright © 2017 by Frommer Media LLC. All rights reserved. No part
of this publication may be reproduced, stored in a retrieval system, or
transmitted in any form or by any means, electronic, mechanical, photo-
copying, recording, scanning or otherwise, except as permitted under
Sections 107 or 108 of the 1976 United States Copyright Act, without
the prior written permission of the Publisher. Requests to the Publisher
for permission should be addressed to support@frommermedia.com.

Frommer's is a registered trademark of Arthur Frommer. Frommer
Media LLC is not associated with any product or vendor mentioned in
this book.

ISBN 978-1-628-87374-0 (paper), 978-1-628-87375-7 (e-book)

Editorial Director: Pauline Frommer
Editor: Alexis Lipsitz Flippin
Production Editor: Heather Wilcox
Photo Editor: Meghan Lamb
Cartographer: Roberta Stockwell

Front cover photos, left to right: Florence © Sergey Novikov; Vineyards
in Tuscany © cate_89; Siena © leoks
Back cover photo: San Gimignano © Emi Cristea

For information on our other products or services, see www.frommers.com.

Frommer Media LLC also publishes its books in a variety of electronic
formats. Some content that appears in print may not be available in
electronic formats.

Manufactured in China

5 4 3 2 1

About This Guide

Organizing your time. That's what this guide is all about.

Other guides give you long lists of things to see and do and then expect you to fit the pieces together. The Day by Day guides are different. These guides tell you the best of everything, and then they show you how to see it in the smartest, most time-efficient way. Our authors have designed detailed itineraries organized by time, neighborhood, or special interest. And each tour comes with a bulleted map that takes you from stop to stop.

Hoping to relive the glory days of the Florentine Renaissance, or to tour the highlights of Siena? Planning a drive through Chianti country, or a tour of Tuscany's most charming small towns? Whatever your interest or schedule, the Day by Days give you the smartest routes to follow. Not only do we take you to the top attractions, hotels, and restaurants, but we also help you access those special moments that locals get to experience—those "finds" that turn tourists into travelers.

The Day by Days are also your top choice if you're looking for one complete guide for all your travel needs. The best hotels and restaurants for every budget, the greatest shopping values, the wildest nightlife—it's all here.

Why should you trust our judgment? Because our authors personally visit each place they write about. They're an independent lot who say what they think and would never include places they wouldn't recommend to their best friends. They're also open to suggestions from readers. If you'd like to contact them, please send your comments our way at feedback@frommers.com, and we'll pass them on.

Enjoy your Day by Day guide—the most helpful travel companion you can buy. And have the trip of a lifetime.

About the Author

Donald Strachan is a travel writer and journalist who has written about Italy and Europe for publications worldwide, including *National Geographic Traveller, The Guardian, Telegraph,* and *CNN.com.* He lives in London, England.

Stephen Brewer has been writing travel guides for three decades. As an editor and writer, he has focused on European coverage for such magazines as *Esquire, Connoisseur* and *Geo,* and he was a producer of a popular radio travel show for many years. He has written several previous guides for Frommer's, Insight, and other companies, as well as authoring *Beautiful Small Coastal Towns* for Rizzoli. Stephen divides his time between Manhattan and Italy.

An Additional Note

Please be advised that travel information is subject to change at any time—and this is especially true of prices. We therefore suggest that you write or call ahead for confirmation when making your travel plans. The authors, editors, and publisher cannot be held responsible for the experiences of readers while traveling. Your safety is important to us, however, so we encourage you to stay alert and be aware of your surroundings.

Star Ratings, Icons & Abbreviations

Every hotel, restaurant, and attraction listing in this guide has been ranked for quality, value, service, amenities, and special features using a **star-rating system.** Hotels, restaurants, attractions, shopping, and nightlife are rated on a scale of zero stars (recommended) to three stars (exceptional). In addition to the star-rating system, we also use a **kids icon** to point out the best bets for families. Within each tour, we recommend cafes, bars, or restaurants where you can take a break. Each of these stops appears in a shaded box marked with a coffee-cup-shaped bullet .

The following **abbreviations** are used for credit cards:

AE	American Express	DISC	Discover	V	Visa
DC	Diners Club	MC	MasterCard		

Frommers.com

Now that you have this guidebook to help you plan a great trip, visit our website at **www.frommers.com** for additional travel information on more than 4,000 destinations. We update features regularly to give you instant access to the most current trip-planning information available. At Frommers.com, you'll find scoops on the best airfares, lodging rates, and car rental bargains. You can even book your travel online through our reliable travel booking partners. Other popular features include:

- Online updates of our most popular guidebooks

- Vacation sweepstakes and contest giveaways

- Newsletters highlighting the hottest travel trends

- Online travel message boards with featured travel discussions

A Note on Prices

In the "Take a Break" (☕) and "Best Bets" sections of this book, we have used a system of dollar signs to show a range of costs for 1 night in a hotel (the price of a double-occupancy room) or the cost of an entree at a restaurant. Use the following table to decipher the dollar signs:

Cost	Hotels	Restaurants
$	under $100	under $10
$$	$100–$200	$10–$20
$$$	$200–$300	$20–$30
$$$$	$300–$400	$30–$40
$$$$$	over $400	over $40

How to Contact Us

In researching this book, we discovered many wonderful places—hotels, restaurants, shops, and more. We're sure you'll find others. Please tell us about them, so we can share the information with your fellow travelers in upcoming editions. If you were disappointed with a recommendation, we'd love to know that, too. Please write to: Contact@FrommerMedia.com.

18 Favorite
Moments

18 Favorite Moments

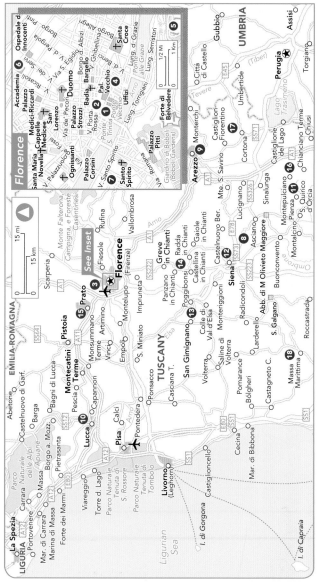

Previous page: The Ponte Vecchio in Florence.

The treasures of the Uffizi and Michelangelo's David are just one part of an unforgettable journey into Tuscany: There is so much more to the region than just the magnificence of Florence. Beyond the city that cradled the Renaissance lie snow-capped peaks, dramatic cypress-studded ridges, the turquoise Tyrrhenian Sea, and hills crowned with silver-green olive groves. With Chianti's vineyards, Pisa's errant Tower, San Gimignano's medieval "skyscrapers," and a wealth of Florentine and Sienese art and architecture, it's difficult to single out 18 highlights. But this list is our attempt to do just that.

1 Eating the world's best gelato. At Florence's **Carapina,** San Gimignano's **"di Piazza,"** or Siena's **Kopakabana,** the ice cream is most definitely not just for kids. You name the flavor, and you'll probably find it somewhere. Vespa-riding ravers and contessas alike come for their daily fix. *See p 19, 163, and 91.*

2 Drinking in the full 360 degrees of Piazza della Signoria. Find a comfortable perch on Florence's grandest square—the site of Savonarola's infamous "Bonfire of the Vanities"—and take in Benvenuto Cellini's *Perseus* with the head of Medusa, a replica of Michelangelo's *David*, the Uffizi, and the

A cone filled with the divine gelato available in Tuscany.

Piazza della Signoria.

Palazzo Vecchio. It's the best free show in town. *See p 13.*

3 Walking the road of the ancients from Fiesole to Florence. Start at Etruscan Fiesole's Piazza Mino and follow the road through San Domenico to Florence, below. Untamed vegetation pours over high walls that line the way past gnarled olive groves, regimented gardens, and 18th-century villas—and a panoramic vista of the city that opens suddenly. *See p 23.*

4 Catching a glimpse of where Tuscan art was born. In Room 2 of the Uffizi, the great *Madonnas* of

Statue of David by Michelangelo in the Galleria dell'Academia.

Cimabue, Duccio, and Giotto are displayed almost side by side. Between them, these three painters shaped Florentine and Sienese art for generations. *See p 24.*

⑤ Basking in the lights of the Renaissance, at twilight, from San Miniato al Monte. The climb up here is a stiff one, but the view of the city twinkling from the steps in front of this ancient church will rank among the greatest you've seen. *See p 34.*

View of Siena.

⑥ Standing in awe at the foot of Michelangelo's *David*. The massive genius of Michelangelo's masterpiece in marble, at the Accademia, may bowl you over—even from behind its Plexiglas shield. After 5 centuries, he is still miraculously alive, embodying the ideals of the Tuscan High Renaissance. *See p 14.*

⑦ Hitting San Frediano after dark. We love the buzz of this fashionable, left-bank neighborhood, which stretches west along the River Arno from the Ponte Santa Trinita to and through the Porta Pisana. Once a working-class artisans' borough, it is now where young Florentines head for the liveliest bars and most creative restaurants in the city. *See p 133.*

⑧ Seeing Siena for the first time—from the hills of Le Crete. The S438 from Asciano to Siena traverses Tuscany's most photogenic landscape. And that first, unmistakable sight of the 102m (335-ft.) Torre del Mangia piercing the horizon in the distance is one you won't forget. *See p 169.*

⑨ Following the Piero della Francesca trail. His iconic work is Tuscany's best fresco cycle, the *Legend of the True Cross* in Arezzo's San Francesco. The Piero trail continues to Monterchi for a rarity in Italian art, a pregnant *Madonna*. His

18 Favorite Moments

Biking in the ancient walled city of Lucca.

hometown of Sanselpolcro still exhibits a work that Aldous Huxley claimed was the greatest ever painted, Piero's 1463 *Resurrection of Christ. See p 125 and 89.*

⑩ Biking the walls of Lucca. Kids and octogenarians alike pedal Tuscany's greatest cycle track, 5km (2¾ miles) in length, on 16th-century ramparts so thick they now function as a tree-lined promenade and public park. The chestnut and ilex trees came compliments of Marie-Louise of Bourbon, planted in the 1800s. *See p 133.*

⑪ Dining alfresco in autumn. What could be finer than a *bistecca alla fiorentina* dripping with olive oil and fresh herbs, grilled over a chestnut-wood fire? One served outdoors, of course, in Tuscany in autumn. When the leaves turn red and gold, regional delicacies—black truffles, roast guinea hen, foraged porcini mushrooms—taste their best. Try La Porta in Montic-chiello, close to Pienza and Montepulciano. *See p 149.*

⑫ Attending the Palio, Italy's grandest medieval spectacle. This breakneck, bareback horse race around Siena's dirt-packed Piazza del Campo takes place twice a year, in July and August, in honor of the Virgin Mary. Alongside the race, it's bacchanalia—with days of parades, pageantry, and parties. *See p 169.*

⑬ Wandering San Gimignano's historic center at dusk. A unique skyline pierced by 14 towers (sometimes nicknamed "skyscrapers") is what makes this place the #1 spot on the hilltown trail. When the tour buses have left, the quiet streets exude a haunted, medieval air quite unlike anywhere else in Tuscany. *See p 160.*

⑭ Tasting the wine in Chianti Country. The vine-studded hills between Florence and Siena

Dining alfresco in Piazza della Signoria in Florence.

Wandering the streets of San Gimignano.

nurture one of Italy's most famous exports. Against a backdrop of ancient villages and crenellated castles from the Middle Ages, you can sample the vino from cantinas around Castellina, Greve, and Radda. *See p 91.*

⑮ Rounding out lunch with *cantuccini* and *vin santo*. Pour a glass of the sweet wine, take one of the hard almond cookies, and dip. Our favorite places just leave the bottle, the biscuits, and plenty of time. For

Renaissance town of Montepulciano.

the originals, correctly known as *biscotti di Prato,* visit Mattei, the best biscuit-maker in its home city. *See p 93.*

⑯ Discovering your favorite Tuscan hilltown. Our vote goes to Montepulciano, not just for its noble red wine first cultivated here by the Etruscans, nor for its *palazzi* by High Renaissance masters like Sangallo. We just love the pace of the place, the welcoming nature of its inhabitants, and the fact that we know we'll find Tuscany's best steak right in the center. *See p 142.*

⑰ Enjoying the views. Most towns in Tuscany have a memorable panorama, and the higher those town walls, the better. Outlooks from Cortona might just get best in show: They extend across the checkerboard fields of the Valdichiana to Lago Trasimeno and Umbria beyond. *See p 128.*

⑱ Squeezing into La Tana del Brillo Parlante for a memorable lunch. This tiny restaurant in sleepy Massa Marittima is the best place to get acquainted with the flavors of the Maremma, the fertile terrain that stretches along Tuscany's coastline. *See p 141.* ●

Strategies for Seeing **Tuscany**

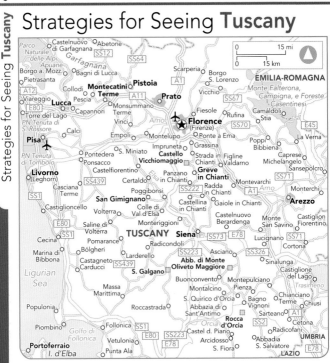

Tuscany isn't Tokyo or New York; racing around trying to "see" everything runs against the grain of the place and might even prevent you from really *experiencing* it. It's tempting to make tracks, given the number of sights in a relatively small region easily traversed by car. But structuring a relaxed itinerary makes for a memorable trip. In the chapters that follow, we show you how to maximize your time in Tuscany. Remember: Just about everywhere in this glorious corner of Italy is improved by taking a little extra time to see it.

Previous page: Horse carriage in Pisa.

Rule #1: Slow down.

Consider the experience of two couples we know who visited the region. One fashioned an aggressive itinerary that encompassed most of the major towns we cover in Chapter 6. And although they could say they saw town after town, church after church, and artwork after artwork, they spent 2 or 3 hours a day in the car, fighting the heat and crazy truck drivers. The other couple decided to take on less turf; naturally, they didn't see as much and even missed Cortona and some of our other favorite towns.

A vineyard in Montalcino.

Instead, they had time to spend an entire afternoon in a Montepulciano cafe, splitting a bottle of Vino Nobile, gazing over a wrought-iron balcony at a church in the distance. In hindsight, they considered that stop the pinnacle of their trip.

Rule #2: Remember, distances between towns are short.

Visiting Tuscany is as easy as traveling around a small U.S. state or mid-size Mediterranean island. You can drive from Florence to San Gimignano, Lucca, Pisa, or Siena in around an hour. The entire Chianti wine country is only 48km (30 miles) from north to south and 32km (20 miles) at its widest point. Once you veer off the autostrada, the roads become slower, but unless you're taking a *strada bianca* (unsurfaced road) to a remote hamlet, they're generally well maintained and signposted (if sometimes erratically). The only problem in the summer will be occasional traffic caused by visitors aiming for the same towns as you.

Rule #3: Consider staying in one place over making a daily hotel hop.

Checking in and out of hotels is often a tedious hassle involving packing and unpacking, registering and checking out, and other technicalities that can drain pleasure from

a trip. Because many Tuscan towns are within easy reach of one another, you can set up camp in the same hotel for 3 nights—in Siena, for example—and venture to smaller towns nearby on day trips. From Siena, you can easily visit San Gimignano, Pienza, Colle di Val d'Elsa, Montepulciano, Montalcino, or the Chianti wine country without wasting too much time in the car. You'll save a lot of wear and tear on your soul with this tack, reserving your energy for hotel switches required by longer hauls.

Rule #4: Plan your excursions around lunch.

If you're driving from town to town, plan to reach your destination by noon, which gives you time to hit the tourist office before it closes for the *riposo*. Restaurants usually serve lunch until 2 or 2:30pm, and you'll also need time to park (which is sometimes tricky) and to locate the address of your restaurant (ditto). If you don't want to be beholden to such a schedule, pack a picnic before setting out.

Rule #5: Every now and then, let the train take the strain.

It's cheaper, greener, and hassle-free arriving in your Tuscan town for the day by train. The Italian network is inexpensive, accessible, and easy

Pick Your Point of Entry

The logical start to your Tuscan adventure is Galileo Galilei airport in Pisa. Flights on regular and budget airlines connect it with most of Europe's major hubs—and there's sometimes a direct summer flight from New York a few days a week. If you're already touring near Milan, Venice, or Rome, there's no need to think about connecting to Tuscany by air. All are well linked by rail or autostrada. Rome and Milan are alternative, hassle-free intercontinental air gateways, both just over 1½ hr. from Florence by high-speed train. From Rome, a 277km (172-mile) drive north to Florence on the fast-moving A1 takes you past some of the highlights of southern and eastern Tuscany: Break up your trip in Montepulciano, Cortona, or Arezzo. Milan is slightly farther—298km (183 miles) northwest of Florence—but worth the extra distance if you find a cheaper flight there; a drive to Florence can pleasantly be broken in Pisa or Lucca. For more about reaching Tuscany by plane and traveling between airports and your final destination, see the "By Plane" section in "Getting There & Getting Around," on p 187.

to use. Not every town is handily reached by rail, but the highlights of the region's northwest, such as Lucca, Pisa, Pistoia, and Prato, are all perfect for seeing by train.

Rule #6: The tourist office is the best (and often the friendliest) free resource in any town—so use it.
This guidebook arms you with just about everything you need to plan an amazing trip to Tuscany. But there's no substitute for the 100% local savvy you'll find in most Tuscan destinations, particularly for information on what's happening around town on the day you show up. See p 190 for contact details of Tuscany's tourist offices.

Rule #7: Don't follow these ideas to the letter; use them as building blocks for your trip.
This is a *guidebook*, not a rulebook, designed to help you piece together your own getaway. Plan

your time in Florence using one section and then hop about Tuscany in the next few days using another. It's like an à la carte menu—select one item from column A and another from column B, and then mix according to your own tastes and interests to make the most of our advice. ●

Peppers in a market in Tuscany.

Florence in One Day

1 Uffizi
2 Piazza della Signoria
3 I Due Fratellini
4 Battistero San Giovanni
5 Cattedrale di Santa Maria del Fiore (Duomo)
6 Museo dell'Opera del Duomo
7 Galleria dell'Accademia
8 Piazzale Michelangiolo
9 San Miniato al Monte
10 Il Rifrullo
11 Ponte Vecchio

i Tourist Information

Previous page: Arcades beside the Piazza Repubblica.

Florence in a day? "Impossibile," a Florentine might tell you before throwing up her hands in despair and striding away, convinced you are mad. But 1 day in Florence is better than none—provided you rise with the roosters and move with discipline and stamina to make the most of it. This "greatest-hits" itinerary begins with the highlights of the Uffizi, the most rewarding and time-consuming stop. After lunch in the Centro Storico, you'll take in the city's majestic ecclesiastical complex, including the Duomo and Baptistery. Round out the day with a trek to Michelangelo's *David* at the Accademia, followed by an *aperitivo* on the city's lively Left Bank and a stroll across the Ponte Vecchio as night falls. START: **Bus C1 to the Uffizi.**

1 ★★★ Uffizi. This is one of the world's great museums, and the single-best repository of Renaissance art. In room after room, you'll view masterpiece after masterpiece—including Leonardo da Vinci's *Annunciation* (with an angel who could be Mona Lisa's brother), Michelangelo's *Holy Family*, Botticelli's *Birth of Venus*, Giotto's *Ognissanti Madonna,* and more. In old Florentine, *uffizi* means "offices," and that's what Vasari deigned this building to be in 1550. But it's come a long way, *bambino.* These Uffizi will dazzle you. (Serious art devotees may want to spend an entire day here.) ⏱ *3 hr. See p 24.*

2 ★★ Piazza della Signoria. The monumental heart of Florence (and Tuscany's most famous square) is an open-air museum of sculpture, dominated by Michelangelo's *David* (a copy of the original that used to stand here). The powerful mass of the Palazzo Vecchio lords over one side of the square; another is defined by the 14th-century **Loggia dei Lanzi,** filled with ancient and Renaissance statues (the most striking being Benvenuto Cellini's bronze *Perseus* holding aloft the severed head of Medusa). Also check out Giambologna's *Rape of the Sabines,* which marks the point (1584) when Tuscan tastes abandoned drama in favor of melodrama. ⏱ *30 min.*

3 ★ I Due Fratellini. This old-fashioned hole-in-the-wall fiaschetteria sells central Florence's favorite lunch on the move. Choose a tasty sandwich from the long list, wash it down with a "shot" of Chianti, and continue on the sightseeing trail. *Via dei Cimatori 38R.* ☎ *055-2396096. www.iduefratellini.it. $. Bus: C2.*

4 ★★★ Battistero San Giovanni. On a hurried first-day tour of Florence, you need to invade the inner precincts of the Baptistery only to take in the magnificent 13th-century mosaics lining

Uffizi Gallery.

The Best of Florence

Piazza della Signoria.

the inner dome. The major excitement is outside, on the world-famous bronze doors that face the Duomo. Sure, they're replicas (the originals are in the Museo dell'Opera del Duomo; see **6**, below), but even the copies are masterpieces. Ghiberti's north doors—a commission he won in 1401 in a public competition against Brunelleschi, Donatello, and Jacopo Della Quercia—are said to mark the start of the Renaissance. 🕐 *30 min. See p 30,* **9**.

5 ★★ **Cattedrale di Santa Maria del Fiore (Duomo).**

Cattedrale di Santa Maria del Fiore.

Consecrated in 1436, one of Europe's most majestic cathedrals rests under Filippo Brunelleschi's revolutionary dome, a triumph of engineering over gravity. As the symbol of Florence itself, it's a tourist stamping ground of horrendous proportions—but justifiably so. It's part church, part candy cane, part zebra—in stripes of marble-white, bottle-green, and pink. The interior, by contrast, is spartan but has one of Europe's classic views from the top of the cupola. 🕐 *45 min. See p 30,* **7**.

6 ★★ **Museo dell'Opera del Duomo.** For connoisseurs of Renaissance sculpture, this museum opposite the rear of the Duomo is a shrine, hosting everything from an unfinished, heart-wrenching *Pietà* by Michelangelo to its premier attraction: the restored panels of Lorenzo Ghiberti's *Gates of Paradise*. The works here were deemed too precious to be left to the elements and so were moved inside from their positions adorning the ecclesiastical monuments. 🕐 *1 hr. See p 42,* **7**.

7 ★★ **Galleria dell'Accademia.** You've seen replicas of Michelangelo's *David* all over the world. This gallery has the real thing (1501–04)—a monumental icon of youthful

The view of Florence from Piazzale Michelangiolo.

male beauty and a stellar example of Michelangelo's humanism. His four unfinished *Slaves* are equally expressive. Admission can require an hour-long wait, unless you reserve tickets. ⏱ *30 min., without wait. Via Ricasoll 58–60.* ☎ *050-294883 to reserve tickets (in English). www.firenzemusei.it. Admission 6.50€–12.50€ (higher price is during regular special exhibitions). Tues–Sun 8:15am–6:50pm. Bus: C1, 14, 23.*

Ride bus 23 from Piazza San Marco across the Arno to alight at the Porta San Niccolò, and then walk directly uphill.

❽ ★ Piazzale Michelangiolo.

For a fine view over Florence, head for its panoramic piazza, laid out in 1885. From the balustraded terrace, the city of the Renaissance unfurls before you. In the center of the square is yet another replica *David*. ⏱ *15 min. Bus: 12, 13.*

❾ ★★★ San Miniato al Monte.

As the shadows lengthen, there's no better spot to drink in the views, and the silence, than this ancient Romanesque church surrounded by its monumental graveyard. Time it right, and you'll catch the Benedictine monks who still inhabit the complex celebrating Vespers with Gregorian chants. ⏱ *30 min. See p 34,* ❶.

🔟 ★ Il Rifrullo. This laid-back bar is right at the social center of a buzzy Oltrarno corner just downhill from Piazzale Michelangelo. Join locals and visitors for an aperitivo. *Via San Niccolò 55R.* ☎ *055-2342621. www.ilrifrullo.com. $–$$. Bus: 12, 13.*

⓫ ★ Ponte Vecchio.

The Ponte Vecchio, as its name suggests, is the city's oldest bridge; its latest incarnation dates to 1345, but the shops along it have been taking advantage of the foot traffic since at least the 12th century. Originally occupied by blacksmiths, butchers, and tanners, the shops that flank the bridge have mostly sold gold and silver since the reign of the Medici dukes. Sunset is the ideal time to cross. ⏱ *15 min. Bus: C3, D.*

Church of San Miniato in Florence.

Florence in Two Days

Palacongressi

Palaffari

Stazione Centrale S. Maria Novella

Piazza Adua

Via Guelfa

Via Faenza

Via Nazionale

Via Panicale

Via Fiume

Piazza del Mercato Centrale

6 La Divina Enoteca

San Marco

Piazza San Marco

Galleria dell'Accademia

Via S. Reparata

Via S. Gallo

Via San Gallo

Via Cavour

Via de' Ginori

Via Guelfa

Via Ricasoli

Via dei Servi

Piazza Brunelleschi

Piazza della Stazione

Via Luigi Alamanni

Via S. Antonino

Piazza dell'Unità Italiana

Cappelle Medicee

Piazza S. Lorenzo

7 San Lorenzo

Palazzo Medici-Riccardi

Via de' Martelli

Palazzo Pucci

Via dei Pucci

Ospedale S. Maria Nuova

(i) S. Maria Novella

Piazza S. Maria Novella

Via della Scala

Via de' Panzani

Via de' Cerretani

Piazza S. Giovanni

Campanile

Duomo

Piazza S. M. Nuova

H

Via de' Pecori

(i) Piazza del Duomo

Via dell'Oriuolo

Via de' Fossi

Via de' Pecori

Piazza Goldoni

Via del Moro

Via della Vigna Nuova

Via de' Tornabuoni

Via d. Campidoglio

CENTRO

Via Roma

Via dei Calzaiuoli

Via S. Elisabetta

V. S. Studio

DUOMO

Via del Corso

Borgo degli Albizi

Via de' Pandolfini

Casa di Dante

Via D. Alighieri

Via de' Cimatori

Badia

Palazzo Corsini

Via d. Parione

Via del Moro

Santa Trinita

Piazza Strozzi

Palazzo Strozzi

Piazza della Repubblica

Orsanmichele

Via Porta Rossa

V. Calimala

Bargello

V. d. Vigna Vecchia

Ponte alla Carraia

Lung. Corsini

Piazza Trinita

Palazzo Davanzati

Piazza della Signoria

SIGNORIA

Borgo de' Greci

Via de' Benci

Lungarno Guicciardini

Borgo Ss. Apostoli

Lungarno Acciaiuoli

4 Ponte Santa Trinita

Palazzo Vecchio

10 Loggia dei Lanzi

Uffizi

Via de' Neri

Via S. Giacomo

Via Vellutini

3

Santo Spirito

Piazza S. Spirito

OLTRARNO

Via Guicciardini

Piazza S. Felicita

Piazza S. Maria Soprarno

Ponte Vecchio

Piazza Mentana

Lung. Gen. Diaz

Arno

Lungarno Torrigiani

Via de' Bardi

Ponte alle Grazie

Lung. Serristori

Borgo Tegolaio

Via Maggio

Piazza dei Pitti

1 Palazzo Pitti

Costa d. S. Giorgio

Forte di Belvedere

2

Giardino di Boboli (Boboli Garden)

0   1/8 mi
0   200 km

1 Palazzo Pitti
2 Giardino di Boboli
3 Santa Felicita
4 Ponte Santa Trinita
5 Santa Trinita
6 La Divina Enoteca
7 Cappelle Medicee
8 Museo di San Marco
9 Palazzo Vecchio
10 Carapina

(i) Tourist Information

On your second day in Florence, spend the morning wandering the Oltrarno, the district on the left bank of the Arno. The set-piece attraction here is the Palazzo Pitti and adjacent Giardino di Boboli. Even if you take all morning, you will see only a part of the Pitti Palace's great collection of art, which encompasses not only Renaissance works but painting and sculpture by later European masters. Stroll through the Boboli Garden before heading back to the Centro Storico for the Medici Chapels (with Michelangelo's sculptures), the artistic delights of Fra' Angelico at San Marco, and Florence's Gothic town hall, the Palazzo Vecchio. START: **Bus D to Piazza de' Pitti.**

❶ ★★ Palazzo Pitti. This vast 15th-century Medici palace on the south side of the Arno is second only to the Uffizi in its wealth of artwork. The **Galleria Palatina** on the second floor is reason enough to come to Florence; visit for the Raphaels alone. And the Palatina also has a decent supporting cast if you have more time on your hands: the city's most extensive coterie of museums, including exhibitions of costumes, modern art, and even the royal family's private digs. ⏱ *2 hr. See p 38,* ❸.

Medici Skywalk.

After Cosimo I moved to the Pitti Palace, he commissioned Giorgio Vasari to build a private, aboveground tunnel to the Uffizi and Palazzo Vecchio. The Corridoio Vasariano, built in just 5 months in 1565, runs from the Pitti Palace past the Boboli and above Santa Felicita to the Ponte Vecchio, crosses the river above the bridge's shops, then continues to the museum that once served as the Medici offices. Lined with self-portraits, it was for years open for prebooked guided visits only, and regularly shut completely for restoration. But a major policy change brings back admission from inside the Uffizi. *Note: Ticketing plans are not clear at time of writing, with reopening scheduled for mid-2018.*

❷ ★ Giardino di Boboli. Laid out between 1549 and 1656, this is the grandest Renaissance garden of Italy. Before departing, take a stroll down the Viottolone, a stunning avenue of pines and cypresses, to the Isolotto, a complex of water and statuary laid out in 1612. ⏱ *45 min. See p 37,* ❷.

❸ ★★ Santa Felicita. The star works in this tiny Oltrarno church are in the first chapel on your right, paintings by Mannerist master Pontormo (1525–27). A *Deposition* and frescoed *Annunciation* are rife with his garish color palette of oranges, pinks, golds, lime greens, and sky blues and exhibit his trademark

The Galleria Palatina at Palazzo Pitti.

Grotto Buontalenti in the Boboli Garden.

surreal sense of figure. ⏱ *15 min. Piazza Santa Felicita.* ☎ *055-213018. Free admission. Daily 9:30am–1:30pm & 3:30–5:30pm. Bus: C3, D.*

❹ ★★ Ponte Santa Trìnita. Cross the Arno by way of Florence's most elegant bridge (but certainly not its most famous one). Built in 1567 by Ammannati, it was destroyed by retreating Germans in 1944 and rebuilt using 16th-century tools and methods in 1957. It is guarded at both ends by statues representing the seasons. ⏱ *10 min. Bus: C3, D.*

❺ ★★ Santa Trìnita. There aren't many corners of Florence

The domes of the Cappelle Medicee.

where you can admire the finest works of the Quattrocento (1400s) in peace, but the historic church of Santa Trìnita is one of them. The frescoed chapels are by Lorenzo Monaco (1370–1425) and Domenico Ghirlandaio (1449–94), Michelangelo's first teacher. The marble tomb of Benozzo Federighi was sculpted in 1454 by Luca Della Robbia. ⏱ *20 min. See p 47,* ❾.

Browse your way north along Florence's upscale shopping street, Via de' Tornabuoni (p 63), then through San Lorenzo street market to:

❻ La Divina Enoteca. Stop in for a panino tartufato (truffled sandwich) or anything from a long, filling menu that employs only the best ingredients. There's a long list of wine by the glass, too. *Via Panicale 19R. www.ladivinaenoteca.it.* ☎ *055-292723. $.*

❼ ★★ Cappelle Medicee. The key sights here are the celebrated Medici tombs by Michelangelo— two of his grandest creations that, alas, honored scurrilous members of the clan. Nevertheless, the great artist portrayed them as idealized

Museo di San Marco.

princes of the Renaissance. Allegorical figures representing *Night* and *Day* and *Dawn* and *Dusk* face each other across his perfectly proportioned Renaissance sacristy. ① *1 hr. See p 44,* ❷.

❽ ★★★ Museo di San Marco. This Dominican convent has been converted to a unique museum honoring Florence's gentlest painter of the "International Gothic" style, Fra' Angelico (1395–1455). Angelico's art is touched with a pacifying power, especially his iconic *Annunciation,* as are the walls of the 44 friars' cells upstairs, which he frescoed with scenes (and plenty of Dominican saints) to foster meditation. Don't leave without stopping in at the Pilgrim's Hospice, now a mini-museum to Angelico, centered on his beatific, weightless *Deposition.* ① *1 hr. Piazza San Marco 3.* ☎ *055-2388608. Admission 4€ (7€ with temporary exhibition). Mon–Fri 8:30am–1:50pm; Sat–Sun 8:30am–4:50pm; closed 1st, 3rd, & 5th Sun & 2nd & 4th Mon of month. Bus: C1, 1, 6, 7, 11, 14, 17, 20, 23, 25.*

❾ ★ Palazzo Vecchio. The civic heart of Florence, this crenellated 13th-century palace is still the city hall. The highlight inside is the **Salone dei Cinquecento,** or "Hall of the 500," where the great council met. It's decorated with gaudy Vasari frescoes but houses Michelangelo's *Genius of Victory*, a statue originally intended for the tomb of Pope Julius II. ① *1 hr. See p 29,* ❹.

❿ ★★★ Carapina. The strictly seasonal fruit flavors at this backstreet gelateria are sensational. *Via Lambertesca 18R. www.carapina.it.* ☎ *055-291128. $.*

Ponte Santa Trinita.

Florence in Three Days

1 Santa Croce
2 Casa Buonarroti
3 Museo Nazionale del Bargello
4 Mario
5 Campanile di Giotto
6 Orsanmichele
7 Santa Maria Novella
8 Fiesole
9 Cave di Maiano

i Tourist Information

A third day in Florence yields another glimpse of the city's treasures. The Bargello is the world's greatest museum of Renaissance sculpture. Combine it with the city headquarters of the Dominicans and Franciscans—Santa Maria Novella and Santa Croce, respectively—to form the cultural core of your day. (Michelangelo and Galileo, among others, are buried in the latter.) As dusk approaches, head for the hills for a stroll and a romantic dinner in the Etruscan hilltown of Fiesole. START: **Bus C1, C2, or C3 to Piazza Santa Croce.**

❶ ★★ Santa Croce. Victorian critic John Ruskin had the right idea: "Wait then for an entirely light morning: rise with the sun and go to Santa Croce, with a good opera glass in your pocket." Travelers call it "the Westminster Abbey of Tuscany," because this 14th-century church contains the tombs of the Renaissance's brightest lights— notably Michelangelo and Galileo. The great Giotto di Bondone (ca. 1267–1337) frescoed two tiny, time-worn chapels in the right transept but is almost outshone by better-preserved works by his own student, Taddeo Gaddi, who frescoed *Scenes from the Life of the Virgin* between 1332 and 1338, including the first night scene ever painted. ⏱ *1 hr. Piazza Santa Croce. www. santacroceopera.it.* ☎ *055-2466105. Admission 8€. Mon–Sat 9:30am–5pm; Sun 2–5pm. Bus: C1, C3.*

❷ Casa Buonarroti. The house inhabited by Michelangelo's nephew Lionardo is preserved as a shrine to the master. Michelangelo's earliest sculptures are here, including the Donatello-esque *Madonna of the Steps,* carved before 1492 when he was a teenage student in the Medici school. A few months later, the prodigy carved another marble, a confused, almost Pisano-like tangle of bodies known as the *Battle of the Centaurs and Lapiths.* ⏱ *45 min. Via Ghibellina 70. www. casabuonarroti.it.* ☎ *055-241752. Admission 6.50€. Wed–Mon 10am– 5pm (Nov–Feb until 4pm). Bus: C2, C3.*

❸ ★★ Museo Nazionale del Bargello. This Gothic fortress is now a vast repository holding some of the finest sculpture created during the Renaissance and later,

Santa Croce.

Some of the many gelato flavors you'll find in Florence.

including Donatello's *St. George*, originally sculpted for Orsanmichele, and his own bronze *David*. The Bargello also houses, along with countless other works, another Michelangelo *David*—created 3 decades after the version in the Accademia. ⓘ *90 min. See p 30,* ⑥.

🍴 ★ **Mario.** A tiny trattoria that has become a lunchtime institution: Expect uncompromising Florentine food, communal tables, competitive prices, and a smiling crush of local workers, tourists, and market

Niche in Orsanmichele, built in 1337.

traders. *Via Rosina 2R (at Piazza del Mercato Centrale).* ☎ *055-218550. www.trattoriamario.com. $$.*

⑤ ★★ **Campanile di Giotto.** An ideal counterpoint to Brunelleschi's dome, this Gothic bell tower was completed at the end of the 14th century, long after Giotto, its designer, had died. Walk 414 steps to the top of the campanile for a panoramic view of the dome and all of central Florence. Queues here are usually much shorter than those for the Duomo. ⓘ *30 min. See p 31,* ⑧.

⑥ ★★ **Orsanmichele.** Although the upstairs museum is usually closed every day apart from Monday, a circuit around the outside of this grain-warehouse-turned-church reveals a gallery of sculpted saints. Each of the niches was commissioned by one of Florence's great trade guilds, including the powerful Arte della Lana (wool manufacturers). After you've toured the outside, take a quick look inside. ⓘ *15 min. See p 46,* ⑦.

⑦ ★★ **Santa Maria Novella.** The Dominicans began construction on this church in 1246, and it is filled with some of Tuscany's most important frescoes, notably Masaccio's epoch-defining 1427 *Trinity*. The *Scenes from the Lives of the Virgin Mary and St. John the Baptist* (1485–90) in the apse were painted by Michelangelo's teacher, Domenico Ghirlandaio. Twelve years later, Filippino Lippi, the illegitimate son of Filippo and nun Lucrezia Buti, decorated the **Cappella Filippo Strozzi** with scenes from the life of his patron saint, St. Philip. Other treasures include a carved *Crucifix* by Filippo Brunelleschi. ⏱ *45 min.*

⑧ ★ **Fiesole.** As well as its archaeological (mostly Roman) attractions, the ancient hilltop settlement of Fiesole supplies a welcome change of pace, and an escape from the oppressive heat and crowds of Florence. The little town was here long before its neighbor down in the valley: It was already an important Etruscan settlement in the 8th century B.C. The best thing to do is stroll: A route along Via Marini, Via delle Mura Etrusche, then uphill on Via Giovanni and Via del Cimitero skirts the Roman ruins, takes in the splendid little Franciscan convent, and ends up at the most spectacular

Santa Maria Novella.

balcony above Florence. ⏱ *90 min. www.museidifiesole.it. Bus: 7 (20 min. from Santa Maria Novella).*

☕ ★ **Cave di Maiano.** For a final goodbye to the city, take the short ride to this converted farmhouse. Expect hearty regional cuisine, such as chicken roasted under a brick with peppers, and succulent pastas, such as green tortellini. Adventurous diners might like to walk the entire 8km (5 miles) back to Florence, with the city lights twinkling in the distance to lead the way. You can stop at any point along the way and board bus #7 back to the center. *Via delle Cave 16, Maiano.* ☎ *055-59133. $$–$$$.*

The Duomo in Fiesole.

The Best of the Uffizi

Ground Floor

- Foreign Artists
- 15th Century Tuscans
- Ademollo
- Modern Mannerisms
- Verone
- Caravaggesque Rooms
- 17th C Florentines

Piazzale degli Uffizi

90 88
95
96 18 91
97
98   83 17
99 92
100 93

75
74 16
71
68

66 15
65
64 14
61 62 63
60
59
58 57 56

55
52 53 54
49 12 50 51
11 47
46 48

Second Floor

South (Second) Corridor

8
17

9
35

Exit

15 7

6
10-14

9 5 4
7 3 8

5-6 1
2

4 2 3

Entrance 1

Piazzale degli Uffizi

East (First) Corridor

West (Third) Corridor

41

42

43 44
45

Café 10

1. Cimabue, Duccio & Giotto
2. Sienese School
3. International Gothic
4. Masaccio & Uccello
5. Piero della Francesca
6. Botticelli
7. Leonardo & Verrochio
8. La Tribuna
9. Michelangelo & Del Sarto
10. Uffizi café
11. El Greco, Goya & Velazquez
12. Rembrandt
13. Florentine Mannerism
14. Bronzino portraits
15. Raphael
16. Parmigianino
17. Titian
18. Caravaggio & Gentileschi

Once the Medici business offices, the **Galleria degli Uffizi** is now the world's finest museum of Renaissance painting. If you don't have a Firenze Card (p 30), reserving tickets is essential: Without reservations, expect to queue for up to 6 hours during peak periods. **Firenze Musei** takes reservations in advance, in English over the phone and online (www.firenzemusei.it; ☎ **055-294883**), and at the teller window on the façade of Orsanmichele. START: **Bus C1 to Piazza dei Giudici. Trip length: 3 hr. Admission: 13€ plus booking fee 4€. Opening hours: Tues–Sun 8:15am–6:50pm.**

❶ ★★★ **Room 2.** This opening gallery introduces a trio of great Madonnas. Although still with its roots in Byzantine artistic conventions, Cimabue's *Santa Trinita Maestà* (ca. 1280) takes tentative steps toward realism. Duccio di Buoninsegna's *Rucellai Madonna* (1285) influenced a generation of Sienese art. Three decades later, Giotto (1276–1337) painted the most solid *Maestà* (Virgin in majesty) of them all, the *Ognissanti Madonna*.

❷ ★★★ **Room 3.** This room gives a taste of 14th-century Sienese painting—none finer than Simone Martini's ethereal *Annunciation* (1333), showing a horrified Mary learning of her Immaculate Conception. The Lorenzetti brothers, Pietro and Ambrogio, also

The Uffizi's Loggia dei Lanzi.

created masterpieces displayed here, before the Black Death of 1348 claimed their lives; the most sophisticated (and much emulated) work is Ambrogio's *Presentation at the Temple* (1342).

❸ ★★ **Room 7.** The iconic work in the hyperdecorative style known as "International Gothic," Gentile da Fabriano's *Procession of the Magi* (1423), dominates here. The line to see the baby Jesus is full of comic elements and even longer than the one waiting outside the Uffizi.

❹ ★★ **Room 8.** Renaissance innovations in painting were possible in part because of Masaccio (1401–28) and Paolo Uccello (1397–1475) and their revolutionary use of perspective. Look at the characteristically chaotic foreshortening in Uccello's *Battle of San Romano* (1440), depicting a Florentine victory over the Sienese army. A rare piece by Masaccio (he was dead at 27) is *Madonna and Child with St. Anne* (1424). Paintings by Fra' Filippo Lippi (1406–69) are also displayed here. His *Madonna and Child with Two Young Angels* is an overtly romantic portrait of the amorous monk's mistress.

❺ ★★ **Room 9.** Piero della Francesca's *Portrait of Federico da Montefeltro and Battista Sforza* (1472) is as famed for the perspective Tuscan landscape as for the profiles of the duke and duchess of Urbino.

Botticelli's Allegory of Spring.

6 ★★★ **Rooms 10–14.** Sandro Botticelli (1445–1510) authored perhaps the most visited paintings in Florence: his *Birth of Venus* and the enigmatic *Primavera (Allegory of Spring)*. *Primavera*'s varied cast includes (from the left) Mercury, the Three Graces, Venus, and Flora—the goddess of spring who was known as Chloris, before her rape by Zephyr (the West Wind), the scene on the right of the panel.

7 ★★ **Room 15.** Leonardo da Vinci (1452–1519) is the main man here, not least for an unfinished *Adoration of the Magi*. His *Annunciation* (1472) is known for its tricky use of a vanishing point (look at it from the lower-right corner). The *Baptism of Christ* is by his teacher, Andrea del Verrocchio (1435–88).

8 ★★ **Room 18.** The octagonal *La Tribuna* is the Uffizi's most lavish salon, decorated with lapis lazuli for air, red walls for fire, green *pietre dure* for earth, and mother-of-pearl for water. Its focus is the *Medici Venus*, a medieval copy of a Greek original whose pose was copied by Botticelli for his own Venus.

9 ★★ **Room 35.** Michelangelo's only painting in Florence, a tondo (round painting) of the *Holy Family*, was commissioned by the Doni family and so nicknamed the *Doni Tondo* (1506–08). Perfectionist Michelangelo even designed the frame. The family's muscular forms and contorted poses suggest Michelangelo's preference for sculpture. Florentines who followed in the master's wake, including Andrea del Sarto (1486–1530), are also represented here.

10 **The Uffizi café,** a bar with a view atop the loggia, serves drinks and snacks at prices not so out of line with central Florence. *Piazzale degli Uffizi. No phone.* $–$$.

11 ★★ **Room 46.** The *Sale Blu* (Blue Rooms) were inaugurated in 2011 to exhibit the best of the Uffizi's large foreign painting collection, much of it commissioned or bought by the Medici. Restored in 2010, El Greco's *St. John the Evangelist and St. Francis* (ca. 1600) is rich in symbolism, including a chalice (for the

Church) and dragon (the Devil). This small Spanish room also has works by Goya and Velázquez.

⑫ ★ Room 49. Four paintings by Dutch Old Master Rembrandt van Rijn hang side by side here, spanning the period 1639 to 1669, the year of his death.

⑬ ★ Rooms 58–61. Florentine Mannerism reaches fever pitch in rooms dedicated to Andrea del Sarto and Rosso Fiorentino (1485–1541), his pupil. Fiorentino is best appreciated in his *Madonna with Four Saints* (1515) and his workshop's *Moses Defends the Daughters of Jethro* (1523), which owes a heavy debt to Michelangelo. See *Supper at Emmaus* (1525) by Del Sarto's other renowned pupil, Jacopo Pontormo (1494–1557).

⑭ ★ Rooms 64–65. Agnolo Bronzino (1503–72) was a talented baroque portrait painter who became court artist to the Medici dukes. He is most famous for the portrait of Eleonora of Toledo, wife of Cosimo I displayed here. When the Medici tombs were opened in 1857, her body was discovered buried in the same satin dress she wore in the painting. Around 1542, he also painted Cosimo's illegitimate daughter Bia, just before she died, age just 5.

⑮ ★★ Room 66. The epitome of High Renaissance composition is

Raphael's *Madonna del Cardellino (Madonna of the Goldfinch),* in which his usual triangular, hierarchical layout is enlivened by a goldfinch. Raphael portraits here include *Pope Leo X with Cardinals Giulio de' Medici and Luigi de' Rossi* (1518), a shifty-looking bunch of Renaissance power players.

⑯ ★ Room 74. The late Mannerist painter Parmigianino (1503–40) is the star of this gallery. His *Madonna and Child* is more usually known as the *Madonna with the Long Neck,* for obvious reasons (but to be fair, it is unfinished).

⑰ ★★ Room 83. This *sala* is dedicated to Venetian visionary and master colorist, Titian (1488–1566). The highlight is his 1538 *Venus of Urbino*. It's no coincidence that the edge of the curtain, the angle of her hand and leg, and the line splitting floor and bed all intersect in the forbidden part of her body.

⑱ ★ Rooms 90–93. Bad boy of the baroque, Caravaggio (1571–1610) is the star of the refurbished *Sale Gialle* (Yellow Rooms). His screeching circular *Medusa* (1599), mounted on a circular shield, is a typically deranged self-portrait. His fondness for extreme *chiaroscuro* (light and shade) shaped art for a generation. Artemisia Gentileschi's violent *Judith Slaying Holofernes* (1621) shows that she was his most worthy heir.

Leonardo da Vinci's Annunciation.

The Heart of the Centro Storico

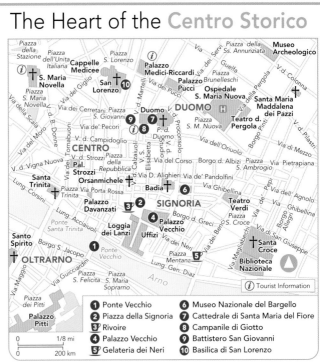

1 Ponte Vecchio
2 Piazza della Signoria
3 Rivoire
4 Palazzo Vecchio
5 Gelateria dei Neri
6 Museo Nazionale del Bargello
7 Cattedrale di Santa Maria del Fiore
8 Campanile di Giotto
9 Battistero San Giovanni
10 Basilica di San Lorenzo

In Florence's flat, compact historic core, you can wander stone streets that remain essentially the same as they were when Michelangelo, Leonardo da Vinci, and Galileo trod them. The few blocks that make up this Centro Storico tell the history of the city itself, and of its art and architecture above all. This is a demanding full-day itinerary, so wear comfortable shoes and bring water. If you're traveling in July or August, be aware that walking the hot, crowded streets can be a draining experience. START: Bus C3 or D to Ponte Vecchio.

1 ★ **Ponte Vecchio.** Built in 1345 across the Arno's narrowest stretch, the Ponte Vecchio was the only bridge spared destruction by the retreating Nazi army in 1944. Florence's greatest goldsmith, Benvenuto Cellini, ran his business in the middle of the bridge—one of many jewelers to have replaced the medieval butchers and tanners who

originally traded here. ⓘ *10 min. Bus: C3, D.*

2 ★★ **Piazza della Signoria.** The center of civic life in Florence for centuries, this landmark square in the shadow of Arnolfo di Cambio's massive Palazzo Vecchio was the site of Savonarola's "Bonfire of the Vanities" in 1497, and then the

Rowers passing under the Ponte Vecchio.

Dominican zealot's own pyre a year later at the same spot (now marked with a small plaque). Away from the crowd-pulling blockbusters, less celebrated statuary includes Giambologna's equestrian *Cosimo I* and Bartolomeo Ammannati's controversial *Fountain of Neptune*, which inspired a 16th-century chant: "*Ammannato, Ammannato, che bel marmo hai rovinato!* (What beautiful marble you've ruined!)" ⏱ *30 min. Bus: C1, C2.*

3 **Rivoire.** If you can (just this once) bear the inflated prices, pause for a coffee and a snack at this landmark cafe—the best positioned in Florence for taking in the glories of the piazza. *Piazza della Signoria. www.rivoire.it. ☎ 055-212412. $–$$$.*

4 ★ **Palazzo Vecchio.** Florence's "Old Palace" became home to Cosimo I and the Medici in 1540, but it dates to the 13th century, when it was built by Gothic master builder Arnolfo di Cambio. (Di Cambio's 92m/308-ft. landmark tower, which visitors can also climb, was an engineering feat in its day.)

The highlight of the interior is the "Hall of the 500" (*Salone dei Cinquecento*), frescoed by Giorgio Vasari and his assistants in the 16th century. Wax-pigment frescoes by Leonardo melted when braziers were brought in to speed up the drying process (their remains are still being hunted to this day). Michelangelo's sculpture *Genius of Victory* survives, thankfully, along with Donatello's bronze group upstairs, *Judith Slaying Holofernes*, cast in 1455. You can also visit the private apartments of Eleanor of Toledo, the Spanish wife of Cosimo I, and the chamber where religious zealot Girolamo Savonarola endured a dozen torture sessions, including "twists" on the rack. ⏱ *90 min. Piazza della Signoria. ☎ 055-2768325. Admission 10€. Fri–Wed 9am–7pm (Apr–Sept open until 11pm), Thurs 9am–2pm. Ticket office closes 1 hr. before palace. Bus: C1, C2.*

5 ★ **Gelateria dei Neri.** Plenty of locals think this, rather than the more famous names, is the best ice-cream stop in town. *Via dei Neri 9R. ☎ 055-210034. $.*

The Fountain of Neptune.

Discount Sightseeing Passes

The Firenze Card (www.firenzecard.it) is valid for 72 hours, costs 72€, and includes entrance to more than 60 sites, including the Uffizi, Accademia, Cappella Brancacci, Palazzo Pitti, and San Marco. It also gets you into shorter lines, making prebooking tickets unnecessary. The **FirenzeCard+** add-on (5€) includes up to 3 days' bus travel (which you likely won't use) and free Wi-Fi (which you might). Don't buy a Firenze Card for anyone ages 17 and under: They can always enter via the express queue with you. They gain free admission to civic museums (such as the Palazzo Vecchio) and pay only the "reservation fee" at state-owned museums (it's 4€ at the Uffizi, for example). The **Grande Museo del Duomo** ticket covers all the sights of Piazza del Duomo: Brunelleschi's dome (including the obligatory booking of a time slot), the Baptistery, Campanile di Giotto, and revamped Museo dell'Opera. It costs 15€; buy at the ticket office in Piazza San Giovanni.

⑥ ★★ Museo Nazionale del Bargello. This grim Gothic fortress—once a site of public executions—centers on a courtyard with a vaulted loggia and portico. Its sculpture collection is the Renaissance's finest, including Donatello's *David* (the first free-standing nude since the Roman era) and side-by-side bronze reliefs depicting the

Museo Nazionale del Bargello.

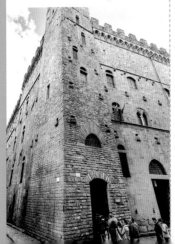

Sacrifice of Isaac by Brunelleschi and Ghiberti. They were judged in a 1401 competition to decide who should get the commission for the north doors of the Baptistery; Ghiberti won. Downstairs, the 1500s room features works by Giambologna and Cellini, and another *David* by Michelangelo. ⏱ *90 min. Via del Proconsolo 4 (at Via Ghibellina). www.polomuseale.firenze.it.* ☎ *055-2388606. Admission 4€ (8€ during temporary exhibition). Daily 8:15am–1:50pm (sometimes until 5pm in summer). Closed 2nd & 4th Sun & 1st, 3rd & 5th Mon of month. Bus: C1, C2.*

⑦ ★★ Cattedrale di Santa Maria del Fiore. From 1294 to 1436, builders labored to construct what was (in its day) the largest cathedral on the planet, but the flamboyant neo-Gothic facade wasn't added until the 19th century. It's a polychrome jumble of marble stripes in sugarcane colors, but few fault the dome Brunelleschi imposed over it, 105m (351 ft.) off the ground; climbing it is one of the joys of Florence. You mount 463 spiraling steps and pass through the ribbed dome for a sublime panoramic view. Afterward, you needn't spend too much time inside; much of the art, frescoes, offerings, and memorials were swept away or moved elsewhere for safekeeping. The most noted is Paolo Uccello's 1436 frescoed "statue" of English mercenary Sir John Hawkwood, on the wall of the left aisle. 🕒 *45 min. Piazza del Duomo. www.ilgrande museodelduomo.it. Free admission to cathedral; 15€ dome on Grande Museo del Duomo combination ticket. Cathedral Mon–Wed, Fri 10am–5pm; Thurs 10am–4:30pm; Sat 10am–4:45pm; Sun 1:30–4:45pm. Dome Mon–Fri 8:30am–7pm; Sat 8:30am–5pm; Sun 1–4pm. Bus: C1.*

❽ ★★ Campanile di Giotto.

Giotto, Andrea Pisano, and Francesco Talenti collaborated to build this 81m (269-ft.) tricolor marble bell tower next to the Duomo. Its lower-level reliefs and statues—by Andrea Pisano, Donatello, Luca della Robbia, and others—are all now copies. Climb the tower's 414 steps for a panoramic view of Florence and a unique perspective on Brunelleschi's dome. When others are queuing around the block waiting to scale the dome, there's often no one waiting here. 🕒 *30 min.*

Cathedral Santa Maria del Fiore.

Campanile di Giotto.

Piazza del Duomo (at Via dei Calzaiuoli). ☎ *055-2302885. Admission 15€ on Grande Museo del Duomo combination ticket. Daily 8:15am–7:20pm. Bus: C1, C2.*

❾ ★★★ Battistero San Giovanni.

This 9th- to 12th-century octagonal baptistery, named after San Giovanni (St. John the Baptist, patron of the city), is visited mainly for the gilded bronze doors on three of its eight sides. The most photographed are Lorenzo Ghiberti's east doors, facing the Duomo, which the typically critical Michelangelo dubbed "The Gates of Paradise." The panels illustrate scenes from the Old Testament.

The "Gates of Paradise": Ghiberti's Baptistery doors.

These are copies hung in 1990; originals are exhibited in the Museo dell'Opera del Duomo (p 42, **7**). Ghiberti also cast the north doors, beating Brunelleschi in a 1401 competition for the commission; the job took him 21 years. Andrea Pisano made the Gothic south doors in 1336. Dominated by a figure of Christ, and packed with imaginative detail, the 13th-century mosaics inside are very much worth a look. ⏱ *15 min. Piazza San Giovanni.* ☎ *055-2302885. Admission 15€ on Grande Museo del Duomo combination ticket. Mon–Sat 8:15–10:15am & 11:15am–7:30pm; Sun & 1st Sat of month 1am–1:30pm. Bus: C1, C2.*

10 ★ San Lorenzo. The overall effect of this basilica, which houses the tombs of many a Medici, is almost Byzantine; one Bulgarian visitor called it "a Florentine Hagia Sophia looming over a souk" (a reference to the tourist-oriented Mercato di San Lorenzo, which fills the nearby streets). The Medici shelled

The Medici

One family, originally pharmacists from the Mugello, has come to symbolize Florence's Renaissance: the **Medici.** Excluding a brief republican interlude, they controlled Florence (often as brutal despots) for 3 centuries. The first to rise to public prominence was **Cosimo "il Vecchio"** (1389–1464), papal banker and patron of Donatello, Fra' Angelico, and Filippo Lippi. His grandson **Lorenzo "The Magnificent"** (1449–92), who survived an assassination attempt at Easter Mass (the Pazzi Conspiracy), knew Botticelli and Michelangelo, dabbled in poetry, and funded a Platonic academy. His death signaled the end of Florence's golden age—the baton passed to Rome. **Cosimo I** (1519–74), the first Grand Duke of Tuscany, built the Uffizi and bought the Pitti Palace. The family also spawned three popes, including **Leo X** and his nephew **Clement VII**—nepotism was the other great family business. Long years of dissolute decline ended with the death of drunkard Giangastone in 1737, and Medici treasures passed to Tuscany.

Piazza della Signoria Statuary

When the medieval Guelph party came out on top after a long political struggle with the Ghibellines, they razed part of the old city center to build a new palace for civic government. The space around what we now call the **Palazzo Vecchio** (❹) became the new civic center of town. **Piazza della Signoria** (❷) is today an outdoor sculpture gallery, teeming with tourists, horses and buggies, and pricey outdoor cafes. The statuary on the piazza is particularly beautiful, starting on the far left (as you're facing the palazzo) with Giambologna's equestrian statue of **"Grand Duke Cosimo I"** (1594). To its right is one of Florence's favorite sculptures to hate, the **"Fontana del Nettuno"** ("Neptune Fountain"; 1560–75). On the far-left corner of Neptune is a copy (original in the Bargello) of Donatello's **"Marzocco,"** symbol of the city. Farther down is a man who needs little introduction, Michelangelo's **"David,"** a 19th-century copy of the original now in the Accademia. Near enough to David to look truly ugly in comparison is Baccio Bandinelli's **"Hercules and Cacus"** (1534). At the piazza's south end is the **Loggia dei Lanzi** ★★ (1376–82). At the front left stands Benvenuto Cellini's masterpiece in bronze, **"Perseus"** ★★★ (1545), holding the head of Medusa. On the far right is Giambologna's **"Rape of the Sabines"** ★★, one of the most successful Mannerist sculptures in existence.

out big bags of gold for it, however. The taller of the two domes at the chancel shelters the **Cappella dei Principi,** the shallower cupola covering Michelangelo's **New Sacristy** (p 45, ❷). Commissioned in 1516, Michelangelo's model for the facade was deemed unacceptable to the Medici. Brunelleschi

designed the **Old Sacristy** at the end of the north transept. In the nave, Donatello created two pulpits with dramatic bronze panels. ◷ *30 min. Piazza San Lorenzo. www.opera medicealaurenziana.org.* ☎ *055-214042. Admission 6€. Mon–Sat 10am–5pm; Mar–Oct also Sun 1:30–5pm. Bus: C1.*

Church of San Lorenzo.

Oltrarno

1 San Miniato al Monte
2 Piazzale Michelangelo
3 Giardino delle Rose
4 Casa Siviero
5 Via dell'Olmo
6 Santa Felicita
7 Santo Spirito
8 A Crudo
9 Cappella Brancacci
10 La Carraia
11 La Specola
12 Giardino di Boboli
13 Palazzo Pitti
ℹ️ Tourist Information

Oltrarno, Florence's "other side of the Arno," was once the artisan heart of the city. You'll see signs that tradition dies hard in the craft and antique shops lining Borgo San Jacopo and Via Maggio. But workshops and studios aren't all the neighborhood has to offer. This tour starts with one of the finest views over Florence, before taking in the very peaks of Renaissance art and architecture, and quiet corners of a district that still has a real, working feel. START: Bus 12 or 13 to Viale Galileo Galilei.

1 ★★★ San Miniato al Monte. This most spiritual of Florentine churches is one of the city's truly ancient places. Built from 1018 in the Pisan–Romanesque style, inside and out, it takes its name from Florence's first Christian martyr. St. Minias apparently picked up his severed head and carried it to this spot in A.D. 250. The nave and aisles are decorated with Taddeo Gaddi's fading frescoes (from 1341)

of the Gospel witnesses, and topped with a soaring, intricate inlaid wooden ceiling. Upstairs, off the raised choir, the Gothic sacristy was frescoed in 1387 with *Stories of the Legend of St. Benedict* by Spinello Aretino, a follower of Giotto. 🕐 45 min. Viale Galileo. ☎ 055-2342731. Free admission (1€ sacristy). Mon–Sat 9:30am–1pm & 3–5:30pm; Sun 1–5:30pm. Bus: 12, 13.

Observation deck at Piazzale Michelangelo.

❷ ★ Piazzale Michelangelo.
Tacky, perhaps; touristy, certainly, but this grand balcony over the city is *the* essential photo stop on any tour of Florence's Left Bank. From where (another) *David* looks out over his city, right at the Palazzo Vecchio that was his first home, you can do the same. ⏱ *15 min. Bus: 12, 13.*

❸ Giardino delle Rose. This little oasis of peace, planted with more than 1,000 varieties of rose, makes a perfect pause halfway down the hill from Piazzale Michelangelo. There's also a

Pink roses at Giardino delle Rose.

little Japanese garden donated to Florence by the city of Kyoto. ⏱ *15 min. Viale Poggi 2. No phone. Free admission. Daily 9am–sunset. Bus: 12, 13.*

❹ ★ Casa Siviero. Inside a colonial villa right on the Arno is the private collection of resistance fighter and art historian Rodolfo Siviero (1911–83). The bulk of the paintings are minor works, ancient and modern. Of particular interest is a set of medallions Siviero commissioned after World War II to honor those who helped liberate his city, including Winston Churchill and Dwight D. Eisenhower. ⏱ *30 min. Lungarno Serristori 1–3 (at Piazza Poggi). www.museocasa siviero.it.* ☎ *055-2345219. Free admission. Sat 10am–2pm & 3–7pm (Sept–Jun 10am–6pm); Sun–Mon 10am–1pm. Bus: C3, D, 23.*

❺ Via dell'Olmo. High on a wall on the western side of this tiny street is a sign that reads: QUI ARRIVA LA PIENA DEL ARNO IL 4 NOVEMBRE 1966. That's the height the flood waters reached in November 1966 before they began to subside that evening. Countless of the city's treasures were damaged, most famously Cimabue's *Crucifix* in Santa Croce, and more than 30

Santo Spirito.

Florentines lost their lives. ⏱ *5 min. Bus: D, 23.*

6 ★★ **Santa Felicita.** The 2nd-century Greek sailors who lived in this neighborhood brought Christianity to Florence, and this little church was probably the second to be established in the city, the first edition of it rising in the late 4th century. The current version was built in the 1730s. Stop by to view paintings by Mannerist Pontormo (1525–27), particularly his emotive *Deposition.* ⏱ *15 min. See p 17,* **3**. *Bus: C3, D.*

7 ★ **Santo Spirito.** This outwardly plain church is where Brunelleschi's ordered architectural style reached its apotheosis. The nave and transept are supported by an unbroken chain of columns and supplemented with 38 peripheral chapels. The whole effect is of a space filled with light and grandeur, one that's only partly spoiled by a baroque canopy above the altar. The sacristy houses a carved wooden *Crucifix* attributed to Michelangelo. ⏱ *30 min. Piazza Santo Spirito.* ☎ *055-210030. Free admission. Mon–Tues & Thurs–Sat 10am–12:30pm & 4–5:30pm; Sun 4–5:30pm. Bus: C3, D, 11, 36, 37.*

8 ★ **A Crudo.** The name means "raw," which provides a clue to this small restaurant's strengths: carpaccio, traditional and creative tartare, and host of fish and vegetarian options. *Via Mazzetta 5.* ☎ *055-2657483. $$.*

9 ★★★ **Cappella Brancacci.** The frescoes in the right transept chapel of Florence's Carmelite church stand on the brink of what we now call "the Renaissance." Originally painted by Masaccio and Masolino between 1424 and 1427, the *Scenes from the Life of St. Peter* were finished off by Filippino Lippi in the 1480s (spot the stylistic differences). It was Masaccio's vivid realism and mastery of linear perspective, especially in his *Expulsion from Eden* and *Tribute Money*, that artists were still coming to study a century later. It's a miracle any of this is still here: Almost the entire remainder of the church was destroyed by fire in 1771. Outside peak season, despite what it says on the door, you may not need a reservation; otherwise, book a slot by phone. ⏱ *30 min. Piazza del Carmine.* ☎ *055-2382195. Admission 6€. Mon, Wed–Sat 10am–5pm; Sun 1–5pm. Bus: D.*

10 ★★ **La Carraia.** The left bank's best gelateria is rightly popular with locals, all day and late into the evening. *Piazza N. Sauro 25R.* ☎ *055-280695. $.*

11 ★ **La Specola.** This former headquarters of Oltrarno's World War II resistance now houses the Museo di Storia Naturale's zoology exhibits. In addition to the thousands of stuffed and pickled beasts, there's a touch of gore that's perhaps suited to older kids only. The **Cere Anatomiche** are lifelike waxworks of the human body spliced and diced 500 different ways, used to teach anatomy in the 18th century. Grislier still are Giulio Zumbo's 17th-century models of Florence during the plague, showing the dead and decomposing strewn across the city streets. ◷ *1 hr. Via Romana 17. www.msn.unifi.it.* ☎ *055-2755100. Admission 6€. Tues–Sun 10:30am–5:30pm (Oct–May 9:30am–4:30pm). Bus: C3, D, 11, 36, 37.*

12 ★ **Giardino di Boboli.** Court architect and artist Niccolò Tribolo (1500–1550) laid out these Renaissance gardens, through which the Medici romped, in the mid-16th

Giardino di Boboli.

century. Since opening to the public in 1776, the Boboli has become the most dazzling (and busiest) garden in Tuscany, with splashing fountains and elegant statuary such as *Venus* by Giambologna inside the Buontalenti grotto. The nearby, much-photographed fountain—an obese *Bacchus* astride a turtle—is a copy of a statue depicting Pietro Barbino, Cosimo I's court jester. Your ticket also includes entrance to the adjacent **Giardino Bardini.** ◷ *30 min. Piazza de' Pitti.* ☎ *055-2388791. Admission 7€ including entrance to Museo degli Argenti,*

The frescoes of Cappella Brancacci.

Palatina Gallery in Palazzo Pitti.

Giardino Bardini & Galleria del Costume. Jun–Aug daily 8:15am–7:30pm; Apr–May & Sept–Oct daily 8:15am–6:30pm; Mar daily 8:15am–5:30pm; Nov–Feb daily 8:15am–4:30pm. Closed 1st & last Mon of each month. Bus: C3, D.

⑬ ★★ **Palazzo Pitti.** Luca Pitti, a wealthy importer of French fabrics, wanted a palace to outclass the Medici—and he got his wish. Niccolò Macchiavelli hailed the palazzo as "grander than any other erected in Florence by a private citizen." When the Pitti family sold up, the Medici moved in, transforming it into the most opulent palace in Europe until Louis XIV built Versailles outside Paris. In the 19th century, the palazzo housed the Italian royal family, when Florence was briefly the country's capital. Victor Emmanuel III gave it to the state in 1919, which turned it into a series of museums.

Fresco on the ceiling of the Pitti Palace.

Pitti Palace

Giardino di Boboli
(Boboli Garden)

Boboli
Amphitheater

Fontana del
Carciofo

Ammannati's
Courtyard

Galleria
Palatina
13A

Galleria del
Costume
13D

Museo degli
Argenti
(Ground Floor)
13E

Appartamenti
Reali
13B

13C

Entrance

Galleria
d'Arte Moderna
(Second Floor)

Ticket
Office

Piazza dei Pitti

Galleria Palatina
Appartamenti Reali

0 ——— 50 m
0 ——— 200 ft

After climbing 140 steps, you enter the **5A** ★★★ **Galleria Palatina.** Head here if you have to skip everything else. It's filled with masterpieces from the High Renaissance and later eras, collected by the Medici and later the ruling dukes of Lorraine. Perhaps the most famous resident in the collection is Raphael, whose *Madonna of the Chair* graces the Sala di Saturno and *La Velata* the Sala di Giove. Raphael is accompanied by several works by Venetian Titian and Flemish Peter Paul Rubens, whose giant *Consequences of War* dominates the Sala di Marte. Rococo excesses define the **5B** **Appartamenti Reali,** former home to the Kings of Savoy, the first rulers of a united Italy. Note Caravaggio's *Portrait of a Knight of Malta,* painted before his expulsion from the island in 1608. In the shadow of the Renaissance rooms, the **5C** ★ **Galleria**

d'Arte Moderna showcases the Macchiaioli, the 19th-century Tuscan school of pre-Impressionist painters who revolted against academicism. The movement's key figure was Livornese artist Giovanni Fattori. The **5D** **Galleria del Costume** is filled with 18th- to 20th-century Florentine fashions, plus historic wardrobes such as Eleanor of Toledo's burial dress. The ground-floor **5E** **Museo degli Argenti** is a camp glorification of the Medici household wares, with treasures in ivory and silver, among other metals. It's ostentatious but fun.

🕐 *2 hr. Piazza de' Pitti. www.polo museale.firenze.it.* ☎ *055-2388614. Galleria Palatina 13€ including Appartamenti Reali & Galleria d'Arte Moderna (13€ during temporary exhibition). Tues–Sun 8:15am– 6:50pm. Bus: C3, D.*

Florence's Best Small Museums

1. Museo Horne
2. Museo di Mineralogia e Litologia
3. Museo Archeologico
4. Museo Opificio delle Pietre Dure
5. Museo Antropologico
6. Coquinarius
7. Museo dell'Opera del Duomo
8. Museo Galileo
9. Il Gelato Gourmet
10. Museo di Orsanmichele
11. Museo di Palazza Davanzati
12. Museo Stibbert

ast into shadow by the marvels of the Uffizi and Palazzo Pitti, the small museums of Florence are often overlooked. But the city has even more to offer than its vast repositories of great art: Away from the tourist-trodden paths are one of Italy's most intriguing archaeological collections, offbeat museums of science, and private museums housing lesser-known Renaissance masterpieces. Because many of these collections are open mornings only, plan an intensive viewing session before lunch. START: **Bus C3 to Via dei Benci.**

1 ★ Museo Horne. English-born Herbert Horne, an art historian, immortalized himself by building the nucleus of this collection, including minor masterpieces by some top-rank artists. Works are displayed in his preserved Renaissance home, round a porticoed courtyard. Horne's greatest acquisitions were Giotto's *St. Stephen*,

dating from the early 14th century, and a small 1320s diptych by Simone Martini depicting the *Man of Sorrows*. ⏱ 45 min. Via dei Benci 6 (at Corso dei Tintori). www.museo horne.it. ☎ 055-244661. Admission 7€. Thurs–Tues 10am–2pm. Bus: C3, 23.

Take bus #23 to Piazza San Marco.

The Arezzo Chimera, circa 400 B.C.

② Museo di Mineralogia e Litologia. This outpost of Florence's multicenter Museo di Storia Naturale (Natural History Museum) is a treasure trove for aspiring (or actual) gemologists and geologists. Hundreds of curious, colorful rocks from all corners of the planet are displayed in detailed, illuminated cross-section; kids are free to touch and handle some of them. ⏱ *30 min. Via La Pira 4. www.msn.unifi.it.* ☎ *055-234-6760. Admission 6€; 10€ with Museo Antropologico (**⑤**, below). June–Sept daily 10:30am–5:30pm; Oct–May Mon–Tues & Thurs–Fri 9:30am–4:30pm, Sat–Sun 10am–4:30pm. Bus: C1, 1, 7, 25.*

③ ★ Museo Archeologico. A marvelous *palazzo* is home to one of Italy's best (if slightly haphazard) collections of Egyptian and Etruscan artifacts, much of it gathered by the Medici and later Leopold II of Lorraine, in the 1830s. The collection is regularly rearranged, but the highlights are usually upstairs, including eerie Egyptian sarcophagi. The 4th-century *Arezzo Chimera* (a bronze lion with a serpent

for a tail) is the prize exhibit. Look out, too, for a couple of precious bronzes: the Roman *Idolino*, whose provenance is a little mysterious, and the Etruscan *Arringatore*, found near Perugia in Umbria. ⏱ *1 hr. Via della Colonna 38 (at Piazza della SS. Annunziata).* ☎ *055-23575. Admission 4€. Tues–Fri 8:30am–7pm, Sat–Mon 8:30am–2pm. Closed 2nd, 4th & 5th Sun of month. Bus: 6, 19, 23, 31, 32.*

④ Museo Opificio delle Pietre Dure. This unique collection grew out of the Medici's passion for *pietre dure*, a type of mosaic work made from semiprecious stones and marble, popular in the 16th century. (The craft is sometimes called "Florentine Mosaic.") Since 1796 this workshop has been dedicated to restoring *pietre dure* works. Attached is a small museum with some examples of the art form, including intricate Tuscan landscapes. ⏱ *30 min. Via degli Alfani 78 (at Via Ricasoli).* ☎ *055-2651348. Admission 4€. Mon–Sat 8:15am–1:30pm. Bus: C1.*

42

The Best of Florence

❺ Museo Antropologico.
Extend your timeout from the
Renaissance at this fascinating little
anthropological enclave of the University of Florence. Inuit canoes,
Japanese *kabuki* masks, Sumatran
spears, and Inca mummies from
Cuzco, Peru, were all collected during the heyday of European imperi-
alism in the 19th century. Displays
are mostly in Italian. ⏱ *45 min. Via
del Proconsolo 12. www.msn.unifi.it.*
☎ *055-2756444. Admission 6€; 10€
with Museo della Mineralogia (❷,
above). Same hours as Museo della
Mineralogia. Bus: C1, C2.*

☕ ★ Coquinarius. Enjoy a plate
of mixed cold cuts or something
tasty from a lengthy carpaccio list at
this traditional brick-walled enoteca.
*Via delle Oche 11R. www.coquinarius.
com.* ☎ *055-2302153. $$.*

**❼ ★★ Museo dell'Opera del
Duomo.** Reorganized and
enlarged for a grand relaunch in
2015, the former workshop where
Michelangelo carved his iconic
David is now a repository for the
loot from the Duomo and Baptis-
tery, and all the external sculptures
from Giotto's Campanile. Undis-
puted stars of the collection are Ghi-
berti's restored and reassembled
"Gates of Paradise," from the

Baptistery. There's also a couple of
Michelangelos, including his *Pietà*,
originally intended for the artist's
tomb. Elsewhere are joyous 1430s
cantorie (singing galleries)—one by
Donatello, the other by Luca della
Robbia—and Donatello's *Mary Mag-
dalene*, one of his most celebrated
penitent works, from 1455. ⏱ *1 hr.
Piazza del Duomo 9.* ☎ *055-
2302885. Admission 15€ on Grande
Museo del Duomo combination ticket.
Wed–Mon 9am–7pm. Bus: C1, C2.*

❽ ★ Museo Galileo. The city's
renamed and revamped Museo di
Storia della Scienza (History of Sci-
ence Museum) houses such trea-
sures as the lens Galileo used to
discover the four moons of Jupiter
and the great scientist's right-hand
middle finger, stolen before his
burial at Santa Croce. The collec-
tion was started by the science-
minded later Medici dukes, and a
hands-on multimedia approach
(including an interactive website)
really appeals to older kids. ⏱ *1 hr.
Piazza dei Giudici 1. www.museo
galileo.it.* ☎ *055-265311. Admission
9€. Wed–Mon 9:30am–6pm, Tues
9:30am–1pm. Bus: C1, C3, D.*

**☕ ★ Il Gelato Gourmet di
Marco Ottaviano.** Seasonal, pro-
duce-led flavors can include sub-
lime Sicilian pistachio. *Via Palmieri
34R.* ☎ *055-2341036. $.*

Museo dell'Opera del Duomo.

Catching a Show at the Strozzi

The two spaces inside the Renaissance Palazzo Strozzi, Piazza Strozzi (www.palazzostrozzi.org; ☎ **055-2645155**)—known as the Piano Nobile and the basement Strozzina—are Florence's major spaces for temporary and contemporary art shows and have been experiencing a 21st-century renaissance of their own under energetic directorship. Recent hits have included 2017's "Bill Viola: Electronic Renaissance." Plus, look for talks, one-off events, and discovery trails aimed at 5- to 9-year-olds. It's usually open late on Thursdays.

⑩ ★ Museo di Orsanmichele. The former granary rooms above Orsanmichele now house the statues that once surrounded the Gothic church's exterior—though sadly, it's usually open just 1 day per week. Many of the original sculptures are here, well labeled, including Donatello's marble *St. Mark* (1411–13); Ghiberti's *St. John the Baptist* (1413–16), the first life-size bronze of the Renaissance; and Verrocchio's *Incredulity of St. Thomas* (1473–83). ⏲ *20 min. Via Arte della Lana.* ☎ *055-210305. Free admission. Mon 10am–5pm. Bus: C2.*

⑪ ★★ Museo di Palazzo Davanzati. One of Florence's best-preserved 14th-century palaces was originally built for the Davizzi family, then bought by the Davanzati clan. The emphasis is not on the decor but on giving visitors insight into medieval life for a noble Florentine family: feasts and festivities in the Sala Madornale; a private, internal well for a secure water supply; and magnificent bedchamber frescoes dating to the 1350s, which recount, comic-strip style, "The Chatelaine of Vergy," a 13th-century morality tale. ⏲ *30 min. Via Porta Rossa 13.* ☎ *055-2388610. Admission 6€. Daily 8:15am–1:50pm. Closed 2nd & 4th Sun & 1st, 3rd & 5th Mon of each month. Bus: C2.*

Friday through Sunday, make the 5-min. walk northwest to Piazza dell'Unità Italiana to catch bus #4. After 8 stops, get out at Gioia to snag the last time slot of the day (5pm) at:

⑫ Museo Stibbert. Frederick Stibbert (1838–1906), half-Italian, half-Brit, was an eclectic collector, as the 50,000 *objets d'art* (tapestries, antiques, porcelain, paintings) in these 57 rooms testify. Stibbert also had a fetish about war and weaponry: Expect lances, swords, and suits of Japanese, European, and Middle Eastern armor. ⏲ *45 min. Via Stibbert 26. www.museostibbert. it.* ☎ *055-475520. Admission 8€. Mon–Wed 10am–1pm; Fri–Sun 10am–5pm. Bus: 4.*

Museo di Palazzo Davanzati.

Florence's Masters of the Renaissance

① Basilica di Santa Maria Novella
② Cappelle Medicee
③ Cenacolo di Sant'Appolonia
④ Santissima Annunziata
⑤ Pugi
⑥ Palazzo Medici-Riccardi
⑦ Orsanmichele
⑧ Palazzo Rucellai
⑨ Santa Trinita
⑩ Galleria degli Uffizi

ⓘ Tourist Information

For over a century, Florence was the center of the world. The period we now call the Renaissance ("the rebirth") is often dated from Lorenzo Ghiberti's commission for the north doors of the Baptistery, in 1401, until Michelangelo's final departure for Rome, in the 1530s. This remarkable period of artistic and architectural development, initially led by such figures as Masaccio, Donatello, and Brunelleschi, created the city we see today. On this tour, we take you to the best works left behind by the sculptors, painters, and architects who changed art forever. START: **Piazza Santa Maria Novella.**

① ★★ **Basilica di Santa Maria Novella.** This basilica's iconic green and white marble facade was completed in 1470 by the Renaissance's key architectural theorist, L. B. Alberti, while the interior dates to the 13th century. (Writer

Boccaccio used it for scenes in his *Decameron*.) Of the many interior frescoes, Masaccio's *Trinity* is the most significant in the history of art and astonished onlookers when it was unveiled in 1427: They'd never seen such realistic perspective painted onto a flat wall. Domenico Ghirlandaio's sumptuous frescoes adorning the **Cappella Tornabuoni** ostensibly depict *Scenes from the Lives of the Virgin and St. John the Baptist*, but they're also a unique snapshot of wealthy society in 1490 Florence. The multi-talented Brunelleschi carved the *Crucifix* in the **Cappella Gondi.** By the 1800s, Santa Maria Novella had become Florence's "church for foreigners," attracting expatriate literati, including the poet Percy Bysshe Shelley. ⏱ *45 min. Piazza Santa Maria Novella. www.smn.it. ☎ 055-219257. Admission 5€. Mon–Thurs 9am–7pm, Fri 11am–7pm, Sat 9am–5:30pm, Sun 1–5:30pm. Bus: C2, 6, 11.*

Basilica di Santa Maria Novella.

❷ ★★ **Cappelle Medicee (Medici Chapels).** Make a fast trek to the **Sagrestia Nuova (New Sacristy),** Michelangelo's first realized architectural work—begun in 1520, but left unfinished until 1534. As an architectural space, it echoes Brunelleschi's Pazzi Chapel in Santa Croce. From the door, on the left, the tomb of Lorenzo, duke of Urbino, bears the artist's reclining figures representing *Dawn* and *Dusk.* On the right, the tomb of Giuliano, duke of Nemours (and youngest son of Lorenzo the Magnificent), features Michelangelo's allegorical figures of *Day* and *Night.* Shrewd observers will note that Michelangelo obviously hadn't seen many naked female bodies. The artist never completed two other tombs commissioned to him, but in 1521 he did finish a moving *Madonna and Child,* for the tomb of Lorenzo "The Magnificent." ⏱ *40 min. Piazza Madonna degli Aldobrandini 6 (behind San Lorenzo). ☎ 055-2388602. Admission 8€. Daily 8:15am–1:50pm. Closed 2nd & 4th Sun & 1st, 3rd & 5th Mon of each month. Bus: C1.*

❸ ★ **Cenacolo di Sant'Appolonia.** Andrea del Castagno (1421–57) first rose to prominence when he was employed to paint the faces of condemned men on the walls of the Bargello. He went on to become, alongside Piero della Francesca (1412–92), one of the great perspective painters of the mid-Quattrocento (1400s). Here, in what remains of the Benedictine convent of Sant'Appolonia, he gives his intense, rather dark take on the *Last Supper* (1447). No prizes for naming the only diner without his halo. ⏱ *15 min. Via XX Aprile 1. ☎ 055-2388607. Free admission. Daily 8:15am–1:50pm. Closed 1st, 3rd & 5th Sat–Sun of each month. Bus: 1, 6, 11, 14, 17, 23.*

❹ ★ **Santissima Annunziata.** As the artistic style we now call "Renaissance" waned, Florence hosted its last great artistic movement before the action moved south to Rome: Mannerism. Behind this church's Michelozzo-designed portico, the **Chiostro dei Voti (Votive Cloister)** has some of the city's finest Mannerist frescoes. Rosso Fiorentino provided an

Assumption (1513) and Pontormo a *Visitation* (1515) just to the right of the door, but the highlights are by their master, Andrea del Sarto. His *Birth of the Virgin* (1513), in the far right corner, is one of his finest works, and his *Coming of the Magi* (1514) includes a self-portrait at the far right, looking out at us from under his blue hat. ⏱ *20 min. Piazza SS Annunziata.* ☎ *055-266181. Free admission. Daily 7:30am–12:30pm & 4–6:30pm. Bus: 6, 19, 23, 31, 32.*

5̲ ★ Pugi. Choose your topping, and your portion size, of freshly baked schiacciata (flatbread) and munch it in the square across the street. Closed Sunday. *Piazza San Marco 9. www.fornopugi.it.* ☎ *055-280981. $.*

6 ★ Palazzo Medici-Riccardi. The onset of the Florentine Renaissance didn't totally kill off the decorative style of painting known as "International Gothic," as a tiny chapel frescoed in 1459 by Benozzo Gozzoli shows. Gozzoli's *Procession of the Magi* includes a pageant of Medici friends and family, accompanied by a beautifully rendered menagerie of creatures. This Michelozzo-designed palace (1444) was originally built as the Medici family home for Cosimo "il Vecchio." ⏱ *30 min. Via Cavour 3. www.palazzo-medici.it.* ☎ *055-2760340. Admission 7€ (10€ during temporary exhibition). Thurs–Tues 8:30am–6:30pm. Bus: C1.*

7 ★ Orsanmichele. This 1337 Gothic grain warehouse was converted into a church in medieval times. The external niches were adorned with statuary commissioned by Florence's trade guilds. (Most of the originals are now inside the rarely-open Museo di Orsanmichele; see p 43, **10**.) The sculptors chosen included such luminaries of the early Renaissance as Lorenzo Ghiberti, Nanni di Banco, and Donatello, whose pathbreaking *St George* is now in the Bargello. Inside is Andrea Orcagna's elaborate Gothic Tabernacle (1349–59), housing a *Virgin and Child* (1346) by Giotto's student, Bernardo Daddi. ⏱ *30 min. Via Arte della Lana 1.* ☎ *055-210305. Free admission. Daily 10am–5pm. Bus: C2.*

8 Palazzo Rucellai. Although it stands somewhat uncelebrated on

Andrea del Sarto masterpiece in the Basilica of Santissima Annunziata.

Orsanmichele church.

a quiet shopping street, this was perhaps the most influential *palazzo* ever built in Florence. Harmoniously designed by Alberti and built by Bernardo Rossellino (who more famously worked in Pienza; see p 87), it was the first Renaissance building to feature classical pilasters on its facade. ⏱ *5 min. Via della Vigna Nuova. Bus: 6, 11.*

❾ ★★ Santa Trìnita. This oft-missed church, founded in the 11th century, was the original home of Gentile da Fabriano's Gothic icon, *Procession of the Magi,* now in the Uffizi. Lorenzo Monaco frescoed the **Cappella Bartolini Salimbeni** in the 1420s with *Scenes from the Life of the Virgin;* Domenico Ghirlandaio, in uncharacteristically pious mood, frescoed the **Cappella Sassetti** in the 1480s with a *Life of St Francis.* Comparing them side by side paints a picture of progress made in the depiction of space during the early Renaissance. Opposite the church, across the tiny piazza, is Baccio d'Agnolo's 1523 **Palazzo Bartolini Salimbeni,** one of the city's most handsome late Renaissance palaces. ⏱ *40 min. Piazza di Santa Trìnita.* ☎ *055-216912. Free admission. Mon–Sat 8:30am–noon & 4–5:45pm; Sun 8:30–10:45am & 4–5:45pm. Bus: C3, D.*

❿ ★★★ Galleria degli Uffizi. If you've still got energy for more Renaissance, finish your day at the planet's greatest repository of 13th-, 14th-, and 15th-century painting. Here you'll find influential works by such important Renaissance figures as Leonardo da Vinci, Paolo Uccello, Raphael, and Piero della Francesca. One weeknight in summer it often stays open until 10pm (exact days change). *See p 24. Bus: C1.*

The Best Dining in Florence

Bottega del Buon Caffè **25**
Brac **23**
Cantina Barbagianni **17**
Cantinetta Antinori **9**
Cibrèo **20**
Cipolla Rossa **10**
Da Rocco **22**
Da Tito **1**
Fishing Lab **16**
GustaPizza **12**
Il Santo Bevitore **8**
iO: Osteria Personale **7**

Palacongressi

Via Guelfa

Stazione
Centrale
S. Maria
Novella

Palaffari

Piazza
Adua

Via Faenza

Via Nazionale

Via Panicale

Piazza del
Mercato
Centrale

Via

Via Fiume

Via Luigi Alamanni

Piazza
della Stazione

Via S. Antonino

Cappelle
Medicee

Piazza S.
Lorenzo

Piazza
dell'Unità
Italiana

S. Maria
Novella

Via della Scala

Via de' Panzani

Via del Giglio

San
Lorenzo

Piazza
S. Maria
Novella

Via dei Cerretani

Piazza
S. Giovanni

Via Palazzuolo

Ognissanti

Piazza
d'Ognissanti

Lungarno Amerigo Vespucci

Via del Porcellana

Via de' Fossi

Via del Moro

Via delle B. Donne

Via de' Pecori

V. d. Campidoglio

CENTRO

Via Roma

Piazza
della
Repubblica

Ponte
A. Vespucci

Lungarno

Piazza
Goldoni

Via della Vigna Nuova

V. d. Parione

Santa
Trinita

Palazzo
Strozzi

Via d. Strozzi

Via dei Tornabuoni

Orsan-
michele

V. Calimala

Piazza
di Cestello Soderini

Ponte
alla Carraia

Palazzo
Corsini

Lung. Corsini

Piazza
Trinita

Via Porta Rossa

Palazzo
Davanzati

Borgo San Frediano

Arno

Borgo SS. Apostoli

Lungarno Acciaiuoli

Loggia
dei Lanzi

SAN FREDIANO

Lungarno Guicciardini

Via dell'Orto

Piazza
del Carmine

Via Santo Spirito

SANTO
SPIRITO

Ponte
Santa Trinita

Ponte
Vecchio

Santa Maria
del Carmine

Via dell'Ardiglione

Via Sant'Agostino

Borgo S. Jacopo

Via della Chiesa

Via de' Serragli

Santo
Spirito

V. Vellutini

Via Guicciardini

Piazza
S. Felicita

Piazza
S. Maria
Soprarno

Via del Campuccio

Via d. Caldaie

Piazza
S. Spirito

Via Mazzetta

Via Maggio

Piazza
dei Pitti

OLTRARNO

Giardino
Torrigiani

Borgo Tegolaio

Via Romana

Palazzo
Pitti

Giardino di Boboli
(Boboli Garden)

Forte di
Belvedere

Costa di S. Giorgio

Konnubio **11**
Koto Ramen **19**
La Gratella **2**
Le Mossacce **15**
Lobs **5**
Mercato Centrale **3**
Nerbone **4**

Ora d'Aria **14**
Osteria del
  Caffè Italiano **18**
Osteria Pastella **6**
Quattro Leoni **13**
Santarpia **21**
Zeb **24**

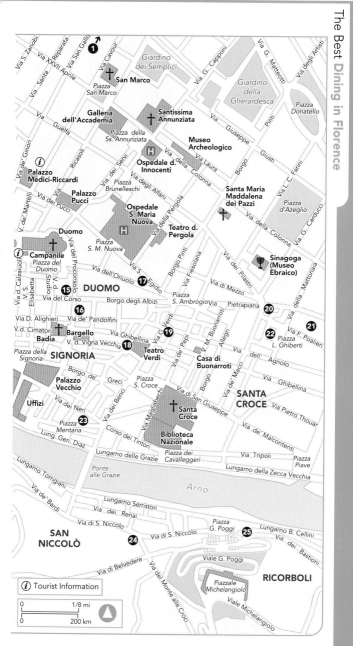

San Marco
Piazza San Marco
Via S. Zanobi
Via S. Reparata
Via XXVII Aprile
Via. Santa
Via San Gallo
Via Cavour
Giardino dei Semplici
Via G. Capponi
Via G. Matteotti
Via degli Artisti
Giardino della Gherardesca
Piazza Donatello
Galleria dell'Accademia
Via Guelfa
Santissima Annunziata
Piazza della Ss. Annunziata
Museo Archeologico
Via della Colonna
Via Giuseppe
Giusti
Borgo
Via L. C. Farini
Via de' Ginori
Ricasoli
Via dei Servi
Via della Laura
Palazzo Medici-Riccardi
Via de' Pucci
Palazzo Pucci
Ospedale d. Innocenti
Piazza Brunelleschi
Via degli Alfani
Santa Maria Maddalena dei Pazzi
Via della Colonna
Piazza d'Azeglio
Via G. Carducci
V. de' Martelli
Duomo
Ospedale S. Maria Nuova
Via della Pergola
Piazza S. M. Nuova
Teatro d. Pergola
Borgo Pinti
Via Fiesolana
Via de' Plastri
Sinagoga (Museo Ebraico)
Via della Mattonaia
Campanile
Piazza del Duomo
Via dello Proconsolo
Via dell'Oriuolo
❶⑦
DUOMO
Piazza S. Ambrogio
Via
Pietrapiana
⑳
Via di Calzaiuoli
V. S. Elisabetta
Studio
Via del Corso
⑮ ⑯
Borgo degli Albizi
Borgo Pinti
Via di Mezzo
Via de' Pandolfini
Via D. Alighieri
V.d. Cimatore
Bargello
Badia
Via G. Verdi
⑲
Via Ghibellina
V. d. Vigna Vecchia ⑱
Via M. Buonarroti
Alleg ri
Via F. Poalleri
㉑
Piazza L. Ghiberti ㉒
Piazza della Signoria
SIGNORIA
Borgo de' Greci
Piazza S. Croce
Via de' pepi
Casa di Buonarroti
Via dell' Agnolo
Palazzo Vecchio
Via dei Neri
Borgo de' Greci
Via de' Benci
Via di San Giuseppe
Borgo
Via de' Macci
SANTA CROCE
Via Ghibellina
Via Pietro Thouar
Uffizi
㉓
Piazza Mentana
Lung. Gen. Diaz
Corso dei Tintori
Santa Croce
Biblioteca Nazionale
Via Maddalena
Piazza dei Cavalleggeri
Via Tripoli
Via de' Malcontenti
Piazza Piave
Lungarno delle Grazie
Lungarno della Zecca Vecchia
Lungarno Torrigiani
Ponte alle Grazie
Arno
Via de' Bardi
Lungarno Serristori
Via dei Renai
Via di S. Niccolò
SAN NICCOLÒ
㉔
Via di S. Niccolò
Piazza G. Poggi
㉕
Lungarno B. Cellini
Via dei Bastioni
Via di Belvedere
Viale G. Poggi
RICORBOLI
Via di Monte alle Croci
Piazzale Michelangiolo
Viale Michelangiolo

ⓘ Tourist Information

| 0 | 1/8 mi |
| 0 | 200 km |

Dining Best Bets

Best for a Romantic Evening
★★ Osteria Pastella $$–$$$ Via della Scala 17R (p 53)

Best for a Budget Dinner Close to the Duomo
★ Le Mossacce $$ Via del Proconsolo 55R (p 52)

Best for Seafood
★★ Fishing Lab $$–$$$ Via del Proconsolo 16R (p 52)

Best Steaks
★★ La Gratella $$–$$$ Via Guelfa 81R (p 52)

Best for Relaxed Family Dining
★ Quattro Leoni $$–$$$ Via dei Vellutini 1R (p 53)

Best Pizza
★★ Santarpia $$ Largo Annigoni 9c (p 53)

Best Sandwich
★ Nerbone $ Mercato Centrale (p 53)

Best Vegetarian Food
★★ Brac $$ Via dei Vagellai 18R (p 51)

Best for a Filling Budget Lunch
★ Da Rocco $ Mercato di Sant'Ambrogio (p 51)

Most Creative Contemporary Cooking
★★★ Bottega del Buon Caffè $$$$$ Lungarno Cellini 69R (p 51); and ★★★ iO: Osteria Personale $$$ Borgo San Frediano 167R (p 52)

Mercato Centrale.

Best for All-day Eating with Fussy Kids
★★ Mercato Centrale $$ Piazza Mercato Centrale (p 53)

Most Refined Deli Dining
★★ Zeb $$ Via San Miniato 2R (p 53)

Best for a Business Lunch
★ Cantinetta Antinori $$$$ Piazza Antinori 3 (p 51)

Best Gelato
★★★ Carapina $ Via Lambertesca 18R (p 19)

★★★ Bottega del Buon Caffè

SAN NICCOLÒ *CREATIVE TUS-CAN* The city's ultimate contemporary fine-dining destination (with a value lunch deal). Dishes from stellar head chef Antonello Sardi are ingredient-led and sourced from the best artisan butchers and their own kitchen garden. *Lungarno Cellini 69R. www.borgointhecity.com.* ☎ *055-5535677. Entrees 42€–49€. AE, MC, V. Lunch Tues–Sat, dinner Mon–Sat. Bus: C3, D.*

★★ Brac

SANTA CROCE *VEGE-TARIAN/VEGAN* Seasonal salads, creative pastas, and the *piatto unico* combo plate, which has both plus *pane carasau* (Sardinian flatbread). Artsy venue that doubles as a cafe-bookshop. *Via dei Vagellai 18R. www.libreriabrac.net.* ☎ *055-2341330. Entrees 10€–14€. MC, V. Lunch, dinner daily. Bus: C1, C3, 23.*

★ Cantina Barbagianni

SANTA CROCE *MODERN TUSCAN* A romantic spot that successfully combines the traditional and the contemporary in mood and food. Seasonal Tuscan dishes like *filetto di manzo ai mirtilli* (beef filet with blueberries) are given a light, inventive interpretation. *Via Sant'Egidio 13R. www.cantinabarbagianni.it.* ☎ *055-2480508. Entrees 16€–23€. AE, MC, V. Dinner Mon–Sat. Bus: C1, C2.*

★ Cantinetta Antinori

CENTRO STORICO *TUSCAN* For 600 years, the Antinori family has dazzled with ingredients and wines from their own farms and vineyards, served in a 15th-century *palazzo. Palazzo Antinori, Piazza Antinori 3. www.cantinetta-antinori.com.* ☎ *055-292234. Entrees 27€–31€. AE, DC, MC, V. Lunch, dinner Mon–Sat. Closed Aug. Bus: C3, D, 6, 11.*

★★ Cibrèo

SANT'AMBROGIO *MEDITERRANEAN* Fabio Picchi's innovative restaurant remains one of Florence's finest. Simple soups share the menu with ventures like fricasseed roosters' combs and innards in an egg. *Via Verrocchio 8R. www.cibreo.com.* ☎ *055-2341100. Entrees 40€. DC, MC, V. Lunch, dinner Tues–Sun. Closed late July to early Sept. Bus: C3.*

Cipolla Rossa

SAN LORENZO *MODERN TUSCAN/GRILL* A modern-rustic dining room with a honed, contemporary take on combining Tuscan ingredients. Beef (Chianina) and pork (Cinta Senese) steaks are the kings. *Via dei Conti 53R. www.osteriacipollarossa.com.* ☎ *055-214210. Entrees 15€–20€. MC, V. Lunch, dinner daily. Bus: C1.*

★ Da Rocco

SANT'AMBROGIO *ITALIAN* Simple, market-fresh plates served to hungry local workers. Expect the likes of lasagna or roasted rabbit. *Inside Mercato di Sant'Ambrogio. No phone. Entrees 5.50€. AE, MC, V. Lunch Mon–Sat. Bus: C3.*

The well-stocked bar at Cibrèo.

Fresh pasta dishes are among the culinary treasures of the region.

★ **Da Tito** SAN MARCO *TUSCAN* A beloved (and busy) century-old trattoria where the staff is as welcoming as the food, which sticks to well-executed Italian classics like lombatina di vitella (thick veal chop). *Via San Gallo 112R. www. trattoriadatito.it.* ☎ *055-472475. Entrees 10€–18€. MC, V. Lunch, dinner Mon–Sat. Bus: C1, 1, 17, 25.*

★★ **Fishing Lab** CENTRO STORICO *SEAFOOD* Young, lively seafood restaurant that takes fish pretty much everywhere it can go, from carpaccio to grills. *Via del Proconsolo 16R. www.fishinglab.it.* ☎ *055-240618. Entrees 10€–18€. MC, V. Lunch, dinner daily. Bus: C1, C2.*

★ **GustaPizza** OLTRARNO *PIZZA* The city's best takeout pizzeria, with very limited seating. Pizzas are in doughy Neapolitan style and come in classic combos only, such as margherita (mozzarella, tomato, basil). *Via Maggio 46R.* ☎ *055-285068. Pizzas 4.50€–8€. MC, V. Lunch, dinner daily. Bus: C3, D, 11, 36, 37.*

★ **Il Santo Bevitore** SAN FREDIANO *MODERN ITALIAN* Left Bank foodies patronize the candle-lit interior of this new-generation eatery. Flavors originate from across Italy. *Via Santo Spirito 66R. www. ilsantobevitore.com.* ☎ *055-211264. Entrees 10€–25€. MC, V. Lunch Mon–Sat, dinner daily. Closed 10 days in Aug. Bus: C3, D, 6, 11, 36, 37.*

★★★ **iO: Osteria Personale** SAN FREDIANO *MODERN TUSCAN* The best Tuscan ingredients cooked creatively on a modular menu with meat, fish, and vegetarian choices. Fresh, friendly, and fashionable. *Borgo San Frediano 167R. www.io-osteriapersonale.it.* ☎ *055-9331341. Entrees 15€–22€. AE, DC, MC, V. Dinner Mon–Sat. Closed Aug & 10 days in Jan. Bus: D.*

★ **Konnubio** SAN LORENZO *MODERN ITALIAN* Affordable dining with a refined feel. Creative Tuscan dishes made with traditional ingredients, plus an inviting range of gluten-free and vegan food. *Via dei Conti 6R. www.konnubio.it.* ☎ *055-2381189. Entrees 13€–27€. MC, V. Lunch, dinner daily. Bus: C1.*

★ **Koto Ramen** SANTA CROCE *JAPANESE* Authentic ramen with rich broth that's homemade. Sides gyoza and kara-age (fried chicken). No reservations. *Via Verdi 42R. www.kotoramen.it.* ☎ *055-2479477. Entrees 9€–16€. MC, V. Dinner Wed–Mon. Bus: C3.*

★★ **La Gratella** SAN LORENZO *TUSCAN* Simple sides like Tuscan beans support the star of the show: bistecca alla fiorentina, a large grilled T-bonelike cut brought to the table over coals. *Via Guelfa 81Rwww.lagratella.it. .* ☎ *055-211292. Entrees 9€–18€. MC, V. Lunch, dinner daily. Bus: C1.*

★ **Le Mossacce** CENTRO STORICO *FLORENTINE* This noisy former workers' trattoria features basics like ribollita (hearty veg soup/stew) and spezzatino (veal stew). *Via del Proconsolo 55R.*

www.trattorialemossacce.it. ☎ 055-294361. Entrees 7€–13€. MC, V. Lunch, dinner Mon–Fri. Closed Aug. Bus: C1, C2.

★ **Lobs** SAN LORENZO SEA-FOOD   This shack-style Mediterranean trattoria serves up some of the city's most reliable fish dishes. Pasta plates like orecchiete con pesce persico (with perch) are a great value. Via Faenza 75. ☎ 055-212478. Entrees 16€–25€. AE, DC, MC, V. Lunch, dinner daily (closed Sun lunch in Aug). Bus: C1.

★★ **Mercato Centrale** SAN LORENZO STREET FOOD   A bustling shrine to modern Italian street food, with pasta, Neapolitan pizza, fresh fish, Chianina beef burgers, and more. Piazza Mercato Centrale. www.mercatocentrale.it. ☎ 055-2399798. Dishes 5€–20€. MC, V. Lunch, dinner daily. Bus: C1.

★ **Nerbone** SAN LORENZO FLO-RENTINE   Visit this 1872 market counter for the bagnato (boiled beef sandwich dipped in meat juices). Mercato Centrale (at Via dell'Ariento, stand #292). ☎ 055-219949. Entrees 4€–8.50€. No credit cards. Lunch Mon–Sat. Closed 3 weeks in Aug. Bus: C1.

★★ **Ora d'Aria** CENTRO STORICO MODERN TUSCAN   Florence's most creative chef, Marco Stabile, has worked in Sonoma and France, but the seasonal flavors in

Mixed antipasti platter.

his design-savvy restaurant are staunchly Tuscan. Via dei Georgofili 11R. www.oradariaristorante.com. ☎ 055-2001699. Entrees 38€–45€. AE, MC, V. Lunch Tues–Sat, dinner Mon–Sat. Bus: C3, D.

★ **Osteria del Caffè Italiano** SANTA CROCE TUSCAN   In a 13th-century palazzo, this lively enoteca-restaurant has some of the city's best Tuscan meat dishes. Via Isola delle Stinche 11R–13R. www. caffeitaliano.it. ☎ 055-289368. Entrees 12€–22€. MC, V. Lunch, dinner daily. Bus: C3.

★★ **Osteria Pastella** SANTA MARIA NOVELLA MODERN TUS-CAN   Sophisticated dining using classic ingredients, such as hand-made tortelloni, and some of the city's best beefsteaks. Via della Scala 17R. www.osteriapastella.it. ☎ 055-2670240. Entrees 16€–24€. MC, V. Lunch, dinner daily. Bus: C2, D.

★ **Quattro Leoni** OLTRARNO TUSCAN   A lively tourist crowd packs this trattoria on a pretty piazza for well-executed Tuscan dishes. Via dei Vellutini 1R. www.4leoni.com. ☎ 055-218562. Entrees 14€–24€. MC, V. Lunch, dinner daily. Bus: C3, D.

★★ **Santarpia** SANT'AMBROGIO PIZZA   Lively modern pizzeria from renowned pizzaiolo Giovanni Santarpia. Look for creative combos like burrata cheese and truffle. Largo Annigoni 9c. www.santarpia.biz. ☎ 055-245829. Pizzas 8.50€–15€. MC, V. Dinner Wed–Mon. Bus: C3.

★★ **Zeb** SAN NICCOLÒ MOD-ERN ITALIAN   Intimate dining right at the deli counter, from the finest ingredients. Via San Miniato 2R. www.zebgastronomia.com. ☎ 055-2342864. Entrees 9€–15€. MC, V. Lunch Thurs–Tues, dinner Thurs–Sat (Apr–Oct also Mon–Tues). Bus: D, 23.

The Best Lodging in Florence

Palacongressi
Palaffari
Stazione Centrale S. Maria Novella
Piazza Adua
Via Guelfa
Via Faenza
Via Nazionale
Via Luigi Alamanni
Via Fiume
Piazza della Stazione
Via Panicale
Piazza del Mercato Centrale
Piazza della Stazione
Piazza dell'Unità Italiana
Via S. Antonino
Cappelle Medicee
Piazza S. Lorenzo
S. Maria Novella
Via de' Panzani
Via del Giglio
San Lorenzo
Via della Scala
Piazza S. Maria Novella
Via dei Cerretani
Piazza S. Giovanni
Via Palazzuolo
Via delle B. Donne
Via de' Pecori
Ognissanti
Piazza d'Ognissanti
Lungarno Amerigo Vespucci
Borgo Ognissanti
Via de' Fossi
Via del Moro
Via della Vigna Nuova
V. d. Campidoglio
CENTRO
Piazza della Repubblica
Via Roma
Ponte A. Vespucci
Lungarno
Piazza di Cestello
Soderini
Piazza Goldoni
V. d. Parione
Via d. Strozzi
Via de' Tornabuoni
Palazzo Strozzi
Orsan-michele
V. Calimala
Borgo San Frediano
Ponte alla Carraia
Palazzo Corsini
Santa Trinita
Lung. Corsini
Piazza Trinita
Via Porta Rossa
Pal. Davanzati
SAN FREDIANO
Arno
Lungarno Guicciardini
Lungarno Acciaiuoli
Borgo S. Apostoli
Via dell'Orto
Piazza del Carmine
Via Santo Spirito
SANTO SPIRITO
Ponte Santa Trinita
Lungarno Acciaiuoli
Loggia dei Lanzi
Santa Maria del Carmine
Via dell'Ardiglione
Via Sant'Agostino
Borgo
S. Jacopo
Ponte Vecchio
Via della Chiesa
Santo Spirito
V. Vellutini
Piazza S. Felicita
Piazza S. Maria Soprarno
Via del Campuccio
Via de' Serragli
Piazza S. Spirito
OLTRARNO
Via Guicciardini
Via Maggio
Via Mazzetta
Borgo Tegolaio
Piazza dei Pitti
Giardino Torrigiani
Via Romana
Palazzo Pitti
Forte di Belvedere
Giardino di Boboli (Boboli Garden)
Costa di S. Giorgio

Hotel Best Bets

A suite at the Four Seasons.

Best for Families
★★ Residence Hilda $$$$ Via dei Servi 40 (p 59)

Best Budget-Friendly Boutique Hotel
★★ Garibaldi Blu $$ Piazza Santa Maria Novella 21 (p 57)

Most Luxurious Address
★★★ Four Seasons Florence $$$$$ Borgo Pinti 99 (p 57)

Best Central Cheap Sleep
★ Locanda Orchidea $ Borgo degli Albizi 11 (p 58)

Best for a Quiet Night
★★ Montebello Splendid $$$$–$$$$$ Via Garibaldi 14 (p 58); and ★ Orto dei Medici $$–$$$ Via San Gallo 30 (p 59)

Best Flashpacking Hostel
★ Plus Florence $ Via Santa Caterina d'Alessandria 15 (p 59)

Best for Bohemian Chic
★★ Antica Dimora Johlea $$–$$$ Via San Gallo 80 (p 57)

Best Piazza Location
★★ Loggiato dei Serviti $$–$$$ Piazza Santissima Annunziata 3 (p 58)

Best for Affordable Contemporary Design
★★ Riva Lofts $$$ Via Bandinelli 98 (p 59)

Most Stylish Rooms
★★★ J. K. Place $$$$$ Piazza Santa Maria Novella 7 (p 58)

Best B&B in the Center
★★★ La Dimora degli Angeli $$ Via Brunelleschi 4 (p 58); and ★★ Alloro $$ Via del Giglio 8 (p 57)

Best for Great Service
★★ Davanzati $$$ Via Porta Rossa 5 (p 57); and ★★ Palazzo Tolomei $$$ Via de' Ginori 19 (p 59)

Most Elegant Palazzo Accommodations at a Reasonable Price
★★ Palazzo Galletti $$ Via Sant'Egidio 12 (p 59)

Florence Hotels A to Z

★ **Alloro** SAN LORENZO   Modern B&B rooms with high ceilings, color-washed walls, and air-conditioning, all overlooking the inner courtyard of a Renaissance palace. Say hi to the friendly resident ghost. *Via del Giglio 8. www. allorobb.it.* ☎ *055-211685. 5 units. Doubles 85€–175€ w/breakfast. MC, V. Bus: C1.*

★★ **Antica Dimora Johlea** SAN MARCO   A regal Florentine *dimora* whose cozy, smallish rooms are tricked out in decor that draws inspiration from East and West. The best roof terrace in the city in this price bracket is a knockout extra. *Via San Gallo 80. www.antichedimore fiorentine.it.* ☎ *055-4633292. 6 units. Doubles 90€–220€ w/breakfast. No credit cards. Bus: C1, 1, 17, 25.*

★ **Antica Dimora Firenze** SAN MARCO   The sister place to Johlea (see above) has the same boho styling, with herringbone tiled floors, color-washed walls, and canopy beds, but no roof terrace. *Via San Gallo 72. www.antichedimore fiorentine.it.* ☎ *055-4627296. 6 units.*

The lounge at J.K. Place.

Doubles 70€–150€ w/breakfast. No credit cards. Bus: C1, 1, 17, 25.

★ **Casci** SAN LORENZO   Gioachino Rossini (*Barber of Seville*) once lived in this old hostelry near the Duomo. Renovations have upgraded it without destroying the vintage charm. Family suites sleep four or five. *Via Cavour 13. www. hotelcasci.com.* ☎ *055-211686. 25 units. Doubles 75€–160€ w/breakfast. Closed 2 weeks in Dec. AE, DC, MC, V. Bus: C1.*

★★ **Davanzati** CENTRO STORICO   From iPads in each of the tasteful rooms to complimentary drinks with the family proprietors each evening, they've thought of it all at this most welcoming of *palazzo* hotels. *Via Porta Rossa 5 (at Piazza Davanzati). www.hotel davanzati.it.* ☎ *055-286666. 27 units. Doubles 122€–211€ w/breakfast. AE, DC, MC, V. Bus: C2.*

★★★ **Four Seasons Florence** NORTH OF CENTER   Should the Medici miraculously return to the city, they would surely lodge here. The best address in Florence comes with frescoes, gardens, a spa, luxurious appointments—and a price tag to match. *Borgo Pinti 99. www.fourseasons.com/florence.* ☎ *055-26261. 116 units. Doubles 500€–920€. AE, DC, MC, V. Bus: 8.*

★ **Gallery Hotel Art** CENTRO STORICO   Florence's original boutique hotel, opened by the Ferragamo fashion family, remains a bastion of designer comfort. *Vicolo dell'Oro 5. www.lungarnocollection. com.* ☎ *055-27263. 74 units. Doubles 190€–545€. AE, DC, MC, V. Bus: C3, D.*

★★ **Garibaldi Blu** SANTA MARIA NOVELLA   The glitterati shell out small fortunes for a room on

Florence's trendiest piazza. At Garibaldi Blu, you can secure one at a fraction of the price without sacrificing (much) style. *Piazza Santa Maria Novella 21. www.hotelgaribaldi blu.com.* ☎ *055-277300. 21 units. Doubles 130€–350€ w/breakfast. MC, V. Bus: C2, 6, 11.*

★★ Il Guelfo Bianco SAN
MARCO Each room in this sympathetically converted 16th-century *palazzo* is different, but the friendly welcome is universal. Deluxe units have a separate seating area. *Via Cavour 29. www.ilguelfobianco.it.* ☎ *055-288330. 40 units. Doubles 99€–280€ w/breakfast. AE, DC, MC, V. Bus: C1, 14, 23.*

★★★ J. K. Place SANTA MARIA
NOVELLA This architectural gem, blending contemporary and Liberty styles, has elegant rooms with four-poster beds and fireplaces, a glass-covered courtyard, a rooftop terrace, and a splendid library. *Piazza Santa Maria Novella 7. www. jkplace.com.* ☎ *055-2645181. 20 units. Doubles 340€–550€ w/breakfast. AE, MC, V. Bus: C2, 6, 11.*

★ La Casa di Morfeo
SANT'AMBROGIO Midsize rooms with modern gadgetry are painted in bright contemporary colors, each scheme corresponding to a flower after which the room is named. Nightlife is right on the doorstep. *Via Ghibellina 51. www.lacasa dimorfeo.it.* ☎ *055-241193. 9 units. Doubles 75€–240€. MC, V. Bus: C2, C3.*

★★★ La Dimora degli Angeli
CENTRO STORICO A blend of contemporary and 19th-century styles in midsize rooms creates a romantic atmosphere at this B&B wedged between the Duomo and Florence's upscale shopping district. *Via Brunelleschi 4. www.dimore deicherubini.it.* ☎ *055-288478. 12 units. Doubles 76€—198€. Breakfast 12€. MC, V. Bus: C2.*

★ Locanda Orchidea SANTA
CROCE If you need to flop on a tight budget but don't want to compromise on location, there's nowhere cleaner and friendlier at the price. *Borgo degli Albizi 11. www.locandaorchidea.it.* ☎ *055-2001410. 7 units. Doubles 45€–112€ w/breakfast. MC, V. Bus: C1, C2.*

★★ Loggiato dei Serviti SAN
MARCO A monastery in 1527, this comfortably elegant hotel has beamed or vaulted ceilings and terracotta floors on an iconic Brunelleschi square. *Piazza SS. Annunziata 3. www.loggiatodei servitihotel.it.* ☎ *055-289592. 37 units. Doubles 120€–330€ w/breakfast. AE, DC, MC, V. Bus: C1, 6, 19, 31, 32.*

★★ Montebello Splendid
WEST OF CENTER A citadel of refinement and a 10-minute walk outside the center, this elegant hideaway offers the most realistically priced luxury rooms in the city. *Via Garibaldi 14. www.montebello splendid.com.* ☎ *055-27471. 60 units. Doubles 199€–550€. AE, DC, MC, V. Bus: C2, C3.*

★★ Morandi alla Crocetta
SAN MARCO In a 16th-century convent, this quaint *pensione* evokes the era when Grand Tourists sought private homelike lodgings

Loggiato dei Serviti.

The Four Seasons Hotel.

with family heirlooms. *Via Laura 50.*www.hotelmorandi.it. ☎ 055-2344747. 12 units. Doubles 90€–177€ w/breakfast. AE, DC, MC, V. Bus: 6, 19, 31, 32.

★ **Orto dei Medici** SAN MARCO   A tranquil *palazzo* with full hotel amenities. Midsize deluxe units have contemporary decor and terraces overlooking a peaceful courtyard garden. *Via San Gallo 30.* www.ortodeimedici.it. ☎ 055-483427. 42 units. Doubles 90€–190€ w/breakfast. AE, DC, MC, V. Bus: 1, 6, 11, 14, 17, 23.

★★ **Palazzo Galletti** SANTA CROCE   Rooms at this converted 18th-century *palazzo* are large (for Florence), and come with high ceilings and grandeur as standard. Upgrade to a suite for restored frescoes, too. *Via Sant'Egidio 12.* www.palazzogalletti.it. ☎ 055-3905750. 11 units. Doubles 100€–170€ w/breakfast. MC, V. Bus: C1, C2.

★★★ **Palazzo Tolomei** SAN LORENZO   Renaissance palace that once hosted Raphael, with large rooms, terracotta floors, and modern furnishings that chime perfectly with baroque decor from the 1600s. *Via de' Ginori 19.*www.palazzo tolomei.it. ☎ 055-292887. 8 units. Doubles 215€–395€ w/breakfast. AE, MC, V. Bus: C1.

★ **Plus Florence** NORTH OF CENTER   Hotel amenities, private rooms sleeping up to three, a swimming pool, Turkish bath, and free Wi-Fi: You'd never think this was a hostel, until you saw the building (ugly) and the price (incredible value). *Via Santa Caterina d'Alessandria 15.* www.plushotels.com/plusflorence. ☎ 055-6286347. 240 units. Doubles 35€–125€. MC, V. Bus: 20.

★★ **Residence Hilda** CENTRO STORICO   These bright, modern apartments with hotel amenities come fully equipped and have a great location between the Duomo and Santissima Annunziata. No minimum stay. *Via dei Servi 40.* www.residencehilda.com. ☎ 055-288021. 12 units. Apartments 150€–450€. AE, MC, V. Bus: C1.

★ **Residence La Contessina** SAN LORENZO   Simple, characterful mini apartments sleeping up to 5, with hotel services and kitchenettes. Superb buffet breakfast. *Via Faenza 71.* www.lacontessina.it. ☎ 055-2670275. 20 units. Doubles 80€–220€ w/breakfast. MC, V. Bus: C1.

★★ **Riva Lofts** WEST OF CENTER   Built into a former stone-built artisan workshop, Riva has a taupe-and-white scheme with laminate flooring, marble bathrooms with rainfall showers, and clever integration of natural materials. *Via Bandinelli 98.* ☎ 055-7130272. www. rivalofts.com. 10 units. Doubles 165€–255€ w/breakfast. MC, V. Bus: 6 / Tram: T1.

★ **Tourist House Ghiberti** CENTRO STORICO   Large rooms with clean lines but a traditional Florentine flavor characterize this modern B&B near the Duomo. There's a shared guest Jacuzzi for tired feet and memory-foam mattresses in each room. *Via Bufalini 1.* www.tourist houseghiberti.com. ☎ 055-284858. 6 units. Doubles 64€–179€ w/breakfast. AE, MC, V. Bus: C1, 14, 23.

60

The Best Shopping in Florence

Alice Atelier 1
Angela Caputi 12
Bojola 5
Coin 16
Emilio Pucci 9
Flor 23
Gucci 8
Il Papiro 18
Il Tamarino 6
La Rinascente 15
Madova 14
Mercato Centrale 2
Mercato di San Lorenzo 3
Mercato di Sant'Ambrogio 21
Mrs Macis 19
Officina Profumo-Farmaceutica di Santa Maria Novella 4
Paperback Exchange 17
Parione 10
Pineider 7
Roberta Firenze 13
Salvatore Ferragamo 11
Scuola del Cuoio 22
Vestri 20

Via S. Zanobi
Via Santa Reparata
Via XXVII Aprile
Via San Gallo
Via Cavour

Giardino dei Semplici

Via G. Capponi
Via degli Artisti
Via G. Matteotti

† San Marco
Piazza San Marco

Giardino della Gherardesca

Piazza Donatello

Galleria dell'Accademia

† Santissima Annunziata

Via
Guelfa
Piazza della Ss. Annunziata

Museo Archeologico

Via Giuseppe
Via della Colonna
Giusti

Borgo
Pinti

(18)

Via de' Ginori
Ricasoli

Via dei Servi

H
Ospedale d. Innocenti

Via della Laura

(i) Palazzo Medici-Riccardi

Via de' Martelli

Piazza Brunelleschi

Via degli Alfani

Santa Maria Maddalena dei Pazzi †

Piazza d'Azeglio

Via dei Pucci
Palazzo Pucci

Ospedale S. Maria Nuova

Via della Pergola

Via della Colonna

Via L. C. Farini

Via G. Carducci

Duomo
Campanile

H
Piazza S. M. Nuova

Teatro d. Pergola

Via dei Pilastri

Sinagoga (Museo Ebraico)

(i) Piazza di Duomo

Via del Proconsolo

Via S. Egidio

Borgo Pinti

Via della Mattonaia

V. d. Studio

(17) DUOMO
Via del Corso

Via dell'Oriuolo

(19) Via Fiesolana
Piazza S. Ambrogio

Via di Mezzo

V. S. Elisabetta

(16)

Borgo degli Albizi

Via Pietrapiana

Via d. Calzaiuoli

Casa di Dante

Via
Via F. Poalieri

(21) Piazza L. Ghiberti

Via D. Alighieri

Via de' Pandolfini

(20)

Via G. Verdi

Via M. Buonarroti

V.d. Cimatori
Bargello

Via Ghibellina

Via dell' Agnolo

† Badia
V. d. Vigna Vecchia

Casa di Buonarroti

Via Ghibellina

Piazza della Signoria
SIGNORIA

Teatro Verdi

Via de' Pepi

Borgo Allegri

SANTA CROCE

Via Pietro Thouar

Palazzo Vecchio

Borgo de' Greci

Piazza S. Croce

Via di San Giuseppe

Via dei Neri

Via de' Benci

† Santa Croce

Via de' Malcontenti

Uffizi

Piazza Mentana

(23)

Via Magliabechi

(22) Biblioteca Nazionale

Piazza Piave

Lung. Gen. Diaz

Corso dei Tintori

Piazza dei Cavalleggeri

Via Tripoli

Lungarno della Zecca Vecchia

Lungarno Torrigiani

Lungarno delle Grazie

Ponte alle Grazie

Arno

Via de' Bardi

Lungarno Serristori

Via dei Renai

SAN NICCOLÒ

Via di S. Niccolò

Via di S. Niccolò

Piazza G. Poggi

Lungarno B. Cellini

Via dei Bastioni

Via di Belvedere

Viale G. Poggi

RICORBOLI

Via del Monte alle Croc.

Piazzale Michelangelo

Viale Michelangiolo

(i) Tourist Information

0 ————— 1/8 mi
0 ————— 200 km

Shopping Best Bets

Handmade stationery makes a great Florentine gift.

Best for **Accessories & Jewelry**
★★ Angela Caputi, Via Santo Spirito 58R (p 63)

Best for **Florentine High Fashion**
★★★ Gucci, Via de' Tornabuoni 73R (p 64)

Best for **Leather Goods**
★★ Scuola del Cuoio, Piazza Santa Croce 16 (p 65)

Best **Food Market**
★★ Mercato Centrale, Piazza del Mercato Centrale (p 65)

Best for **Souvenir Prints**
★★ Il Tamarino, Via del Moro 46R (p 65)

Best for **Paper Goods**
★★ Pineider, Piazza della Signoria (p 65)

Best **Beauty Products**
★★★ Officina Profumo-Farmaceutica di Santa Maria Novella, Via della Scala 16 (p 63)

Best **Shoes for Men and Women**
★★ Salvatore Ferragamo, Via de' Tornabuoni 14R (p 65)

Best for **Souvenir Shopping**
★ Mercato di San Lorenzo, Via dell'Ariento/Via Rosina (p 65)

Best **Local Craftsmanship**
★★ Alice Atelier, Via Faenza 72R (p 64)

VAT Refund

Visitors from non-European Union countries who spend 155€ or more at any one shop are entitled to a value-added tax (VAT) refund worth 4% to 22% of the total. To get a refund, pick up a tax-free form from the retailer. Present your unused purchases and their receipt for inspection at the Customs Office (Dogana) at your point of departure. An inspector will stamp your form, enabling you to pick up a refund (minus commission) from a refunds agent on the spot.

Florence Shopping A to Z

Florence is known for its showrooms of famous designers and for its artisan workshops, turning out jewelry and leather of the highest quality. The most fashionable shops—and the most expensive—are clustered along now pedestrianized **Via de' Tornabuoni.** There you'll find big international names like **Prada** (51R; ☎ 055-283439), **Giorgio Armani** (48R; ☎ 055-219041), **Celine** (26R; ☎ 055-2645521), **MaxMara** (68–70R; ☎ 055-214133), and **Roberto Cavalli** (83R; ☎ 055-2396226). **Via della Vigna Nuova** and **Via degli Strozzi** also pack a high style quotient.

Accessories

★★ Angela Caputi

OLTRARNO   High-concept acrylic jewelry and accessories, especially bracelets and necklaces. Prices 30€ to 100€ and up. *Via Santo Spirito 58R. www.angelacaputi.com.* ☎ 055-212972. MC, V. Bus: C3, D, 11, 36, 37.

★ Madova OLTRARNO   Almost

a century in business selling handmade leather gloves lined with cashmere, silk, or wool. *Via Guicciardini 1R. www.madova.com.* ☎ 055-2396526. MC, V. Bus: C3, D.

Beauty Products

★★ Flor SANTA CROCE   Hand-

crafted fragrances, soaps, and creams sold from the elegant surrounds of a former *deposito. Borgo Santa Croce 6. www.florenceparfum. com.* ☎ 055-2343471. MC, V. Bus: C1, C3, 23.

★★★ Officina Profumo-Farmaceutica di Santa Maria Novella CENTRO

STORICO   Herbal secrets used by the Medici are still sold here in a wonderfully antique atmosphere— potpourris, perfumes, scented soaps, and more. *Via della Scala 16. www.smnovella.it.* ☎ 055-216276. AE, MC, V. Bus: C2.

Books

★ Paperback Exchange CEN-

TRO STORICO   New and used

Perfume in Officina Profumo-Farmaceutica di Santa Maria Novella.

titles, all in English. *Via delle Oche 4R. www.papex.it.* ☎ *055-293460. AE, MC, V. Bus: C1.*

Chocolate

★ **Vestri** SANTA CROCE   There's no mistaking the aroma…cocoa, made into all shapes and sizes, including gelato, granita, and cold drinking chocolate, at this artisan chocolatier. *Borgo degli Albizi 11R. www.vestri.it/en.* ☎ *055-2340374. MC, V. Bus: C1, C2.*

Crafts

★★ **Alice Atelier** SAN LORENZO   Handmade theatrical masks in Venetian *Carnevale* and *Commedia dell'arte* styles. *Via Faenza 72R. www.alicemasks.com.* ☎ *055-287370. AE, MC, V. Bus: C1.*

Department Stores

★ **Coin** CENTRO STORICO   This department store in a 16th-century *palazzo* sells everything from affordable clothing for men, women, and children to Italian-designed kitchenware to cosmetics. *Via dei Calzaiuoli 56R.* ☎ *055-280531. www.coin.it. AE, DC, MC, V. Bus: C2.*

La Rinascente CENTRO STORICO   This six-story emporium sells top Italian designerwear at affordable prices. *Piazza della Repubblica 1. www.rinascente.it.* ☎ *055-219113. AE, DC, MC, V. Bus: C2.*

Fashion

★★ **Emilio Pucci** CENTRO STORICO   Marilyn Monroe left a request to be buried in her favorite Pucci dress, and their bright, busy patterns are in fashion again. *Via de' Tornabuoni 20-22R. www.pucci.com.* ☎ *055-2658082. AE, DC, MC, V. Bus: C3, D.*

Florence's flagship department stores, Coin and La Rinascente, are great places to shop for housewares.

★★ **Mrs Macis** SANTA CROCE   Bold-print dresses and womenswear, plus bags, breezy accessories, and more in a tiny, trendy boutique. *Borgo Pinti 38R.* ☎ *055-2476700. DC, MC, V. Bus: C1, C2.*

★★★ **Gucci** CENTRO STORICO   Unforgettable luxury leather goods and high fashion in the city Gucci calls home. *Via de' Tornabuoni 73R. www.gucci.com.* ☎ *055-264011. AE, DC, MC, V. Bus: C3, D.*

Leather

★ **Roberta Firenze** OLTRARNO   Florentine leather bags and purses at sensible prices. Also accessories for men: belts, ties, wallets. *Borgo San Jacopo 74R. www.robertafirenze.com.* ☎ *055-284017. AE, MC, V. Bus: C3.*

★ **Bojola** CENTRO STORICO   A leading retailer of traditional Florentine leather goods. The store pioneered the 1960s trend of combining leather and cotton fabric. *Via dei Rondinelli 25R.* ☎ *055-211155. www.bojola.it. AE, DC, MC, V. Bus: C2, 22.*

★★ Scuola del Cuoio SANTA CROCE The sales outlet for genuine handcrafted leather goods made at Florence's world-famous leather school. *Piazza Santa Croce 16 (entrance behind church at Via San Giuseppe 5R). www.scuoladel cuoio.com.* ☎ *055-244534. AE, DC, MC, V. Bus: C3.*

Markets

★★ Mercato Centrale SAN LORENZO Wine, olive oil, porcini mushrooms, and pecorino cheese—it's all on sale on two floors of Europe's largest covered food hall. *Piazza del Mercato Centrale. No phone. Bus: C1.*

★ Mercato di San Lorenzo SAN LORENZO A fun place to pick up T-shirts, marbleized paper, or a souvenir. Leather is another popular purchase—be sure to assess the workmanship, and haggle shamelessly. *Via dell'Ariento/Via Rosina. No phone. Bus: C1.*

★ Mercato di Sant'Ambrogio SANT'AMBROGIO Florentines' local market, 6 mornings a week. Fruit, vegetables, costume jewelry, preserves, and end-of-line clothing out on the piazza. Meat, olive oil, **Da Rocco** (p. 51), and a cafe inside the market building. *Piazza Ghiberti. No phone. Bus: C2, C3.*

Produce at the Mercato Centrale.

Paper & Stationery

★ Il Papiro CENTRO STORICO Sumptuous stationery, photo frames, and more at this boutique chain. *Via Cavour 49R. www.ilpapiro firenze.eu.* ☎ *055-215262. AE, MC, V. Bus: C1.*

★★ Parione CENTRO STORICO Venerable stationers with exquisite writing paper and journals in Florence's traditional "busy" style. Also small theatrical dioramas and souvenir marionettes. *Via dello Studio 11R. www.parione.it.* ☎ *055-215684. AE, DC, MC, V. Bus: C1, C2.*

★ Pineider CENTRO STORICO Since 1774 clients from Napoleon to Liz Taylor have ordered personal stationery, greeting cards, and handcrafted diaries here. *Piazza de' Rucellai 4–7R. www. pineider.com.* ☎ *055-284656. AE, DC, MC, V. Bus: 6, 11.*

Prints

★ Il Tamarino CENTRO STORICO Limited-edition prints made and colored by hand from unique copper etchings. Prices start around 15€. *Via del Moro 46R. www. iltamarino.com.* ☎ *055-282457. MC, V. Bus: 6, 11.*

Shoes

★★ Salvatore Ferragamo CENTRO STORICO Shoes (and bags) are big news here, with some world-class fashionwear and accessories for men and women. *Via de' Tornabuoni 4R. www.salvatore ferragamo.it.* ☎ *055-292123. AE, DC, MC, V. Bus: C3, D.*

The Best Nightlife & A&E in Florence

Archea **8**
Bitter Bar **16**
Dolce Vita **7**
Gilli **3**
Il Santino **6**
Jazz Club **18**
Le Volpi e L'Uva **12**
Mostodolce **2**
Moyo **14**
O'Cafe **13**
Opera di Firenze **1**
Pitti Gola e Cantina **11**
Procacci **4**
St. Mark's
  English Church **10**
Tabasco **5**
Teatro della Pergola **17**
Teatro Verdi **15**
Volume **9**

(i) Tourist Information

0 ___ 1/8 mi
0 ___ 200 km

Nightlife/A&E Best Bets

Sweet treats in Gilli Café Firenze.

Best Wine Bar
★★ Le Volpi e l'Uva, Piazza de' Rossi 1 (p 69)

Best Cafe
★★ Procacci, Via de' Tornabuoni 64R (p 70)

Best Aperitivo Hour in the Center
★ O'Cafe, Via dei Bardi 23R (p 69)

Best Gay Club
★ Tabasco, Piazza Santa Cecilia 3 (p 70)

Best for Jazz & Blues
★ Jazz Club, Via Nuova de' Caccini 3 (p 70)

Best Theater
★ Teatro della Pergola, Via della Pergola 12–32 (p 70)

Best Opera & Ballet
★★ Opera di Firenze, Viale Fratelli Rosselli 7R (p 70)

Best Bar for Twentysomething Hipsters
★ Volume, Piazza Santo Spirito 5R (p 69)

Bars & Wine Bars

★ **Archea** OLTRARNO Belgian-style pub and microbrewery with 10 craft beers on tap. Happy hour is 6pm to 8pm, when a couple of their own beers are down to 3€ a pint. *Via de' Serragli 44R.* ☎ 347-7110239. Bus: C3, D, 11, 36, 37.

★★ **Bitter Bar** SANT'AMBROGIO Decor somewhere between a speakeasy and a gentleman's club, with cozy low-watt lighting, Prohibition and creative modern cocktails, and impeccable mixology. *Via di Mezzo 28R. www.bitterbarfirenze.it.* ☎ 340-5499258. Bus: C2, C3.

★★ **Il Santino** SAN FREDIANO Tiny wine bar that stocks niche labels from across Italy and serves exquisite "Florentine tapas" plates to munch while you sip. *Via Santo Spirito 60R.* ☎ 055-2302820. Bus:C3, D, 11, 36, 37.

★★ **Le Volpi e L'Uva** OLTRARNO More than 30 Italian vintages by the glass draw them in to this relaxed wine bar in a tiny piazza behind Santa Felicità church. *Piazza de' Rossi 1. www.levolpieluva. com.* ☎ 055-2398132. Bus: C3, D.

Mostodolce SAN LORENZO A young crowd enjoys artisan beer brewed in nearby Prato, and sports (usually soccer) on the screens. *Via Nazionale 114R.* ☎ 055-2302928. Bus: C1.

★ **Moyo** SANTA CROCE One of the busiest 6:30pm *aperitivo* spots with the expat crowd. Cocktails and pumping tunes flow later. *Via de' Benci 23R. www.moyo.it.* ☎ 055-2479738. Bus: C1, C3, 23.

★ **O'Cafe** OLTRARNO Elegant and minimalist with a refined *aperitivo* buffet (10€–14€ with drink), and jazz 3 nights a week. *Via de' Bardi 56R. www.goldenviewopenbar.com.* ☎ 055-214502. Bus: C3, D.

★ **Pitti Gola e Cantina** OLTRARNO This refined little wine bar opposite the Pitti Palace has a carefully selected list of wines by the glass. *Piazza de' Pitti 16. www.pittigolaecantina.com.* ☎ 055-212704. Bus: C3, D.

★ **Volume** OLTRARNO An artsy cafe-bookshop by day, with cocktails and live acoustic music after dark. *Piazza Santo Spirito 5R. www. volumefirenze.com.* ☎ 055-2381460. Bus: C3, D, 11, 36, 37.

Teatro dell'Opera di Firenze.

Club & Concert Tips

Italian clubs are cliquey—single travelers hoping to find dance partners may be disappointed. If you're clubbing at the cutting edge, pick up a copy of the latest *Firenze Spettacolo* at newsstands (2€) or check the website for **Zero** (http://zero.eu/firenze).

Florence is wanting for the grand old opera houses of Milan, Naples and Venice, but the 2014 opening of the **Opera di Firenze** (see below) may just lift the city into Italy's operatic big leagues. **St. Mark's English Church** (www.concertoclassico.info; ☎ 340-8119192), in Oltrarno, also stages regular opera and classical music concerts. Tickets for cultural events are available through **Boxol** (www.boxol.it; ☎ 055-210804).

Cafes

Gilli CENTRO STORICO Dating from 1733, this is Florence's oldest, most elegant cafe, with prices to match. *Piazza della Repubblica 39R. www.gilli.it.* ☎ 055-213896. Bus: C2.

★★ **Procacci** CENTRO STORICO This darling cafe/bar's specialty is *panini tartufati*, rolls filled with truffle paste. *Via de' Tornabuoni 64R. www. procacci1885.it.* ☎ 055-211656. Bus: C3, D.

Clubs & DJ Bars

★ **Dolce Vita** SAN FREDIANO Going strong after 3 decades and the haunt of fashionable 30-somethings. *Piazza del Carmine. www.dolcevita florence.com.* ☎ 055-284595.Bus: D, 6.

Gay Clubs

Tabasco CENTRO STORICO The oldest gay dance club in Italy lives up to its fiery name. *Piazza Santa Cecilia 3. www.tabascogay.it.* ☎ 055-213000. Bus: C1, C2.

Jazz

★ **Jazz Club** SANTA CROCE The best live jazz and blues in town, in an atmospheric basement. *Via Nuova de' Caccini 3. www.face book.com/jazzclubfirenze.it.* ☎ 055-5271815. Membership 6€. Bus: C1, 6, 14, 19, 23, 31, 32.

Theater

★ **Teatro della Pergola** SANTA CROCE Tuscany's major classic theater, but you'd better know Italian. *Via della Pergola 12–32. www.teatro dellapergola.com.* ☎ 055-22641. Tickets 15€–30€. Bus: C1, 14, 23.

Opera & Ballet

★★ **Opera di Firenze** CASCINE Vast arts complex that seats up to 1,800 in modernist surrounds. *Viale Fratelli Rosselli 7R. www.operadi firenze.it.* ☎ 055-277-9350. Tickets 10€–85€. Tram: T1.

★ **Teatro Verdi** SANTA CROCE Expect everything from Tchaikovsky to *Rocky Horror Show* at the home of the Orchestra della Toscana. *Via Ghibellina 99. www.teatroverdionline. it.* ☎ 055-212320. Tickets 17€–50€. Bus: C1, C3. ●

Florence's bars in the evening.

The Best of Tuscany in Three Days

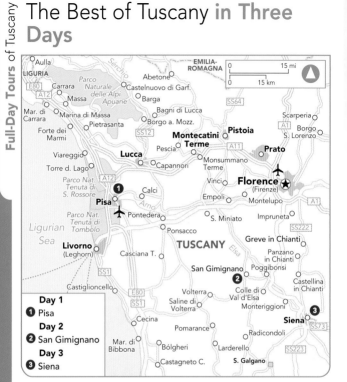

Day 1
❶ Pisa
Day 2
❷ San Gimignano
Day 3
❸ Siena

If you have only 3 days to see Tuscany beyond Florence, focus on Pisa, with its gravity-defying tower; San Gimignano, known for its medieval "skyscrapers"; and Siena, a living repository of Gothic art and architecture. From Florence, you'll shoot 81km (50 miles) west to Pisa, for day 1; 92km (57 miles) southeast to San Gimignano for day 2; and 40km (24 miles) southeast again to Siena. START: **Florence. Trip length: 283km (174 mile) loop.**

Travel Tip

For detailed information on sights and recommended hotels and restaurants in this chapter, see the individual sections on Arezzo, Cortona, Lucca, Montepulciano, Pienza,

Pisa, San Gimignano, Siena, and Volterra in Chapter 6, "Charming Tuscan Towns & Villages." For details of tourist offices in all of Tuscany's major destinations, see p 190.

Previous page: The Leaning Tower of Pisa.

Pisa's Cathedral and Battistero on Campo dei Miracoli.

Pisa is just over an hour west of Florence by car. Follow signs for the four-lane FI–PI–LI *raccordo.*

❶ ★★★ **Pisa.** Pisa is one of the easiest Tuscan cities to explore, both because it's flat and because nearly all the major attractions center on Piazza del Duomo (also known as the Campo dei Miracoli—"Field of Miracles"). Your half-hour in and at the **Leaning Tower,** or Torre Pendente, is a memorable, though expensive, experience. You certainly shouldn't miss the **Duomo** (cathedral) or **Battistero** (baptistery), and the **Camposanto** (burial ground) provides a more contemplative contrast. The **Museo dell'Opera del Duomo** (cathedral museum) and **Museo Nazionale di San Matteo** are must-sees for anyone with a keen interest in painting and sculpture.

For dining and nightlife, head into the heart of the "real" Pisa, closer to the river, where the city's produce market still thrives. After a night of Pisan fare at a local trattoria, bed down and head out the following morning to San Gimignano.

For detailed coverage of sights, hotels, restaurants, shops & nightlife in Pisa, see p 150 of Chapter 6.

Travel Tip

The most economical way to cover the Campo dei Miracoli is with an Opera Pisana pass, available from ticket offices on the piazza. For 10€, you'll get into everything except the Tower. Alternatively, it's 6€ for any two monuments.

From Pisa, head east along the FI–PI–LI *raccordo* until the S429 turn-off at Ponte a Elsa. Take the S429 southeast as far as Certaldo; San Gimignano is signposted on a scenic road south from here. Journey time is approximately 1½ hr.

❷ ★★ **San Gimignano.** Like Pisa, San Gimignano makes for a doable day trip because its major attractions are tightly packed. Once you've parked and dropped off

San Gimignano.

Siena's Piazza del Campo.

your bags at the hotel, you can easily get around the town, with its ancient streets and medieval towers, in a day. The *centro storico* centers round the magnificent twin squares of Piazza del Duomo and Piazza della Cisterna.

Undoubtedly, the art highlight is the frescoed interior of the **Collegiata,** no longer a proper "cathedral" because it doesn't have a bishop's seat. **Sant'Agostino** and the **Museo Civico,** as well as the ascent of the **Torre Grossa,** are all within a few minutes' walk. You should have time left for a real-life

horror show at the **Museo della Tortura.** Teens will love it, although little ones may prefer the enchanting reproduction that is **San Gimignano 1300.**

The first essential culinary pause is for an unforgettable ice cream at **Gelateria "di Piazza."** If you're planning a dose of slow-food heaven at **Dorandó,** be sure to book ahead. After dinner, stroll the historic core: With the day-trippers gone, and just you left in town, it's a place of unparalleled magic.

For detailed coverage of sights, hotels, restaurants, shops & nightlife in San Gimignano, see p 160 in Chapter 6.

Siena is 40km (24 miles) southeast of San Gimignano. Head east on the S324 to meet the Firenze–Siena *raccordo* at Poggibonsi, then south to Siena. Enter town via the "Siena Ovest" exit. You should be out of your car and on the way to the Campo within 45 min.

❸ ★★★ Siena. Seeing Siena in a day will be the biggest challenge of your trip. Begin at the functional and spiritual heart of town, scallop-shaped **Piazza del Campo.** The Lorenzetti and Martini frescoes at the **Museo Civico** (inside the

Santa Maria della Scala church in Siena.

The richly embellished facade of Siena's Duomo.

Palazzo Pubblico) should be your first stop. Serious Sienese art fans should then detour to the **Pinacoteca Nazionale,** Siena's picture gallery, for a more in-depth crash course in Sienese art. After lunch, head for the cathedral complex centered round **Piazza del Duomo.** You can easily spend 3 hours seeing the **Duomo,** the **Museo dell'Opera Metropolitana** (home of Duccio's Maestà), and the **Battistero.** The former hospital of **Santa Maria della Scala,** opposite the Duomo, is a great spot to end your day. (If you have little ones in tow, it's here you'll also find **Bambimus,** the children's art museum.)

If time remains, squeeze in some shopping and cafe time. Siena is renowned for both craftsmanship and bakery products.

With just 1 night in Siena, sleep close to the center to maximize your time. Depending on your budget, the **Antica Residenza Cicogna** or nearby **Campo Regio Relais** could hardly be more central. Take your pick between dinner at **Da Divo** (refined Sienese cuisine) or **L'Osteria** (our favorite neighborhood eatery).

For detailed coverage of sights, hotels, restaurants, shops & nightlife in Siena, see p 166 of Chapter 6.

To return to Florence, where you began this whirlwind tour, take the Firenze–Siena *raccordo* north. Total distance is 70km (43 miles). Journey time is around an hour, depending on Florence traffic.

The Best of Tuscany **in One** Week

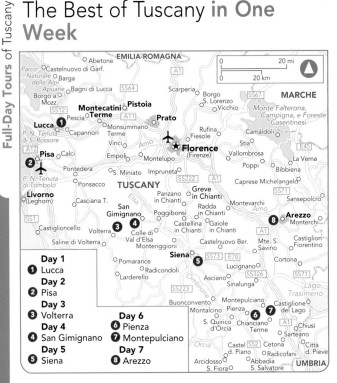

Day 1
❶ Lucca
Day 2
❷ Pisa
Day 3
❸ Volterra
Day 4
❹ San Gimignano
Day 5
❺ Siena

Day 6
❻ Pienza
Day 7
❼ Montepulciano

❽ Arezzo

An extra 4 days in Tuscany means you can experience four more towns, because driving distances in the region are short and manageable. This weeklong itinerary expands on the 3-day tour to include Lucca, with its Roman street plan ensconced behind mighty ramparts; Pienza, the "ideal Renaissance city" commissioned by Pope Pius II in the 15th century; Montepulciano, which yields one of the world's best wines, Vino Nobile; and Arezzo, home of Tuscany's greatest fresco cycle. START: **Florence. Trip length: 407km (282 mile) loop.**

From Florence, Lucca is 72km (45 miles) west on the A11.

❶ ★★ **Lucca.** At one time, Lucca was the unofficial capital of Tuscany, and a Roman colony known to Caesar and Pompey. Today, it's celebrated for the most complete

Renaissance ramparts in Europe. We recommend you start by circumnavigating them on a bicycle.

After your ride, you can see the highlights of Lucca from closer up: Although it's light on truly first-class museums, the town shelters some of Tuscany's loveliest churches. Try

Lucca's San Michele in Foro.

to visit the **Cattedrale di San Martino, San Frediano,** and **San Michele in Foro,** if only to check out their Pisan-Romanesque facades. Leave time for one of Lucca's great pleasures: wandering the main pedestrian shopping street, **Via Fillungo.**

There are plenty of trattorias where you can dine on Lucchese fare that evening, before bedding down for the night. Lodge inside the walls for the most atmosphere.

For detailed coverage of sights, hotels, restaurants, shops & nightlife in Lucca, see p 132 of Chapter 6.

Leave early and drive 22km (14 miles) southwest on the S12r to:

❷ ★★★ **Pisa.** For detailed suggestions on how to make the most of Pisa in a day, see "The Best of Tuscany in Three Days," p 73, ❶.

For detailed coverage of sights, hotels, restaurants, shops & nightlife in Pisa, see p 150 of Chapter 6.

From Pisa, head southeast along the FI–PI–LI *raccordo* to the S439 turnoff at Ponsacco. Take the S439, following signs for Capannoli, then for Volterra. Total journey time for the 69km (43-mile) trip is around 1¼ hr.

❸ ★★ **Volterra.** If you arrive in the morning, you can cover Volterra's attractions in a day. Take in the **Duomo;** a major Etruscan treasure trove in the **Museo Guarnacci;** the frescoed chapel inside **San Francesco;** and best of all, the town's **Pinacoteca,** home of Rosso Fiorentino's iconic *Deposition.*

For detailed coverage of sights, hotels, restaurants, shops & nightlife in Volterra, see p 176 of Chapter 6.

Head east on the S68 as far as Castelsangimignano, then turn north. The journey from Volterra to San Gimignano is 30km (18½ miles).

❹ ★★ **San Gimignano.** Arrive in San Gimignano in the morning and set about exploring the town, with its once-fortified medieval towers. For guidance, see "The Best of Tuscany in Three Days," p 73, ❷.

For detailed coverage of sights, hotels, restaurants, shops & nightlife in San Gimignano, see p 160 of Chapter 6.

Siena is 40km (24 miles) southeast of San Gimignano. Head east on the S324 to meet the Firenze–Siena *raccordo* at Poggibonsi, then

Volterra's Duomo.

San Gimignano's medieval towers.

south to Siena. Enter via the "Siena Ovest" exit.

⑤ ★★★ Siena. There's no Gothic city like it anywhere in the world—follow the outline in "The Best of Tuscany in Three Days," p 72, to see the best of it in a day. Siena's center is more alluring on a summer evening than even Florence, so round off your evening with a gelato at our favorite place in town, **Kopakabana.**

For detailed coverage of sights, hotels, restaurants, shops & nightlife in Siena, see p 166 of Chapter 6.

Travel Tip

This itinerary does not leave you much time to relax at your stops. If you prefer to move more slowly, consider sacrificing one of the stops to spend an extra day in Siena: see Siena, in "The Best of Tuscany in Ten Days," p 81, for suggestions on how to spend your time that day.

Leave Siena early, the morning of your sixth day, and drive southeast 55km (33 miles) on the S2 then S146 to:

⑥ ★ Pienza. You can see all of Pienza's major attractions in about 3 hours, before heading out for your next stopover. The highlights of this model Renaissance town are all in Piazza Pio II, chiefly the **Duomo, Museo Diocesano,** and **Palazzo Piccolomini.** Wine collectors shouldn't depart without at least looking in at the **Enoteca di Ghino.** Grab a *porchetta* sandwich from **Nannetti e Bernardini** and make for your next stop.

For detailed coverage of sights, hotels, restaurants, shops & nightlife in Pienza, see p 146 of Chapter 6.

Montepulciano is 14km (8¾ miles) east, on the S146.

⑦ ★★ Montepulciano. After the morning in Pienza, strike out for an afternoon in Montepulciano. Plan to arrive right after lunch, so you can see Montepulciano's attractions before nightfall. The unmissable sights here are the **Cattedrale,** the **Tempio di San Biagio** (just outside the gates), and the **Palazzo Nobili-Tarugi.** Leave time for tasting some Vino Nobile: **Gattavecchi** is my favorite cellar in town. End your day with one of the best steaks you're ever going to eat, at **Acquacheta.**

For detailed coverage of sights, hotels, restaurants, shops & nightlife in Montepulciano, see p 142 of Chapter 6.

Leave Montepulciano first thing, driving 53km (33 miles) north to Arezzo. Head northeast on the S327 to the Firenze–Roma autostrada, then north until you reach the signposted exit.

⑧ ★★ Arezzo. For your final look at Tuscany, Arezzo won't disappoint; it's the major reason to visit the northeastern part of the region. Its steep medieval streets were made for walking (in sensible shoes), but the chief attraction is painted inside the **Basilica di San Francesco:** Piero della Francesca's *Legend of the True Cross.* Book your timed entrance slot as soon as you hit town. If you're rushed, you can skip the Duomo, but don't miss the **Pieve di Santa Maria,** crazy-sloping **Piazza Grande,** or a trip to the **Casa di Vasari,** native-son Giorgio's old digs. The city goes very quiet during the afternoon *riposo* (Italian siesta), so we try to make lunch at **Gastronomia Il Cervo** stretch through the middle part of the day. If you're not due back in Florence until the following day,

Square in Montepulciano.

Arezzo has a couple of stylish, central boutique accommodations at very fair prices.

For detailed coverage of sights, hotels, restaurants, shops & nightlife in Arezzo, see p 124 of Chapter 6.

Arezzo is only 81km (50 miles) southeast of Florence, an easy drive up the A1.

Pienza's Duomo.

The Best of Tuscany in Ten Days

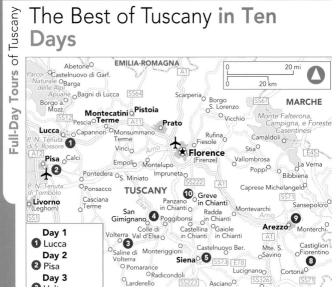

Day 1
❶ Lucca

Day 2
❷ Pisa

Day 3
❸ Volterra

Day 4
❹ San Gimignano

Day 5 & 6
❺ Siena

Day 7
❻ Pienza
❼ Montepulciano

Day 8
❽ Cortona

Day 9
❾ Arezzo

Day 10
❿ Greve in Chianti

This tour is similar to Tuscany in 1 week, with extra days thrown in to allow a few additional stops, notably in Cortona, a steeply pitched throwback to the Middle Ages with two fine museums; and in Chianti Country, where you should have time to visit a vineyard or two before your return to Florence. Those extra days also allow you to take things a little slower. START: **Florence. Trip length: 510km (305 miles) round-trip.**

From Florence, Lucca is 72km (45 miles) west on the A11.

❶ ★★ **Lucca.** Head west from Florence for a 1-day visit to Lucca, where you can circumnavigate its intact Renaissance walls by bike. A 1-day itinerary is detailed in "The Best of Tuscany in One Week," p 76.

For detailed coverage of sights, hotels, restaurants, shops & nightlife in Lucca, see p 132 of Chapter 6.

Leave Lucca early and drive 22km (14 miles) southwest on the S12r to:

❷ ★★★ **Pisa.** If you arrive early enough, you can see Pisa's sights before twilight, and then spend the

Pisa's Duomo and Leaning Tower.

night on the town. See Pisa, in "The Best of Tuscany in Three Days," p 73.

For detailed coverage of sights, hotels, restaurants, shops & nightlife in Pisa, see p 150 in Chapter 6.

From Pisa, head east toward Florence on the FI-PI-LI and take the turn south at Ponsacco signposted for Volterra. Total distance is 65km (40 miles).

❸ ★★ Volterra. If you arrive in the morning, you can cover Volterra's attractions in a day, including the town's **Pinacoteca,** home of Rosso Fiorentino's iconic *Deposition.* See Volterra, in "The Best of Tuscany in One Week," p 77.

For detailed coverage of sights, hotels, restaurants, shops & nightlife in Volterra, see p 176 of Chapter 6.

Head east 17km (11 miles) along the S68 as far as Castelsangimignano, then follow signs 13km (8 miles) north to:

❹ ★★ San Gimignano. Get here early to do San Gimignano in a day. For the 1-day tour, see "The Best of Tuscany in Three Days," p 73, **❷.**

For detailed coverage of sights, hotels, restaurants, shops & nightlife in San Gimignano, see p 160 of Chapter 6.

Siena is 40km (24 miles) southeast of San Gimignano. Head east on the S324 to meet the Firenze–Siena *raccordo* at Poggibonsi, then south to Siena. Enter via the "Siena Ovest" exit.

❺ ★★★ Siena. As a Tuscan destination, Siena is rivaled only by Florence. Because there is so much to see and do, schedule a 2-night stopover. See "The Best of Tuscany in Three Days," p 74, for the best 1-day itinerary—although you can afford to move a little more slowly, leaving a sight or two for your second day.

Start that second day with the **Archivio di Stato,** and you shouldn't miss the **Torre del Mangia,** if you haven't climbed it already. Then visit the **Casa di Santa Caterina,** with mementos of Italy's patron saint, and **San Domenico,** a church also linked with St. Catherine, where you can see her preserved head.

For detailed coverage of sights, hotels, restaurants, shops & nightlife in Siena, see p 166 of Chapter 6.

Leave Siena early, the morning of your seventh day, and drive southeast on the S2 and S146 for 55km (33 miles) to:

The pulpit inside Siena's Duomo.

6 ★ **Pienza.** The Renaissance town is compact enough to cover in a morning. See Pienza, in "The Best of Tuscany in One Week," p 78. After lunch, continue to Montepulciano for the afternoon and night.

For detailed coverage of sights, hotels, restaurants, shops & nightlife in Pienza, see p 146 of Chapter 6.

From Pienza, take the S146 east for 13km (8 miles) to:

7 ★★ **Montepulciano.** For a half-day itinerary in Montepulciano, see Montepulciano in "The Best of Tuscany in One Week," p 78. Spend the night here and head onward in the morning.

For detailed coverage of sights, hotels, restaurants, shops & nightlife in Montepulciano, see p 142 of Chapter 6.

From Montepulciano, head for Cortona, a distance of 45km (28 miles), via Bettolle and the Siena–Perugia *raccordo.*

8 ★★ **Cortona.** This medieval hilltown is major-league steep, but you can still do it in a day. The chief sights are a revamped **Museo dell'Accademia Etrusca e della Città (MAEC)** and sublime panels by Signorelli and Fra' Angelico at the **Museo Diocesano.** If you're fit, take a hike and finish your day with the views from high up on the **Fortezza Medicea.**

For complete coverage of Cortona, see p 128 in Chapter 6.

From Cortona, drive north 34km (22 miles) on the S71 to:

9 ★★ **Arezzo.** Build your day here around the Piero della Francesca frescoes. For a 1-day itinerary, see Arezzo in "The Best of Tuscany in One Week."

For detailed coverage of Arezzo, see p 124 in Chapter 6.

Drive northwest, following signs to Firenze. Take the autostrada northwest toward Florence, to the exit for Figline Valdarno. Follow a signposted route west to:

10 ★ **Greve in Chianti.** On your way back to Florence, make a detour for some good living in Chianti Country. Centered around Piazza Matteotti, **Greve** is riddled with wine shops (*enoteche*), and you'll have time to visit a winery or two in the surrounding hills. Our local favorite is **Vignamaggio,** just south of Greve. Divert 7km (4 miles) south to Panzano for tasting and an entertaining wine education at Chianti's best enoteca, the **Accademia del Buon Gusto.**

For more coverage of Chianti Country, see the dedicated tour on p 112 of Chapter 5.

Florence is 27km (17 miles) north of Greve on the S222. ●

Sangiovese grapes in a Greve vineyard.

4

The Best **Special-Interest Tours** of Tuscany

Tuscany for Art & Architecture Lovers

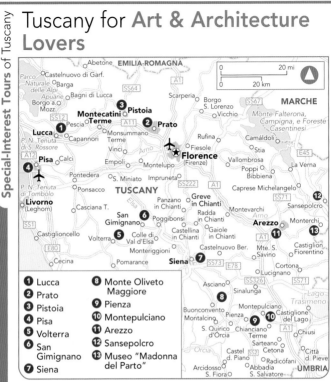

❶ Lucca	❽ Monte Oliveto Maggiore
❷ Prato	❾ Pienza
❸ Pistoia	❿ Montepulciano
❹ Pisa	⓫ Arezzo
❺ Volterra	⓬ Sansepolcro
❻ San Gimignano	⓭ Museo "Madonna del Parto"
❼ Siena	

During the Middle Ages and Renaissance, painters and sculptors who wanted to make a living went to Florence, Pisa, or Siena, where the churches, guilds, and wealthy patrons were. For the most part, the art stayed where it was created. This doesn't mean you won't find great art elsewhere in Tuscany; Arezzo has the region's finest wall paintings, and architecture buffs have a broader playing field: Where the *palazzi* and city plans of Montepulciano and Pienza attracted the stars of the Renaissance, provincial towns such as Lucca mix medieval and Liberty styles. START: **Lucca is 72km (45 miles) west of Florence on the A11. Trip length: 9 days.**

Travel Tip

For recommended hotels and restaurants, see Lucca, Pisa, San Gimignano, Volterra, Montepulciano, Pienza, Arezzo, and Siena in Chapter 6, "Charming Tuscan Towns & Villages."

Previous page: Piazza dei Priori in Volterra.

The Ospedale del Ceppo in Pistoia.

❶ ★ Lucca. While light on the art front, for architecture buffs Lucca is one of the most rewarding stops in Tuscany. The facades of the town's many churches exemplify the Pisan-Romanesque style, richly embroidered with polychrome marble insets and relief carvings, often by visiting Lombard and Pisan sculptors. The finest two are the **Cattedrale di San Martino,** with its green and white marble facade by Guidetto da Como; and the exceptionally tall **San Michele in Foro**—another stellar example of Luccan influence on the Pisan-Romanesque

Lucca's Cattedrale di San Martino.

style, with its twisted columns and many tiers of arcades.

The more restrained "Luccan-Romanesque" style of **San Frediano** is graced with white marble plundered from Lucca's Roman amphitheater and embellished with a giant Byzantine-style gold mosaic by Berlinghieri.

For more on Lucca, see p 132 of Chapter 6.

Lodge 2 nights in Lucca, visiting both Prato and Pistoia on your second day by train.

❷ ★★ Prato. One of central Italy's outstanding fresco cycles, the apse paintings of Prato's **Duomo** were executed between 1452 and 1466 by Fra' Filippo Lippi, a Dominican monk. The dazzlingly restored frescoes tell the life stories of St. Stephen and John the Baptist, completed with a dance of Salome. The cathedral's **Assunta Chapel** also has incomplete frescoes by Florentine pioneer of perspective, Paolo Uccello (painted 1435–36). Designed by Giuliano da Sangallo, **Santa Maria delle Carceri** was the first centrally planned, templelike church of the High Renaissance.

See also p 93, ❻.

❸ ★★ Pistoia. The greatest of the four Gothic pulpits carved by father-and-son team Nicola and Giovanni Pisano (see ④, below) is inside the little Romanesque church of **Sant'Andrea.** Nearby in the compact center are Giovanni della Robbia's terra-cotta frieze on the **Ospedale del Ceppo** and the 1372 frescoes of the **Cappella del Tau.**

For more on Pistoia, see p 156 of Chapter 6.

From Lucca, take the S12r south 21km (13 miles), following signs for:

④ ★★★ **Pisa.** With its **Duomo** and **Leaning Tower,** Pisa introduced the world to the Arab-influenced "Pisan-Romanesque" style of architecture—which flourished from the 11th to the 13th centuries, when the Pisan Republic was a powerful maritime city-state. Gothic sculpture flourished here as well, in the hands of sculptor Nicola Pisano (1220–84) and his son, Giovanni Pisano (1250–1315).

Touring Pisa is easy; its major monuments center round Piazza del Duomo (also known as the **Campo dei Miracoli,** or "Field of Miracles"). Here you'll also find the **Battistero,** with its unusual Gothic dome and Pisano pulpit; and the **Museo dell'Opera del Duomo,** a repository of Gothic sculpture in marble and bronze.

The **Museo Nazionale di San Matteo,** a short trek across town, houses the city's best paintings, notably works by Masaccio (1401–28) and Simone Martini (1284–1344).

For more on Pisa, see p 150 of Chapter 6.

On your fourth morning, after a night in Pisa, head east toward Florence on the Florence–Pisa highway and take the turn south at Ponsacco signposted for Volterra. Total distance is 65km (40 miles).

⑤ ★ **Volterra.** Don't pass by this Etruscan hilltown without stopping in at its picture gallery, the **Pinacoteca.** On the first floor you'll find the exemplar of early Florentine Mannerism, in the form of Rosso Fiorentino's 1521 *Deposition.* It was one of Tuscany's first works of truly "modern" art. Architecture buffs should see the **Palazzo dei Priori,** the oldest Gothic town hall in Tuscany. It was the template for Florence's Palazzo Vecchio.

For more on Volterra, see p 176 of Chapter 6.

Start your fifth day by heading east 17km (11 miles) along the S68 as far as Castelsangimignano, then following signs north to:

⑥ ★★ **San Gimignano.** Although Italy's best-preserved medieval town is today unique in appearance, in the Middle Ages towns throughout central Italy were much like it. San Gimignano's charms are not lost on hordes of day-trippers, and an overnight gives you the opportunity to soak in the medieval ambience in relative peace.

Thirteen of 70+ original towers are left standing from the city's heyday in the decades before the devastating Black Death. More than defensive strongholds, the towers stood as symbols of a family's prestige and worth. Art outposts not to miss include Benozzo Gozzoli's frescoes inside **Sant'Agostino,** and Domenico Ghirlandaio's *Legend of Santa Fina* frescoes inside the **Collegiata.**

For more on San Gimignano, see p 160 of Chapter 6.

Siena is 40km (24 miles) southeast of San Gimignano—set out early to make the most of just one day there. Head east on the S324 to Poggibonsi and take the Firenze–Siena *raccordo* south to the "Siena Ovest" exit.

di Giorgio Martini, Matteo di Giovanni, and Domenico Beccafumi.

For more on Siena, see p 166 in Chapter 6.

Travel Tip

Alongside Florence, the Gothic alleyways of Siena hold more pleasures for art and architecture lovers than any other Tuscan stop. If you have an extra day to allocate, spend it there.

Palazzo Pubblico in Siena.

❼ ★★★ Siena. In the Middle Ages, Siena rivaled, and even outshone, Florence as an art center. Duccio di Buoninsegna and Simone Martini were pioneers in bringing greater realism to the schematic, static Byzantine style, adding flowing lines and expressive human features. Duccio's *Maestà,* inside the **Museo dell'Opera Metropolitana,** is the most important work of this (or any) period in Siena. The Lorenzettis, Pietro and Ambrogio, worked for patrons across Tuscany—and Ambrogio left the greatest work of civic art in Italy on the walls of the **Palazzo Pubblico:** his *Allegories of Good and Bad Government.*

The Black Death of 1348, which decimated Siena's population, also dealt a crippling blow to its artistic aspirations. Florence rose to prominence. But the vitality of Renaissance Siena is evident inside the **Duomo.** The marble intarsia floor, built over centuries, is joined by Pinturicchio's frescoed Libreria Piccolominea as must-sees for any Tuscan art tourist.

The other place to see where Sienese art went with the onset of what we now call "the Renaissance" is the **Pinacoteca Nazionale:** Look for works by Francesco

Your seventh day is spent touring south of Siena before lodging overnight in Montepulciano. Monte Oliveto Maggiore is best reached by the spectacular S438 then S451 via Asciano, at 38km (23½ miles) one of Tuscany's great drives. Afterward head to the S2, then 22km (13 miles) southeast to San Quirico d'Orcia, where you'll turn east on the S146 for 10km (6 miles) to Pienza. Montepulciano is a further 13km (8 miles) to the east.

❽ ★★ Monte Oliveto Maggiore. The open-air frescoes of the **Chiostro Grande** ("Great Cloister") at this most bucolic of rural monasteries were started between 1495 and 1508 by Cortonese painter Luca Signorelli, then completed by Antonio Bazzi, known as Sodoma. (He included a self-portrait, with his pet badger, in panel 3.) They recount *Scenes from the Life of St. Benedict,* based on the biographical *Dialogues* of Gregory the Great. ⏱ *1 hr.* ☎ *0577-707611. Free admission. Daily 9am–noon & 3:15–6pm (until 5pm Oct–Mar).*

❾ ★★ Pienza. This village owes its grandiose look to Pope Pius II, who was born here of Sienese stock in 1405. He set out to transform his modest birthplace of Corsignano

San Biagio, just outside Montepulciano's walls.

into a model Renaissance town: Bernardo Rossellino (1409–64), protégé of the Florentine theorist Leon Battista Alberti, carried out the pope's mandate, creating a **Duomo** with a classicized facade, the adjacent **Palazzo Piccolomini,** and a square, **Piazza Pio II,** that remains a miniature Renaissance jewel. Fifty thousand gold florins poorer, but delighted with the job, Pius renamed the village after himself, hence "Pi-enza."

For more on Pienza, see p 146 of Chapter 6.

⓾ ★ Montepulciano. First on your agenda in this famous wine town should be a parade of the

Renaissance *palazzi* flanking its steep main street, known locally as "Il Corso." The meandering climb ends at **Piazza Grande,** where you'll find Michelozzo's **Palazzo Comunale,** Sangallo's **Palazzo Nobili-Tarugi,** and, inside the **Duomo,** Taddeo di Bartolo's giant *Assumption* altarpiece. Architecture fans mustn't leave town without a short trek outside the gates to the **Tempio di San Biagio,** an architectural masterpiece of the High Renaissance.

For more on Montepulciano, see p 142 of Chapter 6.

On day 8, drive east to the autostrada, taking it north toward Firenze for 53km (33 miles) until the Arezzo turnoff.

⓫ ★★★ Arezzo. This prosperous little jewelry-making town is home to the greatest fresco cycle in Tuscany, justly mentioned in the same breath as Michelangelo's Sistine Chapel and Giotto's Cappella Scrovegni in Padua: Piero della Francesca's *Legend of the True Cross* (1452–66), on the apse walls of **San Francesco.**

Piero was a visionary who imbued his art with an ethereal quality. A pioneering master of perspective, he created human figures

Piazza Grande in Arezzo.

Via Matteotti in Sansepolcro.

that seem to have souls that survive centuries after his death, in the year Columbus reached the Americas. He also painted a small fresco in Arezzo's **Duomo.**

For more on Arezzo, see p 124 of Chapter 6.

On the final morning, head east on the S73 for 39km (24 miles) to Sansepolcro. On the road back, take the turnoff for Monterchi after 13km (8 miles).

⑫ ★★ **Sansepolcro.** There's hardly a Tuscan town more interwoven with art than Sansepolcro. Sienese School painter Matteo di Giovanni was born here, and the **Cattedrale di San Giovanni Evangelista,** Via Matteotti 4 (☎ 0575-742078), has a Perugino *Ascension* (1495). But it's the local boy and Early Renaissance master Piero della Francesca (1420–92) that draws the art lovers.

Head for the **Museo Civico,** Via Aggiunti 65 (☎ 0575-732218), to see his masterpieces. During World War II, the British officer commanding the heights over the town remembered he'd read an essay by

Aldous Huxley—entitled "The Greatest Picture"—which accorded that status to Piero's 1468 *Resurrection of Christ,* still in the same building. He ordered shelling to cease lest a masterpiece be lost, maybe saving Sansepolcro in the process. Also here is Piero's earlier *Polyptych of the Misericordia* (1445–62). *Admission 10€. Daily June 15–Sept 15 10am–1:30pm & 2:30–7pm; Sept 16–June 14 10am–1pm & 2:30–6pm.*

⑬ **Museo "Madonna del Parto."** Art lovers detour to the village of Monterchi for one reason: to see Piero's *Madonna del Parto.* It's almost unique in Italian art in that it depicts the Virgin Mary heavily pregnant—and if *you're* pregnant, admission to the museum is free. It was painted sometime after 1459 (dating Piero is notoriously tricky). ⓧ *45 min. Via Reglia 1.* ☎ *0575-70713. Admission 6.50€. Apr–Oct Daily 9:30am–12:30pm & 2–5pm.*

Follow the S73 back to Arezzo (or continue to Florence) for your final night.

Tuscany for Food & Wine Lovers

1. Siena
2. Chianti Country
3. Montalcino
4. Montepulciano
5. Cortona
6. Prato

Gastronomes celebrate the fertile, sunbaked countryside of Tuscany for its olive groves and the extra-virgin oil they yield; for its Chianina cattle, acclaimed for producing the most succulent beef in Italy; and for its sangiovese grapes, which give forth Chianti, in a region easily explored along the Chiantigiana (the "Chianti Road"). With such a bounty of locally available ingredients, it's only right that Tuscan food be a simply prepared, rural cuisine, known as cucina povera. This moveable feast was designed to help you experience the region at its most delicious. START: **Siena (65km/40 miles south of Florence), where you should stay at least 1 night. Trip length: 7 days.**

Travel Tip

For detailed information on sights and recommended hotels and restaurants, see Montepulciano and Siena in Chapter 6, "Charming Tuscan Towns & Villages," p 166.

❶ ★★ **Siena.** The Sienese are supposedly "cursed with the sweetest teeth in Tuscany." Since the 13th century, locals have been known for their candied fruit-and-almond cakes and other delicious bakery treats.

Panforte and *panpepato* are the two most famous Sienese cakes, baked to ancient recipes. *Panpepato* is a flat, honey-sweetened cake filled with candied fruits and nuts and flavored with spices; the finishing touch is a dusting of ground pepper, cinnamon, and allspice. *Panforte* is dusted with sugar instead. *Ricciarelli* are lozenge-shaped cakes made from almond, sugar, and honey. Originally a jaw-breaker dipped in wine at Christmas, *cavallucci* are made with honey-coated, aniseed-flavored walnuts; for modern tastes, they have been softened.

All are available at family-run bakeries throughout town: **Nannini–Conca d'Oro,** Banchi di Sopra 24 (☎ 0577-41591), is the upscale favorite.

Other Sienese goodies like hung hams, Cinta Senese salami (made from a local breed of pig), and Tuscan wines are available from the city's most extravagant deli: **Pizzicheria de' Miccoli,** Via di Città 95 (☎ 0577-289164).

The town is also home to one of our favorite *gelaterie* in Tuscany. Far too many ice creams later, we still haven't found a flavor we like better than the *panpepato* at

A vineyard in Tuscany.

Kopakabana, Via de' Rossi 52 (☎ 0577-223744).

From Siena, head north on the S222 toward Greve in Chianti, a distance of 42km (26 miles). Stay over a couple of nights to tour the area.

❷ ★★ Chianti Country. Against a quintessential Tuscan landscape— of medieval wine castles and silver-green olive groves—Chianti Country south of Florence is home to some of Italy's finest food producers, restaurants, and markets. And then there's the wine: First codified by Cosimo III in 1716, and with a history that stretches back at least to the A.D. 7th century, Chianti is one of the world's iconic reds. A good base for touring the area is its unofficial capital, **Greve in Chianti.** The town is busiest in September when it hosts the annual Rassegna del Chianti Classico wine fair. You'll find the best local reds at **Vignamaggio,** 5km (3 miles) southeast of town.

Don't leave the Chianti without calling in on one of the region's classic butchers: **Dario Cecchini,** in Panzano, and **Falorni** in Greve are our two favorites.

For more on the Chianti, see the dedicated tour on p 112 of Chapter 5.

Head back to Siena, then drive south down the S2 for 42km (25 miles), following signs into:

❸ ★★★ Montalcino. The hills surrounding (largely south of) this medieval town yield **Brunello di Montalcino,** one of the greatest red wines in the world. Many wineries welcome visitors, and the town itself is filled with *enoteche* (wine shops).

The center of the town's foodstuffs, including gourmet honey and Pecorino cheese, is **Enoteca La Fortezza,** housed in the medieval fortress and one of the few tasting

Pouring Chianti at Castello di Verrazzano.

rooms anywhere with ramparts. While in Montalcino, you can also sample Brunello's "younger brother," the less noble **Rosso di Montalcino,** made of the same sangiovese grapes as its more famous counterpart. Aged for only a year after harvest, this is a fruity red with hints of Brunello's complex flavor at a third of the price.

Our favorite nearby wine estate is **Poggio Antico** (www.poggioan-tico.com; ☎ 0577-848044), 4km (2½ miles), south of town along the Grosseto road. Its Brunellos, especially the *riserva,* are consistently voted among the top wines in the world. Their sangiovese-cabernet "Super Tuscan" Madre is elegant and velvety. *Cantina* visits are free but must be reserved at least a day in advance (more in summer). Tasting onsite costs from 3€ for the Rosso to 22€ for all five of the estate's labels.

For visits to other wineries, check with the **Consorzio del Vino Brunello di Montalcino,** Piazza Cavour 8 (www.consorziobrunellodi-montalcino.it; ☎ 0577-848246;).

For more on Montalcino, including a recommended hotel, see p 117, ❷, & 122.

From Montalcino, head out on your fifth morning via the S146 east 32km (23 miles) to:

❹ ★★ **Montepulciano.** This ancient town of Etruscan origin, which perches like an eyrie above the Valdichiana, is celebrated for its violet-scented, ruby wine, **Vino Nobile di Montepulciano,** known since the 8th century. Although the beefier Brunello is considered number one by many connoisseurs, the silky delights of a good Vino Nobile are well worth sampling. On a tighter budget, as in nearby Montalcino, a younger and less expensive **Rosso di Montepulciano** exists. It is aged less and sold sooner. **Gattavecchi** makes an especially noble selection of wines.

The area is also known for its fine sheep's milk cheese, *pecorino di Pienza.* **Cugusi,** Via della Boccia 8 (2km/1¼ miles outside Montepulciano on the road to Pienza; www.caseificiocugusi.it; ☎ 0578-757558;), sells directly from the farm. The vast range includes artisan pecorino at every aging stage (from *fresco* to *stagionato*) as well as cheeses wrapped in hazelnut leaves or herbs and oil, or infused

Wine tanks at one of Montalcino's vineyards.

Pinocchio puppets at the Parco di Pinocchio, near Pescia.

with grapes (known as *ubriaco*, or "drunk").

For a complete rundown on Montepulciano, including hotels, restaurants & where to taste its wines, see p 142 in Chapter 6.

From Montepulciano, head east across the Val di Chiana on SP17 and SP 10 to Cortona. The trip is only 31km (19 miles), and in good weather you can see one town from the heights of the other.

5 ★★ Cortona. This somber and elegant hilltown has long been known for art (home to such Renaissance luminaries as Luca Signorelli) and, with proud *palazzi*, squares, and stepped streets, can seem like a romantically medieval stage set. An evening on the town includes a walk through the public gardens to take in sweeping views of the Val di Chiana, a stop for a glass of wine at **Enoteca Enotria,** Via Nazionale 81 (☎ 0575-603595), and, the highlight, a steak dinner. When prepared properly, a *bistecca alla fiorentina* is among the best steaks in the world. Authentic versions hail only from the indigenous purebred Chianina cattle, raised in the valley

you've just been regarding below town. Some no-frills places that focus on deliciously simple grills are **Dardona,** Via Dardano 24 (☎ 0575–60194), and **Trattoria la Grotta,** Piazza Badelli 3 (☎ 0575–639271).

For more on Cortona, including recommended hotels, restaurants & sights, see p 128.

Take the A1 north and continue around Florence as far as the junction for the A11, which you'll take to Prato, a 136km (84-mile) journey.

6 ★ Prato. *Cantuccini* (twice-baked almond cookies), which so often round out a Tuscan lunch, in fact originate from Prato. To pick up a bag of these *biscotti di Prato* before your return to Florence, stop by the city's venerable *biscottificio* (biscuit-maker), **Antonio Mattei,** Via Ricasoli 20–22 (☎ 0574-25756; www.antoniomattei.it), which has been selling the famous *cantucci* and the *vin santo* in which to dunk them since 1858.

*For more on Prato, see p 85, **2**, & p 98, **1**.*

Tuscany for **Families**

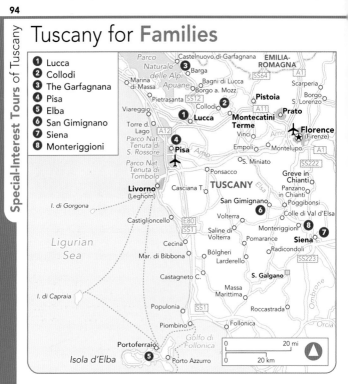

1 Lucca
2 Collodi
3 The Garfagnana
4 Pisa
5 Elba
6 San Gimignano
7 Siena
8 Monteriggioni

With its Renaissance art and architectural wonders, Tuscany isn't the obvious choice as a destination for the kids. Fortunately, many of the region's palaces, castles, and fortified hilltowns look like they were dreamt up by Walt Disney. On this tour, we've created a balance between cultural sites and outdoor activities that will thrill the entire family—and added a trip to Tuscany's most picturesque island sands. START: **Lucca, on the A12 autostrada 71km (44 miles) west of Florence, makes the best base for the first 3 nights of the tour. Trip length: 9 days.**

Travel Tip

For information on sights and recommended hotels and restaurants in Lucca, Pisa, San Gimignano, and Siena, see each town in Chapter 6, "Charming Tuscan Towns & Villages." For details of all local tourist offices, turn to p 190.

1 ★★ **Lucca.** All family members will delight in walking or biking (or even rollerblading) the 5km (2¾ miles) of Renaissance walls that ring the old town.

For more on Lucca, see p 132 in Chapter 6.

For your first, easy day trip from Lucca, head east on the S435 for 15km (9 miles); just before Pescia, is the little town of:

❷ Collodi. This is the hometown of Carlo Lorenzini, who wrote the *Adventures of Pinocchio* in 1881. (He later adopted the name "Carlo Collodi.") The world-famous children's story is celebrated at the **Parco di Pinocchio** (www.pinocchio.it; ☎ 0572-429342), with diversions ranging from a giant mosaic about Geppetto and his fibbing puppet to a fantastical maze and a painting corner. Try to read the book with your kids before you go (the Disney movie is significantly different). The park will enchant tots with imagination. *Admission 13€, 11€ children 5–14, 7€ children 3–5. Daily 8:30am–sunset.*

For a second, fuller day trip, head into the Garfagnana, north of town via the S12 and S445. The total round-trip is 96km (60 miles).

❸ ★★ The Garfagnana. This upland corner of northwestern Tuscany is riddled with chestnut forests, hiking trails, and perfect picnicking pastures tucked between the Apennines and the Apuane Alps. The prettiest town up here is **Barga,** where a climb of the steep, winding streets ends at a mountain panorama outside the 14th-century **Collegiata.** Our favorite lunch spot in town is **Scacciaguai,** Via di Mezzo 23 (☎ 0583-711368).

After lunch explore the **Grotta del Vento,** or "Wind Cave," Vergemoli (www.grottadelvento. com; ☎ 0583-722024), 16km (10 miles) southwest of Barga. Deep under the limestone you'll encounter the most dramatic caves in Tuscany, a subterranean landscape of tunnels, stalactites, stalagmites, and surreal calcite formations. A 1-hour

Climbing the Leaning Tower of Pisa.

tour guides you and your family safely through; take warm clothing because it's always 52°F (11°C) down there. *Tours from 9€. Daily on the hour (except 1pm) 10am–6pm; tours in English sometimes available, English-language audio guide available for free.*

Relocate to Pisa, just 20km (12 miles) southwest of Lucca, along the S12r.

❹ ★★★ Pisa. At the **Campo dei Miracoli** ("Field of Miracles"), all kids will want to make the memorable climb to the top of the **Leaning Tower,** but the minimum age is 8 years old. Young ones who can't make the ascent will find some consolation in romping on the lawn beneath the wonky tower.

Budding scientists can stray into the **Duomo** to follow in the footsteps of Galileo Galilei (1564–1642). He supposedly discovered the laws of pendulum motion right there, while watching the chandelier now known as the "Lamp of Galileo." (Who cares if it's a true story or not?)

For more on Pisa, see p 150 in Chapter 6.

Beachgoers at Sant'Andrea, Elba Island.

From Pisa, head 110km (68 miles) down the coast on the A12, then the S1 to Piombino. From there catch the car ferry (40 min.) to the island of:

⑤ ★★ Elba. The jewel in Tuscany's Mediterranean coast is this island where French emperor Napoleon was exiled after the Treaty of Fontainebleau in 1814. Elba has Tuscany's best beaches, and given the detour required to reach it, you'll want to stay at least 2 nights. Many affordable family apartments come with no minimum rental period (outside Aug). Among the more appealing choices is **Casa Campanella Resort,** near Capoliveri (www.casacampanella.it; ☎ 0565-915740).

Magical strips of sand include the perfect white crescents at **Fetovaia** and **Cavoli** and the little rockpool-and-sand cove of **Sant'Andrea,** all on the island's west side. There are more family beachfront facilities at **Marina di Campo.**

For views right along the arc of the Tuscan coast, kids will love the ride in an open cage to the top of 1,019m (3,343-ft.) Monte Capanne. The **Cabinovia** is just outside Marciana. A round-trip costs 18€, and the cableway is open mornings and afternoons, daily in summer but with seasonal variations.

Elba is best avoided in packed August, when it becomes party central for young Tuscans.

Ferries are run by Moby (www. moby.it) and Toremar (www.toremar.it).

From Piombino, head north on the S1 to Cecina, then east on S68 to Castelsangimignano, from where you'll see signs to San Gimignano. It's a journey of 112km (70 miles).

⑥ ★★ San Gimignano. With its preserved medieval towers, San Gimignano is like a stage set for kids, who love romping through its pedestrian-only historic core. The adventure begins at the **Torre Grossa,** which everyone can climb for a panoramic sweep of the bucolic countryside that surrounds this hilltown. Then decide whether to subject the children to the **Museo della Tortura:** a Tuscan chamber of horrors, with an authentic collection of instruments of torture. Most older kids find the exhibits fascinating, but little ones will prefer the enchanting re-creation of the medieval city in clay at **San Gimignano 1300.**

For more on the town, turn to "San Gimignano" in Chapter 6.

On your eighth morning, travel 11km (7 miles) east on the S324 to Poggibonsi, where you can hook up with the Firenze–Siena *raccordo.* Drive 31km (19 miles) south and exit at "Siena Ovest."

❼ ★★ Siena. The Gothic city of Siena is a place kids will never forget. Climb the **Torre del Mangia,** the bell tower of the **Palazzo Pubblico,** for a dramatic view down into the **Campo,** site of summer pageantry and horse racing at the Palio.

At the converted hospital of **Santa Maria della Scala,** kids have their own art on-site, too: **Bambimus** has art exhibits by and for young children displayed at a child-friendly height.

You'll see a different side of Tuscany, and get to know football Italian-style, if you catch a match at **Società Sportiva Robur Siena,** usually known just as Robur, at Stadio A. Franchi (robursiena.it; ☎ 0577-46649). The team usually plays in Serie A, Italy's top flight, and games are quite genteel by European standards (except those against archrival Fiorentina, or Florence). For the true fan experience,

The towers of Monteriggioni.

ask for a seat in the "Gradinata" (bleachers). *Alternate Sun (occasionally Sat or midweek) Sept–May. Tickets from kiosk next to bus station below Piazza Gramsci; Sogno Siena, Viale dei Mille 3 (☎ 0577-46649). Prices 20€–45€.*

For more on the town, turn to "Siena" in Chapter 6.

❽ ★ Monteriggioni. For an afternoon adventure, drive your kids to Monteriggioni, 18km (11 miles) north along the Florence road. If the Disney empire were to set up shop in Tuscany, it would have some ready-made stage sets in this tiny, perfectly preserved medieval village in its own set of fortified walls (part of which you can scramble onto). The town was once a Sienese outpost, begun in 1213, where soldiers patrolled the walls and kept an eye out for Florentine troops from the towers. All 14 of these vantage points have survived, and you can climb up for a view (admission 3.50€, open Apr–Sept daily 9:30am–1:30pm and 2–7:30pm). A walk from one end of Monteriggioni to the other takes about 5 minutes—as you pass, note the stone houses and garden plots tucked against the walls, which once kept townsfolk nourished during times of siege. Be sure to visit the enchanting **Abbey of San Galgano,** in a grassy meadow on the banks of the River Merse. The abbey is open June to August daily 9am–8pm; March to May and September to October 9am to 7pm, and November to February 10am to 5pm. Admission is 2€.

See p 114, ❻.

Tuscany by Rail & Bus

1 Prato
2 Pistoia
3 Lucca
4 Pisa
5 Siena
6 San Gimignano
7 Pienza
8 Colle di Val d'Elsa
9 Arezzo

Much of this guide has been written for motorists to discover the Tuscan countryside in their own sets of wheels. But increasing numbers of visitors want to travel light and save money in the face of mounting fuel prices, or simply prefer the unique feel you get for somewhere when you arrive by rail. To explore all of Tuscany by train, you'd have to double back to Florence many times. With a few additional connections made by bus, you can easily see many of the region's highlights. We've designed this itinerary to minimize hassle, using Siena as a base for the second half of the trip.

START: **Florence's Santa Maria Novella station. Trip length: 8 days.**

Travel Tip

For detailed information on sights and recommended hotels and restaurants, see the Lucca, Pisa, Pistoia, Siena, San Gimignano, Volterra, Montepulciano, and Arezzo sections of Chapter 6, "Charming Tuscan Towns & Villages."

On your first day, there's time to visit both Prato and Pistoia. Lodge in the latter or take a late train back to Florence or on to Lucca.

❶ ★ **Prato.** Tuscany's second city is your ideal first stop, served by two or three trains per hour and just a half-hour journey from

Florence. Alight at Prato's **Porta al Serraglio** station; the **Duomo** is just a couple of minutes' walk down arrow-straight Via Magnolfi. *See p 85,* ➋.

➋ ★★ **Pistoia.** We love visiting this little city by rail, because the 10-minute walk from the station to Piazza del Duomo takes us through the heart of a "real" working Tuscan town. Around 3 trains an hour run from Prato to Pistoia, just 15 to 20 minutes away. To find the tourist office, walk straight ahead on Via XX Settembre, past the old walls, then take the fifth right on Via degli Orafi into the main square. *See p 156, in Chapter 6.*

Set out early for Lucca, where you'll spend your second night.

➌ ★★ **Lucca.** This lovely walled city receives trains from both Florence and Pistoia approximately every hour, beginning daily before 6am and running up until around 10:30pm. (All pass through Prato.) Trip time from Pistoia is between 45 minutes and 1 hour. Trains pull into the station on **Piazza Ricasoli,** just south of the city walls; exit the station and walk right ahead to reach the center. *See p 132, in Chapter 6.*

Either spend your next night in Pisa, or visit it as an easy day trip from Lucca.

➍ ★★★ **Pisa.** Pisa and Lucca share a convenient rail link: Trains leave Lucca every half-hour daily, from 5:40am to 9:40pm, for the 30-minute trip. If you're heading straight for the Campo dei Miracoli, do *not* get off at Pisa Centrale, at the southern end of town; you want **Pisa San Rossore,** just west of the old wall. *See p 150, in Chapter 6.*

Travel Tip

The golden rule of rail travel in Italy: Don't forget to validate your ticket by inserting it into the yellow machines you find on every platform, often marked "convalida." You may be fined if you forget. Regular tickets are valid for 6 hours from validation, so you are allowed to jump off en route (say, at Prato or Pistoia on the way to Lucca).

Head to Siena, which makes an ideal base for the next 5 days.

➎ ★★★ **Siena.** To reach Siena you have to double back from Pisa toward Florence, changing trains at Empoli. During the day, at least one train an hour makes the connection. Total journey time is about 1¾ hours. Trains arrive in Siena at **Piazza Rosselli,** 15 minutes by frequent bus north of the center. Buy your local bus ticket from the booth inside the station or head up to the old center via a series of escalators.

After seeing the sights of Siena, spend the rest of your time here taking a series of day trips to some of the enchanting towns of central and southern Tuscany, and return to Siena by nightfall. To do this efficiently, you'll have to rely on the bus instead of the train. Bus

Prato's Campanile.

View of Pienza.

services are operated by **Tiemme** (www.tiemmespa.it; ☎ 0577-204111), whose ticket office is below street level at Piazza Gramsci/Via Tozzi. Request a timetable (*un orario*). Many buses also depart from here.

For a complete guide to Siena, see p 166, in Chapter 6.

⑥ ★★ San Gimignano. This hilltop fortress town with its famous towers and medieval lanes is comfortably accessible from Siena. Tiemme runs buses at least hourly (fewer on Sun) linking Siena with San Gimignano. Most require a change at Poggibonsi, so check when you buy your ticket. Total

The Colle di Val d'Elsa.

journey time—including the connection, which is usually slick—is around 1¼ hours. You can see the sights and take a bus back to Siena for dinner. See p 160, in Chapter 6.

⑦ ★★ Pienza. A bus run by **Tiemme** (www.tiemmespa.it; ☎ 0577-204111) is also your best bet for a day trip to this model Renaissance town. Buy your ticket, as before, from below Piazza Gramsci. Bus 112 departs from outside Porta Ovile and reaches Pienza, via Buonconvento, in 70 minutes.

Buses depart Siena for Pienza at the rate of around six a day. You have a choice of overnighting in Pienza or returning to Siena for the night. The last bus departs Pienza just before 6pm, requiring a change to a local service at Monteroni d'Arbia.

See p 146, in Chapter 6.

⑧ Colle di Val d'Elsa. The best-served by bus of all the towns within easy reach of Siena, Colle also lies a little off the regular tourist circuit, and so provides a break from high-season crowds. Lunch at the **Officina della Cucina Popolare** (p 115) is worth the visit alone. Most Tiemme buses linking Siena with Poggibonsi or San Gimignano stop in Colle, as does the hourly "slow" bus to Florence. Services depart Siena's Piazza Gramsci, and journey time is between 30 and 40 minutes. *See p 114,* ⑧.

⑨ ★ **Arezzo.** The art city of Piero della Francesca is comfortably tackled in a day. A Tiemme bus links Siena and Arezzo every couple of hours, departing the bus terminal at Piazza Gramsci. Journey time is 1½ hours. Buses arrive in Arezzo just by the rail station in **Piazza della Repubblica.** After a day seeing the art sights of the city, either return to Siena or hop on one of the frequent rail services back to Florence. *See p 124, in Chapter 6.*

Admiring Arezzo's fetching cityscape.

Rail Passes & Packages

Rail travel in Italy is inexpensive and easy to navigate. Trip planning is simple using the website for the national rail company, **Trenitalia** (www.trenitalia.com; ☎ 892021).

If you're traveling only within Tuscany, it's very unlikely you'll ride enough to get value for any prepaid rail pass. Passes are useful, however, if you're also taking more expensive high-speed routes to Rome, Venice, or farther afield. (**Note:** All high-speed trains must be booked in advance, at a cost of 10€ per booking even if you hold a pass.) It's only worth upgrading to a first-class pass if you're using high-speed trains—many local trains don't even have a first-class carriage.

From the U.S., the **Eurail Italy Pass** offers any 3 days within 2 months for around $175 for second-class travel; additional days, up to 10 days, cost around $25 each. A **Saver** pass offers discounts to two or more people traveling together. The **Italy Rail 'n Drive** package allows you to combine train travel with car rental.

From the U.K., the **InterRail Italy** pass for Italy costs £83 for any 3 days in a month, £134 for any 6 days, second class.

Passes are available from **Eurail** (www.eurail.com), **International Rail** (www.internationalrail.com), **Rail Europe** (www.raileurope.com), **Railpass.com**, and others. Travelers ages 25 and under get discounts on all Italy passes.

Tuscany by Bike

Day 1
1. Oratorio di Santa Caterina
2. Santo Stefano a Tizzano
3. San Polo in Chianti
4. Strada in Chianti
5. La Cantinetta di Spedaluzzo
6. Vicchiomaggio
7. Verrazzano
8. Greve in Chianti

Day 2
9. Panzano in Chianti
10. Fontodi
11. Castellina in Chianti
12. Siena

I f you're someone who feels the need to spike a visit to wineries and old churches with a dose of fresh country air, this is the tour for you. For a guided cycling expedition, or if you only have a single day to spare, you could also contact **I Bike Italy** (www. ibikeitaly.com; ☎ 342-935-2395). Based in Florence, I Bike Italy offers 1- or 2-day tours, with return transportation, including from Florence to Siena. START: **Florence. Trip length: 79km (49 miles)/2 days.**

Travel Tip

We suggest a well-maintained road bike, with at least 24 speeds, for this trip. Our favorite roadside lunch stop is recommended below, but if you prefer to picnic, stock up on supplies in Florence; you'll find dozens of idyllic places along the route. For more on the Chianti, see the dedicated tour starting on p 112 of Chapter 5.

Cross the Ponte San Niccolò, spanning the Arno River at the eastern end of Florence, and follow signs from Piazza Ferrucci to the town of Grassina and the S222. At Ponte a Ema, 4km (2½ miles) southeast of Florence, follow the brown signs to:

1 ★ Oratorio di Santa Caterina. A wall fresco of this church at S. Piero a Ema traces the

Biking in Tuscany.

Life of St. Catherine. Spinello Aretino completed it in 1390, just before he executed his cycle at San Miniato al Monte, in Florence. The apse displays more frescoes of St. Catherine (ca. 1360), by the "Master of Barberino" and Piero Nelli. *Call ahead at ☎ 055-6390356 to book a tour of the interior (3.50€).*

Return to the S222, then take a left at Grassina on a road marked "San Polo." It's a steady, gentle climb to:

❷ Santo Stefano a Tizzano. Four kilometers (2½ miles) south, up a rutted track on the right, you'll come upon this vine-clad Romanesque church. It was built by the Buondemontis, a local ruling family, and offers a spectacular panorama back toward Florence below.

Rejoin the main road and continue to:

❸ San Polo in Chianti. This little town is the center of Tuscany's iris industry—an annual Iris Festival takes place here each May. The main road continues to Strada (**❹**, below), but signposted 2½km (1½ miles) up a steep hill above San Polo is the ancient church of

San Miniato in Robbiana. It was consecrated in 1077 and heavily restored in 1841.

From San Polo a byroad points the way west back toward:

❹ Strada in Chianti. Taking its name, Strada (street), from an old Roman road that ran through here, this town lies 14km (8½ miles) south of Florence. The byroad hits the Chiantigiana south of the center, and there's no need to go in. From this point, it's rolling countryside until lunch.

Continue south on the S222 to:

5️⃣ ★ La Cantinetta di Spedaluzzo. The terrace here, on the brow of a hill south of Strada, is a fine perch to peruse what you've cycled so far. Bowls of pasta are tasty, satisfyingly carb-loaded, and good value. *Via Mugnana 93, Loc. Spedaluzzo.* ☎ *055-0196030. $$–$$$. Closed Mon.*

Continue on the S222 to:

❻ ★ Vicchiomaggio. The **Castello di Vicchiomaggio** (☎ www.vicchiomaggio.it; 055-854661) was

Touring the Tuscan hills by bike.

once a 10th-century Lombard fortress. Tours of the estate (1 hr.) are staged daily March through October, but booking is essential. You can also take part in free tastings at their roadside Cantinetta San Jacopo wine shop, on the S222 at the signposted turnoff to the castle. As well as classic Tuscan red wines, pick up a jar of their acclaimed honey.

⑦ ★★ Verrazzano. This hamlet south of Vicchiomaggio was the birthplace of Giovanni da Verrazzano, the first European colonial to sail into the bay of New York in 1524. His former home, wine estate **Castello di Verrazzano** (www.verrazzano.com; ☎ 055-290684), is in a 10th-century tower surrounded by 15th- and 16th-century buildings. Tours run Monday through Friday, costing from 14€ per person. Booking at least 1 day ahead is essential. If you're more pressed for time and just want to taste their excellent estate wines, stop in at the roadside tasting room.

Continue south on the S222 for 5km (3 miles) to Greve, where you should stay overnight.

Wine at Castello di Verrazzano.

⑧ ★★ Greve in Chianti. On the banks of the Greve River stands wine country's unofficial capital. Head for the central square, **Piazza Matteotti,** and park your bike amid 17th-century buildings, wine bars, and restaurants.

For more on Greve, see p 112, ❶.

Start day 2 with a slow climb 6km (3¾ miles) south of Greve to:

⑨ ★★ Panzano in Chianti. This ancient wine village sits on a crest above the Chianti's most famous winegrowing stretch, the Conca d'Oro, or "Golden Shell." Views over the vineyards from the saddle are among the finest in Tuscany.

For more on Panzano, see p 113, ❸.

⑩ ★ Fontodi. By the roadside just south of Panzano, this aristocratic estate—which in fact owns most of the Conca d'Oro—turns out some of the region's best organic Chianti Classico, although its flagship label, Flaccianello, is a 100% sangiovese sold with IGT status. Visits to the cellars are possible by reservation. The estate also produces sublime extra virgin olive oil. *Via San Leolino. www.fontodi.com.* ☎ *055-852005.*

The remainder of the cycle continues south on the S222 to its end, at Siena.

⑪ ★ Castellina in Chianti. Continue straight down the Chianti Road to this fortified town in the "Sienese Chianti." *See p 114, ❺.*

⑫ ★★★ Siena. At the end of the road lies the most beautiful Gothic city in Italy.

For a complete guide to Siena, see the dedicated tour on p 166, in Chapter 6.

Return to Florence by train (bikes are permitted onboard). ●

5

The Best **Regional Tours** of Tuscany

Northwest Tuscany

Aulla
LIGURIA
Parco Naturale
Carrara
di Garfagnana
E80
A12
Massa delle Alpi
Mar. di
Carrara
Marina di Massa
Forte dei
Marmi
Pietrasanta
Viareggio ❼
Lucca ❶
Torre del Lago ❽
Parco Nat.
Tenuta di
S. Rossore
Pisa ❺
Ligurian
Sea
Parco Nat.
Tenuta di
Tombolo
Livorno ❻
(Leghorn)

Castelnuovo
di Garfagnana
Barga
Apuane ❾
Bagni di Lucca
Borgo a. Mozz.
SS12
Pistoia ❹
Montecatini
Terme ❸
Pescia
Monsummano
Terme
Capannori
Vinci
Calci
Montelupo
Empoli
Arno
Pontedera
S. Miniato
Ponsacco
Casciana T.

EMILIA-ROMAGNA
Abetone
SS64
Scarperia
A1
Borgo
S. Lorenzo
Prato ❷
Florence
(Firenze)
Arno
A1
Impruneta
SS222
TUSCANY
Greve in Chianti
Panzano
in Chianti
Castellina
in Chianti

0 ————— 15 mi
0 ————— 15 km

SS1
Castiglioncello
E80
SS1
Cecina

San Gimignano
Poggibonsi
Volterra
Colle di
Val d'Elsa
Saline di
Volterra
Monteriggioni
Pomarance
Larderello
Radicondoli
SS223
S. Galgano
Monteriggioni
Siena
SS73

❶ Lucca
❷ Prato
❸ Montecatini
   Terme
❹ Pistoia
❺ Pisa
❻ Livorno
❼ Viareggio
❽ Torre del Lago
❾ The Garfagnana

Northwest Tuscany, land of Puccini, is best known for the ancient maritime republic of Pisa. But beyond the city and its wonky Tower, there's Lucca, with its tree-lined Renaissance ramparts; the art and architecture of Prato and Pistoia; and the former Medici port of Livorno, with the best seafood restaurants in Tuscany. Finally, when you've had enough of old churches and want your music loud, your beach crowd raucous, and your nightlife frantic, there is Viareggio. START: **Lucca, 80km (50 miles) west of Florence on the A11. Trip Length: 7 days.**

A Note on Hotels, Restaurants, and Tourist Offices. For hotels, restaurants, and detailed information on attractions in Lucca, see p 132; for Pisa, see p 150. We suggest you use the former as an

Previous page: Lucca's Piazza del Anfiteatro.

accommodation base and visit everywhere on this tour as day trips from there. For details on all of Tuscany's local tourist offices, see p 190.

❶ ★★ **Lucca.** The Lucchese say their city—with its 5km (2¾ miles) of stone ramparts—is more impressive than Florence, Pisa, or Siena, rivals since the Middle Ages. A leisurely look is worth at least a day of your time. Bike the walls, admire the ornate Romanesque facades of its churches, and leave time to join the evening *passeggiata* along **Via Fillungo.**

For more on Lucca, see p 132.

On day 2, you have time to visit both Prato (66km/41 miles east of Lucca) and Montecatini Terme (33km/20½ miles northeast of Lucca) by car or train. By rail, alight at Prato Porta al Serraglio for Prato and Montecatini Centro for Montecatini.

❷ ★★ **Prato.** Known since the 13th century for its textiles, Prato has long lived in the shadow of nearby Florence. The city's reputation for business was well-established before Francesco di Marco Datini, the 14th-century "Merchant of Prato," made his money trading with the Papal entourage in Avignon, France. You can visit his former home, the **Palazzo Datini,** Via Mazzei 43 (www.museocasadatini.it; ☎ 0574-21391), where much of the frescoed interior commissioned by Datini survives. *Free admission. Mon–Fri 9am–12:30pm & 3–6pm, Sat 9am–12:30pm (summer hrs. vary).*

The modern city is home to Italy's largest Chinese community, but it's Prato's Romanesque **Duomo,** Piazza del Duomo (☎ 0574-26234), that supplies the principal reason to visit. Housed in an elaborate chapel left of the entrance is the *Sacro Cingolo* (Holy Girdle), reputedly presented to the Apostle "Doubting" Thomas during the Virgin's Assumption. More dazzling still, after a restoration completed in 2007, are the apse frescoes by Fra' Filippo Lippi. Executed between 1452 and 1466, they recount the lives and martyrdoms

of St. Stephen and John the Baptist. Prato was the setting for Lippi's seduction of nun Lucrezia Buti, and the birthplace of their son, High Renaissance painter Filippino (1457–1504). *Admission to chapel with Filippo Lippi frescoes is 3€. Mon–Sat 10am–5pm; Sun 1–5pm.*

The cathedral facade sports a circular pulpit by Donatello and his workshop, from which the Holy Girdle is displayed to the public five times a year. What you see today is a copy: The original forms the centerpiece of the **Museo dell'Opera del Duomo,** Piazza del Duomo 49 (☎ 0574-29339), next door. Michelozzo's bronze pulpit capital also returned here after restoration in 2011. The collection is an otherwise modest one, but your ticket also gets you into the 12th-century cathedral cloister and atmospheric vaults directly below the altar. *Admission 5€. Thurs–Tues 10am–1pm & 2–5pm (Sun 2–5pm only).*

❸ **Montecatini Terme.** Immortalized in Fellini's *8½*, this is Tuscany's most celebrated spa town. Its waters were known by the Romans for their curative powers, and popularized by Grand Duke Pietro

Prato's Piazza del Duomo.

Ancient pool in Montecatini Terme.

Leopoldo I (who later became Holy Roman Emperor Leopold II) in the late 1700s. Most of the buildings sprang up in the early 20th century, and an eclectic, vaguely Art Nouveau style, along with a sense of faded grandeur, is much in evidence along **Viale Verdi.**

Montecatini's waters supposedly have beneficial effects for the liver, intestines, and kidneys. At the oldest and most stately of the thermal houses, **Terme Tettuccio,** Viale Verdi 71 (www.termemontecatini.it; ☎ 0572-778501), clients arrive every morning to enjoy neoclassical grandeur, a live orchestra, a healthy breakfast, and the rapid laxative effects of the mineral-rich water. *Admission from 6€. Daily Easter–Oct.*

From Viale Diaz, a funicular railway ascends to the original Roman settlement, now known as **Montecatini Alto.** Enjoy the summer breezes, an espresso on the piazza, and dramatic views over the Valdinievole. ☎ *0572-766862. Round-trip 7€.*

For a soothing swim in thermal waters, plunge into the outdoor pools at **Grotta Giusti,** just outside Montecatini in Monsummano Terme at Via Grotta Giusti 1411 (www.grottagiustispa.com; ☎ 0572-90771). *Admission 12€; towel, robe & slipper rental extra.*

Spend day 3 in Pistoia, 45km (28 miles) northeast of Lucca. It's easy to reach by both car (via the A11) or train (40 min.–1 hr.).

④ ★★ Pistoia. Around here, if it's green and grows in straight lines, it probably started life somewhere near Pistoia, Tuscany's market garden. The area wasn't always so serene, however: For centuries, the Pistoiesi were known for rudeness and bellicosity. Machiavelli described them as "brought up to slaughter and war," and allegedly the first pistols were made here in the 1540s.

The core of town, **Piazza del Duomo,** centers around the **Cattedrale di San Zeno** and octagonal **Baptistery** opposite. You'll find our favorite Gothic sculptural work in all of Italy, a pulpit by Giovanni Pisano, inside the Romanesque church of **Sant' Andrea.**

For more on Pistoia, including details of a 1-day tour around the center as well as the city's best restaurants, see p 156, in Chapter 6.

On day 4, leave Lucca early by train (30 min.) or drive 22km (14 miles) southwest on the S12r to:

⑤ ★★★ Pisa. The **Duomo** and the **Leaning Tower** are triumphs of the Pisan-Romanesque style—and the city's **Campo dei Miracoli** is rightly among Europe's top tourist magnets.

For more on Pisa, see p 150.

Spend day 5 in Livorno, 50km (31 miles) southwest of Lucca off the A12.

6 ★ Livorno. Called "Leghorn" by the English (a name later immortalized by a type of rooster), the free port of Livorno has a long Anglophile history. Romantic poet Percy Bysshe Shelley wrote *To a Skylark* nearby and sailed to his death from the dock—also built by an Englishman, "Roberto" Dudley. The city, though, was heavily bombed in World War II, and is thus short on traditional "sights." The colonial streets and canals of the ambitiously named **Venezia Nuova** ("New Venice") are the best part of town for a stroll, particularly in the shadow of the 18th-century merchants' palaces along **Via Borra.**

In Piazza Micheli is Livorno's sculptural treasure, the Mannerist **Monumento dei Quattro Mori** (1623–26), the contorted bronze masterpiece of Pietro Tacca, crowned by a statue of Duke Ferdinand I.

Pistoia's Baptistery.

The art highlight is the **Museo Civico** in Villa Mimbelli, Via San Jacopo in Acquaviva 65 (☎ 0586-808001), with an unmatched collection of paintings by the Macchiaioli, 19th-century Tuscan forerunners to Impressionism. Native son Giovanni Fattori, who worked from the 1860s until 1908, is the star attraction. *Admission 3€. Tues–Sun 10am–1pm & 4–7pm.*

The overhaul of the waterfront and its centerpiece, the checkerboard **Terrazza Mascagni,** south of the center, had a profound effect

Monumento dei Quattro Mori.

Viareggio's Carnevale.

on Livornese life. For one thing, bar action has gravitated south to take advantage of the seaside energy. It's also here you'll find the city's best ice cream, at **Gelateria Popolare 2,** Via Meyer 11 (☎ 0586-260354).

7 **Fruits of the Sea.** If you've made it to Livorno, don't leave without trying its seafood, Tuscany's best—and best value. The local specialty is cacciucco—a spicy, tomato-based seafood soup-stew. **Osteria del Mare,** Borgo

Cappuccini 12 (☎ 0586-881027; closed Thurs), is our favorite napkin-and-tablecloth restaurant in the city, with a menu that changes daily based on the freshest catch. **Cantina Senese,** Borgo Cappuccini 95 (☎ 0586-890239; closed Sun), is slightly blue-collar by comparison—but with an equally firm commitment to delivering the best of the seas onto your plate. It's hard to go wrong anywhere in Livorno with a fritto misto, a mixed fry of today's catch, likely to feature some (or all) anchovies, squid, or totani (baby cuttlefish).

Spend your sixth day at the twin (but very different) beach resorts of Viareggio and Torre del Lago. Viareggio is 31km (19 miles) northwest of Lucca off the A11.

8 **Viareggio.** The "Biarritz of the Versilia," an Italian seaside resort *par excellence,* had its heyday in the late 19th century. Its promenade, the **Passeggiata Margherita,** remains one of Italy's most elegant boardwalks—against a backdrop of fashion boutiques, Art Deco bathing establishments (*stablimenti*), cafes, and overpriced seafood restaurants. Its main "sight," the Art

A sea of umbrellas on the beach in Viareggio.

A meal in the Garfagnana valley often begins with antipasti.

Nouveau **Gran Caffè Margherita,** is somewhat of a puffed-up architectural travesty—but it takes a great photo.

What you're really here for is the fine beach—a wide strip of manicured sand with a shallow shelf that's ideal for even little ones to paddle. Viareggio is also one of the few places in Tuscany where you'll find things lively and youth-oriented well into the night, in season at least.

The town hosts Italy's second-most important February **Carnevale** (viareggio.ilcarnevale.com; ☎ 0584-1840750), after Venice.

⑨ Torre del Lago. Music lovers should head 6km (3½ miles) south of Viareggio along pine-lined **Viale dei Tigli,** to pay homage to composer Giacomo Puccini (1858–1924). *Turandot,* his masterpiece and swan song, belongs among the great operas of all time. It is often featured at the annual summer open-air **Festival Pucciniano** (www.puccinifestival.it; ☎ 0584-359322). Tickets range from 20€ to 160€.

Puccini's home on Lago di Massaciuccoli, now the **Museo Villa Puccini** (www.giacomopuccini.it; ☎ 0584-341445), holds mementos, autographed scores, and curios from the daily life of the maestro. The lakeside setting is delightful, with fruit trees and bamboo thickets. *Admission 7€. Tues–Sun 10am–12:40pm & 2–6:40pm (from 4–8pm in July–Aug on days of performances).*

Torre del Lago also has a reputation as one of the most gay-friendly beach resorts in Italy.

On day 7, make a final day trip—this time, into the highlands of the Garfagnana. The main town, Barga, is 37km (23 miles) north of Lucca via the S12 and S445.

⑩ ★★ The Garfagnana. Smothered in chestnut woods and littered with hiking trails, the Garfagnana valley offers a dose of wilderness within easy reach of Lucca. On the way up there, pause in Borgo a Mozzano to view the impossibly narrow, humpbacked 11th-century **Ponte del Diavolo (Devil's Bridge).**

On the return journey to Lucca, stop at the **Antica Locanda di Sesto** to round out your trip to Tuscany's northwest with a special (and affordable) dinner of Lucchese and Garfagnana specialties.

For details on how to spend a day in the Garfagnana, see p 95, ❸.

Chianti & the Val d'Elsa

1. Greve in Chianti
2. Wineries of the Florentine Chianti
3. Panzano
4. Radda in Chianti
5. Castellina in Chianti
6. Monteriggioni
7. San Gimignano
8. Colle di Val d'Elsa

Wedged between Florence and Siena are the most **famous**—and perhaps the most photogenic—hills of Tuscany. The red sangiovese grape is king in the Chianti vineyards, known for wine since the Etruscans were calling the shots in central Italy. Switch to the Val d'Elsa for the atmospheric medieval settlements of Monteriggioni, Colle di Val d'Elsa, and especially San Gimignano. START: **Greve in Chianti, 27km (17 miles) south of Florence, where you'll spend your first 2 nights. Trip Length: 5 days.**

---

1 ★ **Greve in Chianti.** Chianti's "capital" is arranged around triangular **Piazza Matteotti.** All over town you'll see the famous Black Rooster, symbol of the Classico winelands since 1716. A well-stocked wine shop is the **Bottega del Chianti Classico,** Piazza Matteotti 18 (☎ 055-853631). Butcher **Falorni,** nearby at Piazza Matteotti 71 (☎ 055-853029; www.falorni.it),

is a wonderland spot for meat lovers, with every species of salami and fresh cuts inside. ⏱ *1 hr.*

2 ★★ **Wineries of the Florentine Chianti.** Greve makes the best base for exploring the Chianti cantinas—which you could spend anything between a half-day and a lifetime doing. Call in at Greve's **tourist office,** Piazza Matteotti 1

(☎ 055-8546299), for advice and a map. My favorite local tasting spots include **Villa Vignamaggio** (www.vignamaggio.com; ☎ 055-854661), 5km (3 miles) southeast of town off the road to Lamole. The estate where Da Vinci's subject for his *Mona Lisa* was raised was also the first whose wine was recorded as "chianti." Their Riserva is a dark, concentrated delight. Just north of Greve, **Castello di Verrazzano** (www.verrazzano.com; ☎ 055-854243) produces a superlative 100% sangiovese called Sasello and a Super Tuscan with 30% cabernet. Tasting at the roadside cantina is free. Both estates also offer cellar tours and more elaborate food-and-wine tastings, for which you should book a week ahead.

❸ ★ Panzano. This little village is perched on a promontory above the Chianti's most famous stretch—the **Conca d'Oro (Golden Shell).** At **Antica Macelleria Cecchini,** Via XX Luglio 11 (www.dariocecchini.com; ☎ 055-852020), butcher Dario Cecchini entertains visitors with classical music and tastes, or meals, of his excellent produce, while he recites Dante from memory. Uphill in the Old Town is the **Accademia del Buon Gusto,** Piazza Ricasoli 11 (☎ 055-8560159), where

Casks at Castello di Verrazzano.

Stefano Salvadori's enoteca provides a unique wine education and a particular insight into the smaller Chianti estates. Tasting is free and "without obligation." ① *90 min.*

On day 3, divert southeast to Radda before returning to the Chiantigiana, the "Chianti Road," to overnight in Castellina (see p 114). Total distance is 46km (29 miles).

❹ ★ Radda in Chianti. This quaint little town was one of three players in the original Lega del Chianti (Chianti League). At its heart is the 15th-century **Palazzo del Podestà,** studded with the coats of

Radda in Chianti.

Village of Castellina in Chianti.

arms of past rulers. A short drive (8km/5 miles) east of the walls is **Badia a Coltibuono** (www.coltibuono.com; ☎ 0577-749479), a Vallombrosan abbey from the 1100s that's now an estate with a robust Chianti Classico Riserva. *Tasting free at roadside osteria. Mar–Dec daily.* ⏱ *1 hr.*

⑤ ★ Castellina in Chianti. Castellina's central Piazza del Comune is dominated by the crenellated **Rocca,** which now houses the **Museo Archeologico** (www.museoarcheologicochianti.it; ☎ 0577-742090; Apr, May, Sept, Oct open daily 10am–6pm; June–Aug open daily 11am–7pm; Nov–Mar open Sat–Sun 10am–5pm)—after viewing Etruscan artifacts, climb the Torre for sweeping views of the Sienese Chianti. Stroll evocative "tunnel street" **Via delle Volte,** a soldiers' walk from the town's days as a Florentine bastion. **Andrea Rontini,** at no. 36 (☎ 0577-742016), sells stunning photographic prints of Tuscany from 15€. Castellina's gelateria, **Antica Delizia,** Via Fiorentina 4 (www.anticadelizia.it; ☎ 0577-741337; closed Tues), sells the best gelato for miles in any direction. ⏱ *90 min.*

On day 4, switch from the Chianti to the Val d'Elsa. First head south

down the S222 as far as the SI-FI *raccordo,* then turn north. After a short stop in Monteriggioni, head to San Gimignano for 2 nights. Total driving distance is 53km (33 miles).

⑥ ★ Monteriggioni. In his *Commedia,* Dante compared the towers of Monteriggioni to giants. All 14 of the tiny town's turrets and its ring of walls are still here, more or less, and still look like that "circle of titans" guarding the lowest level of Dante's Hell. Scale the ramparts (1.50€; Apr–Sept only), admire the view, wander the two stone streets of this most perfectly preserved fortified village in Italy, grab a *caffè,* and continue on your way. ⏱ *1 hr.*

⑦ ★★★ San Gimignano. For a rundown of how to spend your time here, and where to stay and dine, see p 160, in Chapter 6.

Spend the morning of day 5 in San Gimignano, before driving 15km (10 miles) southeast to:

⑧ ★ Colle di Val d'Elsa. Colle's major marks on the history of Tuscany both happened in the 1200s: The pretty *città alta* ranged along a snaking ridge was the birthplace of master Gothic architect Arnolfo di Cambio (in 1240) and the site of a famous victory for Florence's Guelph army over Sienese Ghibellines, in 1269. Enter the oldest part of town across the viaduct and through Baccio d'Agnolo's **Palazzo Campana** gate (1539), then follow Via Campana to the **Duomo,** Piazza del Duomo. Inside there's a bronze *Crucifix* designed by Giambologna but cast by his student Pietro Tacca in 1608. The small **Museo Civico,** Via del Castello 33 (www.museisenesi.org; ☎ 0577-923095), houses two ethereal Sienese *Madonnas* by near-contemporaries of Duccio. *Admission 4€. Fri–Sun 11:30am–5pm.*

Return to San Gimignano to spend your final night there.

Where to **Stay & Dine**

For hotels and restaurants in San Gimignano, see p 165.

★★ **Albergaccio** CASTELLINA
MODERN TUSCAN Reservations are essential at this outpost of creative, strictly seasonal Tuscan cuisine served in refined-rustic surrounds. *Via Fiorentina 63. www.albergaccio cast.com.* ☎ *0577-741042. Entrees 25€. Lunch, dinner Mon–Sat.*

★★ **Cetinelle** NEAR GREVE A remote and secluded B&B, with unforgettable sunset views over the winelands toward Greve. The good-size rooms are simple yet comfortable with luxurious touches. *Via Canonica 13. www.cetinelle.com.* ☎ *055-8544745. 8 units. Doubles 70€–95€, w/ breakfast. Closed Jan to mid-Mar.*

Colombaio CASTELLINA Great-value roadside inn whose midsize rooms have sloping beam-and-tile ceilings and terracotta floors. Upstairs units are lighter and airier, with views over the vineyards. *Via Chiantigiana 29. www.albergoil colombaio.it.* ☎ *0577-740444. 13 units. Doubles 90€–100€, w/breakfast.*

★ **Dario DOC** PANZANO *FAST FOOD* It's had a few changes of name—and is still best known as MacDario—but the winning formula has never altered: fresh, bread-crumbed beef burger, oven-cooked "fries," sides, and relishes served fast and with a flourish at communal tables. More formal lunches and dinners are also available on the premises, with a daily **Officina della Bistecca** feast. *Via XX Luglio 11. www. dariocecchini.com.* ☎ *055-852020. Set menu 10–20€. Lunch Mon–Sat.*

★★ **Officina della Cucina Popolare** COLLE VAL D'ELSA *TUSCAN* Dine in the stylish modern interior or grab one of a few outside tables. A succinct menu is sustained by local producers and includes simple, tasty fare like pork ribs or sausages on the grill. *Via Gracco del Secco 86. www.ristorante officinacolle.it.* ☎ *0577-921796. Entrees 7€–13€. Dinner Tues–Sun.*

★★ **Vicchiomaggio** NEAR GREVE On this fine-wine estate homey apartments are tucked away in the turrets and salons of a storybook castle, while a converted priory also houses guests amid chic country styling. All share a shady formal garden and a swimming pool that hangs over the vineyards. *Via Vicchiomaggio 4. www.vicchio maggio.it.* ☎ *055-854079. 16 units. Doubles 130€–195€, w/breakfast.*

Cetinelle, near Greve.

The **Val d'Orcia & Valdichiana**

1. Buonconvento
2. Montalcino
3. Sant'Antimo
4. Bagno Vignoni
5. San Quirico d'Orcia
6. Pienza
7. Montepulciano
8. Sarteano
9. Chiusi
10. Lucignano
11. Monte San Savino
12. Castiglion Fiorentino
13. Arezzo
14. Cortona

This road-trip itinerary covering southeastern Tuscany takes in two of the region's great valleys. The silent, cypress-studded landscape of the Val d'Orcia—emerald green in spring, burnt copper in high summer—has become an iconic image that represents Tuscany itself. The sweeping trough cut by the Valdichiana is the only place a true *bistecca alla fiorentina* (T-bone-like beefsteak) can call home: White Chianina cattle are native here. Southeastern Tuscany is also home to fine medieval and Renaissance art, less-visited towns with quiet charm in abundance, and two great wines that surpass even Chianti at its best. START: **Siena, 72km (45 miles) south of Florence. Trip length: 7 days.**

A Note on Hotels & Restaurants
For hotels, restaurants, and detailed information on attractions in Arezzo, see p 124; in Cortona, see p 128; in Montepulciano, see p 142; in Pienza, see p 146. For hotels and restaurants for other overnight stops on the tour, see p 123. For details of Tuscany's major local tourist offices, see p 190.

Head south down the S2 via Buonconvento, to Montalcino (44km/27 miles distant), where you'll spend your first night (see p 122).

❶ ★ Buonconvento. Park right at the roadside outside the well-tended medieval walls of this prim, tidy town—site of the death of Holy Roman Emperor Henry VII in 1313 (his tomb is inside Pisa's Duomo). You'll find work by important Sienese artists such as Matteo di Giovanni, Pietro Lorenzetti, and Sano di Pietro hanging in the town's **Museo d'Arte Sacra della Val d'Arbia,** Via Soccini 18 (www.museisenesi.org; ☎ 0577-807190). The ticket desk doubles as the local tourist information office. *Admission 3€. Fri–Sun 10am–1pm & 3–6pm (until 5pm Sun).*

The nearby church of **SS Pietro e Paolo** was substantially remodeled in the 18th century but still houses 15th-century panels by the prolific Matteo di Giovanni and Pietro di Francesco Orioli.

❷ ★★ Montalcino. As wine lovers well know, this rustic hilltown of cobbled stone streets and narrow stairways is the source of one of the world's greatest red vintages, **Brunello di Montalcino.** The walled town is visible for miles around, with the spires of its medieval buildings studding the air like asparagus. The **Enoteca La Fortezza** (www.enotecalafortezza.com; ☎ 0577-849211) is installed in the town's main attraction, a fortress where the Sienese Republic holed up for 4 years after final defeat by Florence in 1555. As well as wine, its former keep stocks local foodstuffs including pecorino cheese and Montalcino honey (famous among gourmets). Of course, most come here to taste and buy some of more than 200 Brunellos. Mount the ramparts for a wide, sweeping view from the Val d'Orcia to Monte Amiata. *Admission (ramparts) 4€. Apr–Oct daily 9am–8pm; Nov–Mar daily 10am–6pm.*

The town's gathering place is **Fiaschetteria Italiana,** Piazza del Popolo 6 (☎ 0577-849043), an Art Nouveau cafe with comfortable banquettes and marble tables. It has served the celebrated local wine since 1888.

Don't leave town without a stop at one of Tuscany's best small museums, the **Musei di Montalcino,** Via Ricasoli (☎ 0577-864014), with its collection of mostly Sienese sacred art, including four carved Crucifixions from the 1300s. *Admission 5€. Tues–Sun 10am–1pm & 2–5:50pm.*

For details on wine tasting in & around Montalcino, see p 91, ❸.

Old town of Buonconvento.

Wine for sale at the Enoteca La Fortezza.

On day 2, head south of town on the road to Castelnuovo dell'Abate; it's 9km (5½ miles) to:

❸ ★★★ **Sant'Antimo.** An idyllic glade below Castelnuovo dell'Abate is home to the photogenic Romanesque Abbazia di Sant'Antimo. In the 12th century, it became a Cistercian abbey, and today remains Tuscany's most harmonious example of Romanesque architecture in the Lombard French style, with a semicircular apse, intricate carved capitals, and a 30m (100-ft.) bell tower. The French monks worship with chant six times every day, and you're welcome to attend. Services are at 7am, 9am, 12:45pm, 3:30pm, 7pm, and 8:30pm (9pm in the summer). 🕐 *1 hr. www.antimo.it.* ☎ *0577-835659. Free admission. Daily 10am–1pm & 3–6pm.*

Sant'Antimo.

Return to the S2 via the S323 past Castiglione d'Orcia and the Rocca d'Orcia, a prominent medieval watchtower. It's 20km (12 miles) to:

❹ **Bagno Vignoni.** The steaming, sulfurous waters of this curious little village have been frequented since Roman times, notably by Lorenzo de' Medici "the Magnificent" and St. Catherine of Siena. These days it's more likely to be amateur photographers coming to snap the *piazza d'acqua*, a 49m x 29m (161 ft. x 95 ft.) porticoed Renaissance pool built where the main village square used to be. You can no longer take the plunge here, but to soak away your cares, head to **Antiche Terme di Bagno Vignoni,** Piazza del Moretto 12 (www.termedibagnovignoni.it; ☎ **0577–887635**), or **Piscina Val di Sole,** at the Hotel Posta Marcucci (www.piscinavaldisole.it; ☎ **0577–887112**). 🕐 *45 min/2 hrs. with soak.*

Continue north on the S2, for 5km (3 miles) to:

❺ ★ **San Quirico d'Orcia.** This little walled farming town, with its magnificent travertine Gothic-Romanesque **Collegiata dei Santi Quirico e Giulitta,** was once an important stopover along the Via Francigena, the pilgrim route that linked Canterbury (in England) with

Rome. Its quaint streets and formal 1540 gardens, the **Horta Leonini,** Piazza della Libertà, are a delightful spot to kill a couple of hours.

For a taste of 21st-century Tuscany, stop in at **Birrificio San Quirico,** Via Dante Alighieri 93a (www.birrificiosanquirico.it; ☎ 0577-898193). Tuscany's artisan brewing industry is flourishing, and the blonde and amber ales crafted at this little place are among the best in the region. ⏱ *2 hr.*

Strike northeast on the S146 for Pienza, where you should spend your second night. Total distance from San Quirico is 10km (6 miles)

⑥ ★★ Pienza. The architectural jewel of southern Tuscany was rebuilt in the mid-15th century as a model Renaissance city. Pienza is small enough to take in over an afternoon and evening. Don't leave without enjoying the breathtaking view over the entire Val d'Orcia from **Via del Casello.**

For details of hotels, restaurants, & what to see in Pienza, see p 146, in Chapter 6.

On day 3, head east on the S146 for 13km (8 miles) to:

⑦ ★★★ Montepulciano. Take a full day to study the *palazzo* architecture, taste the wine, and sample the excellent restaurants in southern Tuscany's highest hilltown—it might take you all day to make your way up the steep main street to Piazza Grande at the top.

For hotels, restaurants & details on how to spend 1 day in Montepulciano, see p 142, in Chapter 6.

On your fourth morning, head south on the S146 past Chianciano, then follow signs for Sarteano, a total journey of 19km (12 miles).

⑧ ★ Sarteano. Distinctly off the regular tourist trail, this little walled town remains one of our favorite

Ancient thermal baths of Bagno Vignoni.

places to while away a morning (and have lunch; see p 122) in southern Tuscany. Come on a Saturday and you can join a tour run by the **Museo Civico,** Via Roma 24 (www.museosarteano.it; ☎ 0578-269261), to see the **Tomba della Quadriga Infernale.** This unique Etruscan tomb frescoed with a demonic charioteer was only discovered in 2003; visits are strictly limited, but a replica of part of the tomb is downstairs in the museum if the tour is full or you aren't here on a Saturday. Other tombs in the spectacularly sited **Pianacce** necropolis are open daily (and free). *Tour plus museum: Admission 8€; Sat only: June–Sept at 9:30am & 6pm, Oct–May at 11am; booking (by phoning 0578-269261 or e-mailing museo@comune.sarteano.siena.it) is essential. Museum only: Admission 4€; Apr–Oct Tues–Sun 10:30am–12:30pm & 4–7pm; weekends only otherwise.*

Also worth tracking down is a 1546 *Annunciation* by the last great Sienese painter, Mannerist Domenico Beccafumi. It's in the boxy little church of **San Martino,** Piazza San Martino. If the church is locked, as it often is in low season, there's a key at the tiny tourist office (Corso Garibaldi 9; weekends only).

Main square of Montepulciano.

Follow signposts northeast for Chiusi, 12km (7 miles) away. Spend the afternoon and overnight here, your first stop in the Valdichiana.

9 ★ **Chiusi.** If you're on the trail of the Etruscans, head here to see what's left of one of the most powerful cities in their 12-city confederation (the *Dodecapoli*). So powerful was Chiusi, then known as Clevsin, that its king, Lars Porsenna, attacked Rome in 508 B.C. What's left of Clevsin is buried under the little town today. Explore it for yourself with a subterranean tour of the **Labirinto di Porsenna,** Piazza Duomo (lnx.prolocochiusi.it; ☎ 0578-226490). *Admission 3€. Guided visits June–Oct 15 daily 9:45am–12:45pm & 4–6.30pm; Oct 16–Jan 6 daily 9:45am–12:45pm, also Sun 4–6:30pm; Feb–Mar Tues, Thurs, Sat 9:45am–12:45am, Sun 3–5:15pm.*

Chiusi's **Museo Archeologico Nazionale,** Via Porsenna (☎ 0578-20177), is one of Italy's outstanding Etruscan museums. Wander past alabaster funerary urns, black and orange Attic-style ceramics, Bucchero pottery, and a 6th-century-B.C. sphinx. Most were recovered from necropoli around the town; those tombs are also open daily for visits (ask at the museum desk). *Admission 6€. Daily 9am–8pm.*

Day 5 makes a whistlestop tour of the charming, less-visited small towns of the Valdichiana. Start early and take the A1 bound for Florence for 25km (15 miles) until the exit for Sinalunga/Lucignano. Follow signs for another 14km (9 miles) to:

10 ★ **Lucignano.** In an ideal world, you'd get your first sight of this little place from the air: Its elliptical street layout is unique in the annals of Tuscan town planning. Like a simplified maze, the village is laid out in four concentric ellipses with quaint little squares in the center. One is dominated by the **Collegiata,** with its 18th-century double half-oval staircase by Andrea Pozzo.

The highlight of the tiny **Museo di Lucignano,** Piazza del Tribunale (☎ 0575-838001), is the *Albero della Vita* (*Tree of Life*), a complex 14th-century reliquary made by Sienese goldsmiths. The *Tree,* and the frescoed Sala di Buon Governo that houses it, is a popular spot for wedding vows. *Admission 5€. Mid-Mar to Oct Thurs–Sun 10am–1pm & 2:30–6pm; Nov–Feb Fri–Sun 10am–1pm & 2:30–5:30pm.*

Drive a scenic road 8km (5 miles) north to:

11 ★ **Monte San Savino.** The birthplace of High Renaissance sculptor Andrea Sansovino (1460–1529) is another quiet little Valdichiana hilltown that's managed to avoid the perils (and riches) of commercial mass tourism. Dotted with medieval and Renaissance *palazzi*, it invites exploration and aimless wandering.

As you hoof it around the town, you can see some of Sansovino's works, notably his tabernacles at the little church of **Santa Chiara,** Piazza Gamurrini (☎ 0575-849418). There's also some trademark Luca della Robbia glazed terracotta on display. If the church is locked, call at the tourist office (up the stairs immediately to the right) for the key. *Free admission. Wed–Fri (Apr–Oct also Tues) 9am–1pm; Sat–Sun 9am–1pm & 2:30–6pm.*

The 1520 **Loggia dei Mercanti,** Corso Sangallo, with its Corinthian columns, is also attributed to Sansovino. Across the street is Antonio da Sangallo the Elder's **Palazzo di Monte.** Farther up the hill, at the Piazza di Monte, is the church of **Sant'Agostino.** Sansovino renovated the building in 1532, adding the cloister and gallery, and there's a fine stained-glass window of *St. Augustine* by Guillaume de Marcillat. Schedule a late lunch on the panoramic terrace at **Belvedere** (p 122).

Drive 17km (10 miles) east to Castiglion Fiorentino, where you should spend the night (see p 122).

⓬ ★ **Castiglion Fiorentino.** You can't miss it: as you approach, the **Torre del Cassero,** a pronglike tower built in the 1330s by the Perugians, looms over the town's skyline. (You can climb it on weekends May–Sept 10am–12:30pm and 4–6:30pm; admission 1.50€.) Wandering into the little hilltown takes you through a medieval girdle of fortified walls, leading to its hub, **Piazza del Municipio.** Dominating the square is the (now somewhat tattered) **Loggia di Vasari,** reputedly designed by Renaissance man Giorgio Vasari in the 16th century.

The town's best museum is the **Pinacoteca Comunale,** inside the deconsecrated church of Sant'Angelo al Cassero, directly uphill from Piazza del Municipio (☎ 0575-659457). It houses a 13th-century Umbrian Crucifix and a couple of panels by Bartolomeo della Gatta, including his bizarre *St. Francis Receiving the Stigmata.* There's also access to the church's atmospheric crypt. *Admission 3€. May–Sept Tues–Sun 10am–1pm & 4–7pm.*

On day 6, drive north up the S71 for 18km (11 miles) to:

⓭ ★★ **Arezzo.** Make your first stop at **San Francesco,** to reserve a slot to view Tuscany's greatest fresco cycle, before exploring the rest of eastern Tuscany's "capital" and overnighting in the center.

For a detailed rundown of hotels, restaurants & sights in the city, see p 124, in Chapter 6.

On your final morning, head south on the S71 for 29km (18 miles) to:

⓮ ★★ **Cortona.** This steep, cobblestoned art city is your final stopover: There's no better spot to survey the entire Valdichiana, the so-called "breadbasket of Italy," than from the ramparts of its **Fortezza Medicea.**

For a complete rundown of Cortona's attractions, hotels, restaurants, shops & nightlife, see the Cortona section in Chapter 6.

Castiglion Fiorentino.

Where to **Stay & Dine**

★ **Belvedere** MONTE SAN SAVINO *TUSCAN* At this aptly-named rural restaurant with splendid views over olive groves, service is formal—but that's not reflected in the good-value prices. The kitchen specializes in Valdichiana dishes like *polpette di Chianina* (veal meatballs). *Loc. Bano 226. www. ristorante-belvedere.net.* ☎ *0575-844262. Entrees 7€–13€. Lunch, dinner Wed–Sun.*

★ **Casa Toscana** CHIUSI This B&B inside a handsome Liberty villa combines modern amenities with an eye for design: Rooms are color-washed in rich Tuscan tones, mattresses are firm, and furniture is modern but modeled on antique styles. *Via Baldetti 37. www.bandbcasatoscana.it.* ☎ *0578-222227. 8 units. Doubles 75€, w/breakfast. Closed Mon–Wed in winter.*

★ **Da Gagliano** SARTEANO *TUSCAN* At this small dining room, the menu follows the waxing and waning of the seasons—few ingredients are sourced from beyond the local hills. *Secondi* such as *coniglio al tegame con lardo e finocchio selvatico* (pan-fried rabbit with cured ham fat and wild fennel) are memorable. *Via Roma 5.* ☎ *0578-268022. Entrees 9€–13€. Lunch, dinner Thurs–Mon (daily Aug; weekends only Nov–Mar).*

★ **Porta Castellana** MONTALCINO It's well worth booking ahead at this stylish three-room B&B built into brick-vaulted former storehouses on the edge of Montalcino. Breakfast in the garden as the mists rise from the Val d'Orcia below is unforgettable. *Via S. Lucia 20. www.portacastellana.it.* ☎ *0577-839001. 3 units. Doubles 85€, w/breakfast.*

Re di Macchia MONTALCINO *SOUTHERN TUSCAN* Local cooking around here means one thing: meat, especially game such as wild boar and hare, for *antipasto, primo,* and *secondo* if you dare. The powerful flavors and warrenlike setting are just right to chase down a bottle of the iconic Brunello. *Via Saloni 21.* ☎ *0577-846116. Entrees 16€. Lunch, dinner Fri–Wed.*

★★ **Viziottavo** CASTIGLION FIORENTINO Snug, contemporary rooms are themed around the seven deadly sins and come with modern amenities like air-conditioning and chromatherapy showers, but there's just enough terracotta and exposed wood to retain some Tuscan ambience. *Via San Michele 69. www.viziottavo.com.* ☎ *0575-659534. 8 units. Doubles 70€–90€, w/breakfast. Closed some weekdays Jan–Mar, Nov.*

★★ **Zaira** CHIUSI *SOUTHERN TUSCAN/ETRUSCAN* The finest food in a town that punches above its weight when it comes to cooking: Try meat dishes like rabbit with lemon or duck cooked in Vino Nobile. Then ask to see the underground wine cellar, inside an Etruscan well that dates to 500 B.C. *Via Arunte 12. www.zaira.it.* ☎ *0578-20260. Entrees 8€–16€. Lunch, dinner Tues–Sun (daily July–Sept & Dec).* ●

Arezzo

- ⓘ Tourist Information
- Ⓟ Parking

❶ Piazza Grande
❷ Galleria Il Pozzo
❸ Pieve di Santa Maria
❹ Basilica di San Francesco
❺ Casa di Vasari
❻ San Domenico
❼ Duomo
❽ Busatti
❾ Cremí

Where to Stay
Antiche Mura **10**
Graziella Hotel Patio **13**
Vogue **12**

Where to Dine
Gastronomia Il Cervo **11**
L'Agania **14**
La Torre di Gnicche **15**

Map labels: S. Domenico, Piazza S. Domenico, Il Prato, Fortezza Medicea, Duomo, Via Garibaldi, Via XX Settembre, Via Sassoverde, Via Ricasoli, Via d. Pileati, Viale Bruno Buozzi, Via Pellicceria, S. Maria in Gradi, Museo Statale d'Arte Medievale e Moderna, Via S. Lorentino, Piaggia di Murello, Via Saracino, Via Cavour, Via d. Fioraia, Pieve di Sta. Maria, Piazza Grande, Via Cesalpino, Via Mazzini, Piazza San Geminiano, Minerva, Via Cavour, Via G. Oberdan, Via della Garibaldi, Piazza di Badia, Piazza S. Francesco, Badia, Basilica di San Francesco, Sant' Agostino, Piazza Sant'Agostino, Via Porta Buia, Piazza del Popolo, Via Monaco, Via de' Cenci, Via Italia, Via Pietro Aretino, Piazza Guido Monaco, Via Petrarca, Via della Madonna del Prato, Via Roma, Via Francesco Crispi, Anfiteatro Romano, S. Bernardo, Via Guido, Via Corso, Via Spinello, 100 m / 300 ft

Aretines are a proud and prosperous bunch, racing their Vespas through the Etruscan-era streets of their bustling town abutting fertile Valdarno and Valdichiana farmlands. Famous native sons include the poet Petrarch (1304–74); architect and author Giorgio Vasari (1512–74); and director/actor Roberto Benigni (b. 1952), who brought Arezzo to a world audience in *Life Is Beautiful*. Time here is best spent strolling the steep streets of the medieval core and viewing the frescoes by Piero della Francesca in the Basilica di San Francesco. START: **Arezzo is 81km (50 miles) southeast of Florence, well signposted from the A1. Trip length: 1 day.**

❶ ★★ Piazza Grande. This lopsided square began sinking at one end almost as soon as it was laid out around 1200, and it's been unstoppable since. The **Loggia di**

Previous page: Cortona's Palazzo Comunale.

Vasari, on the eastern (high) side, was designed by the legendary art historian, with obvious similarities to Florence's Uffizi. Note the semicircular apse at the rear of the Pieve di Santa Maria, typical of the Romanesque style. ⓘ *15 min.*

Vasari's loggia on the Piazza Grande.

② **Galleria Il Pozzo.** A charming jumble of a shop where you can pick up a *faux*-antique print, small watercolor, photograph of a Tuscan landscape, or bits and pieces of old decorative masonry. *Piazza Grande 40.* ☎ *0575-352704.*

Shopping Tip Diehard shoppers should time their visit to coincide with the Arezzo Antique Market, which takes over Piazza Grande on the first Sunday of each month and the Saturday before. Bargains and rare finds usually disappear by 10am.

③ **★ Pieve di Santa Maria.** This 12th-century church backing onto Piazza Grande is a stellar example of the Romanesque style, with each of 88 external columns on the facade uniquely sculpted and ascending in multiple tiers. The chief treasure inside is Pietro Lorenzetti's 1320 polyptych of the *Madonna and Child with Saints*, on the high altar above the crypt. Notice how St. Luke on the pinnacle panels witnesses the *Annunciation* and writes it down in his Gospel, a unique narrative feature. ⏱ *20 min. Corso Italia 7.* ☎ *0575-22629. Free admission. Daily 8am–noon & 3–6pm.*

④ **★★★ Basilica di San Francesco.** Between 1452 and 1466, Piero della Francesca painted his *Legend of the True Cross* inside San Francesco's Cappella Bacci—a cycle of frescoes based on Jacopo da Varazze's 1260 *Golden Legend.* They are rightly talked about in the same art-historical league as the Sistine Chapel. Each of the 10 panels is remarkable for its grace, ascetic severity, narrative detail, compositional precision, and dramatic light effects—"the most perfect morning light in all Renaissance painting," wrote art historian Kenneth Clark. They also feature some of the strangest hats ever frescoed. ⏱ *45 min. Piazza San Francesco. www.pierodellafrancesca.it.* ☎ *0575-352727. Admission 8€. Mon–Fri 9am–7pm, Sat 9am–6pm, Sun 1pm–6pm.*

⑤ **★ Casa di Vasari.** The first art historian—who chronicled the lives of Michelangelo, da Vinci, Masaccio and others—Vasari (1511–74) bought this house in 1540. He decorated it with Mannerist artworks, often by his students, but executed the allegorical frescoes in the **Sala del Trionfo della Virtù** himself. Clearly he was a much better architect and writer than he was painter,

Ancient water tap in front of Arezzo's church of San Domenico.

but the works do provide a fascinating window into the High Renaissance prosperous lifestyle and the influence of classical ideas on 16th-century Tuscan elites. ① *30 min. Via XX Settembre 55.* ☎ *0575-409040. Admission 4€. Wed–Sat & Mon, 8:30am–7pm; Sun 8:30am–1pm.*

⑥ ★ **San Domenico.** The curious lopsided facade of this 13th-century basilica, which Vasari claimed was by Nicola Pisano, hides one of Arezzo's most ancient treasures: a Crucifix painted around 1260 by a young Cimabue, teacher of Giotto and "father" of Tuscan art. Fragmentary frescoes by local master Spinello Aretino (1350–1410) adorn both walls of the nave. ① *15 min. Piazza San Domenico 7.* ☎ *0575-23255. Free admission. Daily 9am–6:30pm.*

⑦ ★ **Duomo.** At the highest point in town, Arezzo's 13th-century cathedral is a rare Tuscan Gothic construction that symbolically towers over the civic Palazzo del Comune opposite. Don't miss Piero della Francesca's 1459 *Mary Magdalene* and the stained-glass

windows recounting the *Life of Christ,* by Guillaume de Marcillat (1470–29), a French master who spent the last 10 years of his life creating these seven magnificent works in the right aisle. The adjacent park, **Il Prato,** is a good spot to take a breather, or let the kids run about. ① *15 min. Piazza del Duomo.* ☎ *0575-23991. Free admission. Daily 7am–12:30pm & 3–6:30pm.*

⑧ ★ **Busatti.** Since 1842, the Busatti-Sassolini family from Anghiari has been selling exquisite textiles and handmade fabrics—including sumptuous linens; and hemp, cotton, and wool items such as curtains, towels, cushions, tablecloths, and rugs in several colors. *Corso Italia 48. www. busatti.com.* ☎ *0575-355295.*

⑨ **Cremì.** Interrupt your shopping with a stop for the best artisan gelato in town. They also sell pancakes with a choice of sweet fillings. *Corso Italia 100. No phone. $.*

Where to **Stay & Dine**

★★ Antiche Mura CENTRO STORICO   Whitewashed stone-and-plaster walls, parquet floors, and baroque furnishings cut a contemporary *figura* at this stylish B&B just downhill from the Duomo. Rooms are midsize and modern—and ideal for a romantic getaway on a budget. Credit cards not accepted. *Piaggia di Murello 35. www.antichemura.info.* ☎ *0575-20410. 6 units. Doubles 75€–95€, w/ breakfast.*

★★ Gastronomia Il Cervo CENTRO STORICO *MODERN ITALIAN*   There is a good à la carte menu here, but I prefer to pick from the downstairs deli bar, loaded with dishes prepared that morning. Filling, creative salads like pasta with zucchini, speck, and Parmesan, or squid with potato and celery always hit the mark. *Via Cavour 38–40 (at Via Guido Monaco).* ☎ *0575-20872. Entrees 8€–10€. Lunch Tues–Sun, dinner Tues–Sat.*

★★ Graziella Hotel Patio CENTRO STORICO   For atmosphere, this ambitious hotel in the 18th-century Palazzo de' Giudici is our local favorite. Each of the large units is dedicated to one of Bruce Chatwin's travel tales, with furniture from the country it represents—like Emperor Wu-Ti accessories from China. *Via Cavour 23. www.hotel patio.it.* ☎ *0575-401962. 10 units. Doubles 135€–240€, w/breakfast. Closed 2 weeks in Jan.*

★ L'Agania CENTRO STORICO *TRADITIONAL ARETINE*   Locals and visitors have been packing this place since 1905 for rib-sticking *ribollita* (hearty vegetable soup),

hand-rolled pasta, and robust value fare such as *fegatelli* (pig's liver). *Via Mazzini 10. www.agania.com.* ☎ *0575-295381. Entrees 6€–10€. Lunch, dinner Tues–Sun.*

★★ La Torre di Gnicche CENTRO STORICO *TUSCAN/WINE BAR*   The emphasis in this bottle-lined room is on wine, with more than 30 choices available by the glass and hundreds by the bottle. It's accompanied by a huge selection of cheeses and salamis and many local favorites, such as *baccalà in umido* (salt-cod stew). *Piaggia San Martino 8. www.latorre dignicche.it.* ☎ *0575-352-035. Main courses 7€–11€. Lunch, dinner Thurs–Tues. Closed 2 wks in Jan.*

Vogue CENTRO STORICO   An excellent central location couples with style in these large and distinctive rooms, some with nice views over the rooftop of the old city. *Via Guido Monaco 54. www.voguehotel. it.* ☎ *0575-24361. 26 units. Doubles 120€–220€, w/breakfast.*

One of the modern Italian dishes served at Gastronomia Il Cervo.

Cortona

❶ Museo Diocesano

❷ Museo dell'Accademia Etrusca e della Città

❸ L'Antico Cocciaio

❹ Tuscher

❺ Terrabruga

❻ Via Crucis

❼ Fortezza Medicea Girifalco

❽ Santa Maria delle Grazie al Calcinaio

Where to Stay
Il Falconiere 9
Hotel Italia 10
San Michele 11

Where to Dine
Dardano 14
La Loggetta 13
Osteria del Teatro 15
Trattoria la Grotta 12

Nightlife
Enoteca Enotria 16

ⓘ Tourist Information
Ⓟ Parking
Pedestrian Only

Cortona, as much as anywhere in Tuscany, has a fair claim to the title "city of art." Luca Signorelli (1445–1523) and Sassetta (1392–1451) were both Cortonese; Fra' Angelico lived here for a decade. At its peak Cortona rivaled Arezzo and Perugia, and almost Florence, in power and prestige. Memories of its heyday linger in its art collections and medieval architecture, making it one of Tuscany's most romantic hilltowns. Despite this embarrassment of cultural riches, it was a much more recent phenomenon that placed Cortona on the tourist map: Frances Mayes' bestseller *Under the Tuscan Sun*. START: **Cortona is 106km (63 miles) southeast of Florence on the S71. Trip length: 1 day.**

❶ ★★ **Museo Diocesano.** Cortona's small yet outstanding collection of sacred art reflects the town's former glory and its position at the crossroads of influences from Florence, Siena, and the neighboring region of Umbria. Native son Luca Signorelli is the predictable star, in particular his monumental 1502 *Lamentation*, complete with surreal background scenes including the Crucifixion and Resurrection. Elsewhere in this deconsecrated church turned museum, Fra' Angelico's gentle *Annunciation* (1436) over the former baptismal font reveals him

Santa Margherita Via Crucis.

in top form, on his favorite subject. The narrative scenes from the *Life of the Virgin* on the predella are especially charming. Also represented are Sienese master Pietro Lorenzetti (1280–1348) and Florentine Bartolomeo della Gatta (1448–1502), and a fine Greco-Roman sarcophagus from the 2nd century even pops up. ⏱ *1 hr. Piazza del Duomo.* ☎ *0575-4027268. Admission 5€. Daily 10am–7pm (closed Mon Nov–Mar).*

❷ ★★ Museo dell'Accademia Etrusca e della Città (MAEC).

The 13th-century Palazzo Casali shows off the history of the *città*

Artifact in Cortona's Museo dell'Accademia Etrusca e della Città.

from its prehistoric origins through its Etruscan pomp and Roman decline, using a sequence of multimedia displays from the area's many ancient digs. Upstairs, the eclectic collection of the Accademia Etrusca meanders through a collection of Egyptian mummies and a room dedicated to Futurist Gino Severini to 17th-century celestial globes, Quattrocento ivories, and Etruscan bronze figurines. The prize find is an intact Etruscan bronze lamp from the 4th century B.C., in Room 5. ⏱ *1 hr. Piazza Signorelli 9. www.cortonamaec.org.* ☎ *0575-637235. Admission 10€. Apr–Oct daily 10am–7pm; Nov–Mar closed Mon.*

❸ ★ L'Antico Cocciaio.

Cortona is known for its ceramics, and Cocciaio is the oldest of the town's outlets. The traditional patterns in green, cream, and dark yellow are prominent. This shop is unbelievably stuffed—don't bring your pet bull. *Via Benedetti 24. www.lantico cocciaio.com.* ☎ *0575-605294.*

❹ Caffe Tuscher.

Pause for sustenance at Cortona's most elegant bar-cafe, with an attractive mix of visitors and locals. Excellent pastries, snacks, and coffee are available. *Via Nazionale 43. www. caffetuschercortona.com.* ☎ *0575-62053. $.*

Santa Maria delle Grazie al Calcinaio.

❺ ★ Terrabruga. The designs here are slightly more contemporary, but still offer a wide array of ceramics in traditional Cortonese colors and motifs. These authentic craftwares are designed and manufactured by hand in Giulio Lucarini's workshop. *Via Nazionale 56. www. terrabruga.com.* ☎ *0575-604405.*

❻ ★ Via Crucis. The torturous, stepped ascent up Cortona's Via Santa Margherita is known as the "Path of the Cross": Fifteen mosaics by Cortonese Futurist Gino Severini (1883–1966) depicting the *Stations of the Cross* line the route. The climb also passes the Porta Berarda, through which Margherita di Laviano entered Cortona in 1277, on her way to sainthood as St. Margaret of Cortona. Take water, and don't attempt the route if you have

asthma or a heart condition: It's major-league steep. ⏱ *45 min.*

❼ ★ Fortezza Medicea Girifalco. Built in 1556 by a relative of Pope Pius IV, Cortona's fortress has unmatched views over the Valdichiana, as far as Monte Amiata and Lago Trasimeno in Umbria—making the energy-sapping climb worthwhile. ⏱ *20 min. Viale Raimondo Bistacci.* ☎ *0575-637235. Admission 3€. Hours vary but usually Sat–Sun 10am–7pm.*

Drive 3km (2 miles) downhill from Cortona to:

❽ Santa Maria delle Grazie al Calcinaio. This monument to High Renaissance architecture was built for the guild of shoemakers by Sienese artist/architect Francesco di Giorgio Martini between 1485 and 1513. Laid out on a Latin cross plan, the church enjoys a bucolic setting amid olive groves below the ancient walls. The 1516 rose window is by French master Guillaume de Marcillat, who lived and worked in nearby Arezzo. ⏱ *30 min. Via del Calcinaio. No phone. Free admission. Mon–Sat 4–7pm (3–5pm winter).*

☕ After Dark. Warmly rustic **Enoteca Enotria,** Via Nazionale 81 (☎ 0575-603595), might be the most popular watering hole in town, with excellent Tuscan wines by the glass, panini, and other light fare well into the evening.

Where to Stay & Dine

★ **Dardano** CENTRO STORICO *TUSCAN* The cooks at this family-owned, budget trattoria are known for their roasts—duck, chicken, and guinea hen (our favorite), most prepared over a coal fire and accompanied by rich pastas. *Via Dardano 24. www.trattoriadardano.com.* ☎ *0575-601944. Entrees 8€–13€. Lunch, dinner Thurs–Tues (daily in summer). Closed Jan–Feb.*

★★ **Il Falconiere** SAN MAR-TINO Just 4.5km (3 miles) north of Cortona, a restored series of 17th-century buildings have the feeling of a sumptuous house in the Valdichiana countryside, with original furnishings, four-poster iron beds, and a large pool amid an olive grove. A spa adds to the sense of luxury. *Loc. San Martino. www. ilfalconiere.com.* ☎ *0575-612679. 15 units. Doubles 250€–350€, w/ breakfast. Closed 2 weeks in Jan.*

★ **Hotel Italia** CENTRO STORICO This 15th-century palace hits some high notes with spacious high-ceilinged rooms that are plain but nicely atmospheric, with tasteful rustic wood furnishings, beamed ceilings, and other architectural flourishes. *Via Ghibellina 5–7. www.hotelitaliacortona.com.* ☎ *0575/630254. 17 units. 90€–120€, w/breakfast.*

★ **La Loggetta** CENTRO STORICO *TUSCAN* Innovative pasta dishes like *tagliolini* with cabbage and truffle or *pici* (thick, short spaghetti) with duck *ragù* complement the unique setting under a loggia above Piazza della Repubblica. *Piazza di Pescheria 4. www. locandanelloggiato.it.* ☎ *0575-630575. Entrees 7€–16€. Lunch, dinner Thurs–Tues. Closed 2 weeks in Jan.*

★ **Osteria del Teatro** CENTRO STORICO *TUSCAN* An atmospheric alley is the setting for a theatrical take on Cortonese cuisine. Come in season (summer through October-ish), and you can eat a full *porcini* mushroom menu. *Via Maffei 2. www.osteria-del-teatro.it.* ☎ *0575-630556. Entrees 11€–20€. Lunch, dinner Thurs–Tues.*

★★ **San Michele** CENTRO STORICO This central hotel in a barely-altered 11th-century palace has vaulted ceilings with *pietra serena* arches, nice-size rooms under wood-beamed ceilings, and antique furnishings. The tower rooms are ideal for lovers or those who simply want to bask in countryside views. *Via Guelfa 15. www. hotelsanmichele.net.* ☎ *0575-604348. 42 units. Doubles 115€–135€, w/breakfast. Closed Jan–Feb.*

★★ **Trattoria la Grotta** CENTRO STORICO *TUSCAN* Pastas served in these vaulted rooms include light-as-a-feather housemade gnocchi, a delicious prelude to deftly grilled steaks. *Piazza Baldelli 3. trattorialagrotta.it.* ☎ *0575/630271. Entrees 8€–18€. Lunch, dinner Wed–Mon.*

Porcini mushrooms, which can be sampled at Osteria del Teatro.

Lucca

Passeggiata delle Mura
Via de Bacchettoni
San Francesco
Museo Nazionale Villa Guinigi
Porta Elisa
Via Elisa
Via S. Chiara
Porta S. Gervasio
Giardino Botanico
Via Quarquonia
Viale Marti
Porta Santa Maria
Piazza
Via M. Rosi San Jacopo
Via Fillungo
V. del Fosso
Via d. Zecca
Via S. Nicolao
Via A. Mordini
Via della Rosa
Via S. Andrea
Palazzo Bernardini
Via S. Croce
S.M. d. Servi
Piazza Antelminelli S.Botanico
Via Guinigi
Via del Fosso
Via G. Giard
Via del Fosso
Viale G. Giusti
San Frediano
Palazzo C. Pfanner
Via Beccheria
Via S. Giorgio
San Giovanni
Cattedrale di San Martino
Passeggiata delle Mura
Sant' Agostino
San Paolino
Via Vitt. Veneto
Via d. Giglio
S. Martino
d. Rosa
Via del Fosso
Porta San Pietro
Via S. Paolino
Via G.
Via Tassi
San Romano
Via Vitt. Emanuele
Via Tabacchi
Corso Garibaldi
Passeggiata delle Mura
Museo Nazionale di Palazzo Mansi
Viale Carlo del Prete
Viale Papi
Porta Vittorio Emanuele
Viale Carducci

N

0   100 m
0   400 ft

Tourist Information
Parking

Lucca is the most graceful provincial city in Tuscany, set at the heart of one of Italy's richest agricultural regions within a ring of mighty medieval and Renaissance walls. Locals eat and drink well, have a deserved reputation for politeness, and enjoy the honor of living in the hometown of Giacomo Puccini. Bike is the preferred form of local transport, and it's a pleasure to pedal past all the grand *palazzi* and churches. START: Lucca is 72km (45 miles) **west of Florence on the A11, 21km (13 miles) north of Pisa on the S12r. Trip length: 2 days, with an overnight stay in the historic center, to see Lucca properly.**

❶ Cicli Bizzarri. A bike rental shop (next door to the tourist office) might seem like a curious first stop, but you'll need wheels where we're heading. Rent yours here for 4€ per hour; take your passport or a driver's license, and bring cash, since credit cards are not accepted. *Piazza Santa Maria 32. www.ciclibizzarri.net.* ☎ *0583-496682.*

❷ ★★★ Lucca's Walls. Planted with plane, chestnut, and ilex trees, Lucca's ramparts make for one of Tuscany's great bike rides. Now a city park stretching for 5km (2¾ miles), the **Passeggiata delle Mura** gives Lucca its special charm, and walking or cycling the circular route is the best way to get yourselves oriented. The only question is: clockwise or counterclockwise? We prefer the former, starting from Piazza Santa Maria, so our last view before descending is down into the manicured baroque garden of the **Palazzo Pfanner.** ⏱ *90 min.*

❸ ★ San Frediano. The original 6th-century basilica, built to honor an Irish hermit who became Bishop of Lucca, was reconstructed in the 12th century in the Lucchese-Romanesque style, using marble from the dismantled amphitheater. The dazzling 13th-century *Ascension* mosaic on the facade, probably by Bonaventura Berlinghieri, was restored in the 1800s. Just

Via Fillungo, Lucca's main shopping street.

inside the entrance is the church's treasure, a 12th-century Romanesque baptismal font depicting the story of Moses. ⏱ *20 min. Piazza San Frediano.* ☎ *0583-493627. Free admission. Mon–Sat 8:30am–noon & 3–5:30pm; Sun 9–11:30am & 3–5:30pm.*

❹ ★ Piazza Anfiteatro. A 2nd-century Roman amphitheater stood here, off the northern end of the main shopping street, Via Fillungo ("long thread"), until its destruction in the 1100s: Locals used it as a quarry for the stone to construct

Lucca's palaces and churches. The foundations of what were the grandstands today support an ellipse of medieval houses. ⏱ *10 min.*

⑤ ★ Torre Guinigi. This tower, rising 44m (146 ft.) with trademark ilex growing from the roof, was built by the city's ruling family in the 15th century. Climb its 230 steps to get a proper picture of Lucca enclosed by its ring of walls, with the Apennine mountain range beyond. ⏱ *30 min. Via Sant'Andrea (at Via Chiavi d'Oro).* ☎ *347-6270423. Admission 3.50€. Apr–May daily 9am–7:30pm; Jun–Sept daily 9am–6:30pm; Oct & Mar daily 9:30am–5:30pm; Nov–Feb daily 9:30am–4:30pm.*

⑥ ★ Museo Nazionale Villa Guinigi. A palace once owned by Paolo Guinigi, who ruled Lucca from 1400 to 1430, displays the best from local archaeological digs as well as Romanesque, Gothic, and Renaissance sculpture (including a couple of terracottas recently attributed to Donatello). The painting collection is strong on works by regional artists; highlights include three fine panels by Florentine Fra' Bartolomeo. ⏱ *1 hr. Via della Quarquonia. www.luccamuseinazionali.it.*

☎ *0583-496033. Admission 4€; 6.50€ with Palazzo Mansi. Tues–Sat 8:30am–7:30pm.*

⑦ ★ Carli. One of the oldest jewelry stores in Tuscany, from 1655, shows off exquisite gold and silver behind a glorious Renaissance storefront. *Via Fillungo 95.* ☎ *0583-491119.*

⑧ Amedo Giusto. An always crowded bakery is the place to enjoy the focaccia for which Lucca is famous, emerging from the oven here with many different toppings. *Via Santa Lucia 18.* ☎ *0583-496285. $.*

⑨ ★★ Cattedrale di San Martino. Pope Alexander II consecrated Lucca's Duomo in 1070, but it took 4 centuries to finish. This ornate, asymmetrical structure was constructed around its *campanile* (bell tower) with an arched, multitiered facade in the Pisan-Romanesque style. This facade was never completed; the topmost loggia and tympanum have yet to be built. Look for the reliefs under the portico, a stellar example of 13th-century stonework, including a fascinating 12-panel calendar of

Mosaics on the facade of San Frediano.

Lucca After Dark

Lucca is a typically drowsy Tuscan town after dark, with just a few nightspots. Strolling the center with a gelato is perhaps the best way to pass a warm evening. In business since 1927, **Gelateria Veneta,** Via Vittorio Veneto 74 (www.gelateriaveneta.net; ☎ 0583-467037), is the traditional choice. A ride or walk around the walls can include a stop for a drink, or a meal, at **Antico Caffe della Mura,** on the walls at Piazzale Vittorio Emanuele II 2 (☎ 0583-467993), or **Caffetteria Ristorante San Colombano,** at Rampa Baluardo San Colombano 6 (☎ 0583-464641). October to March is the season at the **Teatro del Giglio,** Piazza del Giglio (☎ 0583-467521; www.teatrodelgiglio.it), one of Tuscany's major houses. Rossini premiered *William Tell* here in 1831. The program has a mix of classical dance, theater, opera, and modern musical shows.

peasant life. The interior was given a Gothic dress in the 14th to 15th centuries and is the repository of the *Volto Santo,* a miraculous crucifix. In the sacristy is Jacopo della Quercia's *Tomb of Ilaria del Carretto* (ca. 1406), a tomb of a young wife with a dog, a symbol of faithfulness, at her feet. Ruskin hailed the sculptor's first known work "the loveliest Christian tomb in Italy."

Adjacent to the cathedral is the **Museo della Cattedrale,** housing among its sacred art the golden crown that adorns the *Volto Santo* during a procession on Lucca's Feast of the Luminara, September 13th. ⏱ *1 hr. Piazza San Martino. www.museocattedralelucca.it.* ☎ *0583-490530. Admission 3€ cathedral, 4€ museum, 9€ cathedral, campanile, museum, baptistery & church of San Giovanni e Santa Reparata. Mon–Fri 9:30am–5:45pm (Nov–Mar closes 4:45pm), Sat 9:30am–6:45pm, Sun 9:30–10:45am & noon–6pm (Nov–Mar closes 5pm).*

⑩ ★ San Giovanni e Santa Reparata. The main structure of the present church dates from the 1100s, although the facade is largely from

the 1500s. Its roots, however, stretch much further back: Foundations under the nave, baptistery, and altar have been opened up to exploration and show an archeological history that heads back past the 7th-century Lombard mausoleum, past the Paleochristian 5th-century church to the 1st-century-B.C. mosaic floor of Lucca's Roman baths. ⏱ *30 min. Piazza San Giovanni.* ☎ *0583-490530. Admission 4€ church & baptistery; 9€ church, baptistery, cathedral, campanile & Museo della Cattedrale. Apr–Nov daily 10am–6pm; Dec–Mar Mon–Fri 10am–2pm, Sat–Sun 10am–5pm.*

A statue of Puccini in Lucca.

One of Lucca's many handsome piazzas.

11 ★ **Taddeucci.** This pastry shop, founded in 1881, created a legendary confection called Buccellato Taddeucci, an anise-flavored cake studded with raisins that's still sold today. *Piazza San Michele 34.* ☎ *0583-494933. $.*

12 ★★ **San Michele in Foro.** The *foro* in the name of this 12th-century church comes from the fact that it was built atop the Roman forum. The facade, with its four galleries, blind arcades, and individually unique, almost pagan

San Michele in Foro.

columns, represents the zenith of the form that Romanesque architecture took around here (sometimes called "Luccan-Romanesque"). While the internal architecture is much altered, and disappointing after that blockbuster facade, worth a peek is Filippino Lippi's *Saints* in the right transept. ⏱ *20 min. Piazza San Michele.* ☎ *0583-48459. Free admission. Daily 9am–noon & 3–6pm (summer from 7:30am; Nov–Mar closes 5pm).*

13 ★ **Puccini's Birth Home.** The birthplace of Lucca's most famous son preserves objects and mementoes relating to the great composer's life and works—including some of his paintings. ⏱ *40 min. Corte San Lorenzo 9. www.puccinimuseum. org.* ☎ *0583-584028. Admission 7€. Mar, Apr & Oct daily 10am–6pm; May–Sept, daily, 10am–7pm; & Nov–Feb, Wed–Mon, 10am–1pm & 3–5pm.*

14 **Museo Nazionale Palazzo Mansi.** It's almost a case of the frame outshining the painting at this lavishly decorated 16th-century palace, formerly owned by the powerful Mansi family. Fans of baroque portraiture, though, should head upstairs to the gallery for works by Pontormo, Bronzino,

Puccini: Hometown Composer

Lucca's native son Giacomo Puccini (1858–1924) was the composer of *Tosca, Madame Butterfly,* and *La Bohème,* some of the most romantic operas of all time—works no doubt inspired by the stage-set ambience of the city and its rich history. It's impossible to walk anywhere in Lucca without a Puccini aria or two wafting through your head. The maestro comes most vividly to life in **Piazza Cittadella,** commanded by his bronze statue. Puccini was born around the corner at 9 Corte San Lorenzo, where he lived until he left for Milan in his early 20s. The modest-yet-comfortable rooms of the **Museo Casa Natale di Giacomo Puccini (⓮)** are open for a look at scores, furnishings, and, most notably, the piano on which he composed many of his scores. Every evening throughout the year, the church of **San Giovanni (⓾),** where Puccini was baptized as a baby, hosts an opera recital or orchestral concert dedicated to the composer, in a series called **Puccini e la sua Lucca** (www.puccini elasualucca.com). Tickets are 17€ (13€ for ages 22 and under) and can be purchased all day inside San Giovanni.

Beccafumi, Correggio, Veronese, and others. ⏱ 45 min. *Via Galli Tassi 43 (at Via del Toro). www.lucca museinazionali.it.* ☎ *0583-55570. Admission 4€; 6.50€ with Villa Guinigi. Tues–Sat 8:30am–7:30pm.*

⓯ ★ Tipografia Biagini. The highest-quality paper is turned into bespoke stationery at this traditional typography workshop. Orders are designed and set by hand, and can be shipped home. *Via S. Giustina 20–24. www.antica tipografiabiagini.it.* ☎ *0583-54292.*

⓰ ★★ Enoteca Vanni. Founded in 1965, Lucca's best wine cellar stocks great examples of the respectable local DOC, Montecarlo. Lucca's hills are also acclaimed for olive oil, the best of which is sold here. *Piazza S. Salvatore 7. www. enotecavanni.com.* ☎ *0583-491902.*

Biking is an ideal way to tour Lucca.

Where to Stay

★★ Alla Corte degli Angeli

CENTRO STORICO   A welcoming, warrenlike *palazzo* is blessed with the most romantic rooms in town. Although bedrooms are not enormous, they're well-proportioned, each kitted out with Italian antique furniture and embellished with a unique, hand-painted fresco. *Via degli Angeli 23. www.allacorte degliangeli.com.* ☎ *0583-496204. 10 units. Doubles 120€–210€, w/breakfast. Closed 2 wks in Jan.*

★ A Palazzo Busdraghi

CENTRO STORICO   This *residenza d'epoca* is located on an elegantly crumbling courtyard right in the heart of the city. Rooms vary in size and layout, but all retain their original *palazzo* furnishings and authentic 1600s feel. *Via Fillungo 170. www. apalazzobusdraghi.it.* ☎ *0583-950856. 7 units. Doubles 120€–160€, w/breakfast.*

★★★ B&B Arena di Lucca

CENTRO STORICO   An old apartment overlooking the Arena surrounds guests with atmospheric terracotta floors, oil paintings, and comfy sofas and chairs. Two of the high-ceilinged rooms face the airy piazza below. *Via dell'Anfiteatro 16. www.bbarenalucca.com.* ☎ *0339-678-6299. www.hotellaluna.com. 4 units. Doubles 100€–135€, w/ breakfast.*

★ Piccolo Hotel Puccini

CENTRO STORICO   The composer, who was born across the street, lent his name to this small, friendly, and good-value inn, where clean, cozy bedrooms are nicely done with modern furnishings. *Tip:* Rooms that open out to the front are lighter and airier than the others. *Via di Poggio 9 (off Piazza San Michele). www.hotelpuccini.com.* ☎ *0583-55421. 14 units. Doubles from 100€, w/breakfast.*

★★ San Luca Palace

CENTRO STORICO   A crisp conversion of a 1540 *palazzo* offers spacious, modern, well-equipped rooms that retain their antique character; many have cozy little reading alcoves equipped with an extra bed, perfect for families. *Via San Paolino 103. www.sanlucapalace.com.* ☎ *0583-317446. 26 units. Doubles 85€–150€, w/breakfast.*

Leafy courtyard of A Palazzo Busdraghi.

Where to **Dine**

Buca di Sant'Antonio.

★ **Buca di Sant'Antonio** CEN-TRO STORICO *TUSCAN* The most reliable fine dining in Lucca is served in a 1782 building where Puccini used to eat. Classic local dishes such as *capretto allo spiedo* (spit-roasted kid goat) are prepared with flavor, flair, and superb simplicity. *Via della Cervia 3.* ☎ *www.bucadi santantonio.it. 0583-55881. Entrees 15€. Lunch Tues–Sun, dinner Tues–Sat.*

★★★ **Da Giulio in Pelleria** CENTRO STORICO *LUC-CHESE* There's no more authentic Lucchese dining, or maybe a friend-lier atmosphere, within the city walls. Local specialties include horse tartar, veal snout, and Tuscan sausages with stewed white beans. As ever, there are grilled meats and pasta. *Via delle Conce 45.* ☎ *0583-55948. Entrees 6€–13€. Lunch Sat & 3rd Sun of month, dinner Mon–Sat.*

★★ **Da Leo** CENTRO STORICO *TUSCAN/LUCCHESE* The Buralli family makes everyone feel welcome at their unpretentious tavern in a 16th-century building. Guests come not only for the charming 1930s decor, but also for the affordable regional menu, including homemade

pastas prepared daily and seasonal game roasts. *Via Tegrimi 1 (at Piazza San Salvatore).* ☎ *0583-492236. www. trattoriadaleo.it. Entrees 9€–16€. Lunch, dinner daily.*

★ **Osteria San Giorgio** CENTRO STORICO *LUCCHESE* A courtyard and several informal rooms hung with old photos are a local favorite, with a menu geared to feeding the neighbors with such classics as rab-bit, *baccalà* (salt cod), and *farro* (spelt wheat), as well as many sea-food pastas. *Via San Giorgio 26.* ☎ *0583-953233. Entrees 8€–14€. Lunch, dinner daily.*

★★ **Ristorante Giglio** CENTRO STORICO *LUCCHESE* White tablecloths and fine china do jus-tice to the setting in the 18th-century Palazzo Arnolfini, and the menu follows suit with refined Tus-can classics: *tagliatelle* topped with shaved white truffles, perfectly grilled beef tenderloin with porcini mushrooms, and for dessert, Luc-chese *buccellato* (sweetbread) filled with ice cream and berries. *Piazza del Giglio.* ☎ *0583-494058. Entrees 9€–20€. Lunch, dinner Thurs–Mon, dinner Tues & Wed.*

Massa Marittima

- ⓘ Tourist Information
- Ⓟ Parking

Chiesa di San Francesco

Via dei Bastioni

Convento delle Clarisse

Castello di Monteregio

Sede del Terziere di Cittavecchia

Torre del Candeliere

Arco Senese

Museo d. Organi Meccanici ❻

Piazza XXIV Maggio

Museo d'Arte Sacra

Palazzo Comunale

Palazzo del Podestà

Piazza Garibaldi

Fonti dell' Abbondanza

Duomo ✝

Piazzale Mazzini

Museo della Miniera ❺

| 0 | 200 m |
| 0 | 500 ft |

❶ Duomo
❷ Torre del Candeliere
❸ Museo degli Organi Meccanici
❹ Museo d'Arte Sacra
❺ Museo della Miniera

Where to Stay & Dine
La Fenice Park Hotel 6
La Tana del Brillo Parlante 7

G ripping the side of a hill 350m (1148 ft.) up in the Colline Metallifere (Metaliferrous Hills) is the former mining community and capital of the Alta Maremma. Massa was overrun by Sienese soldiers, then hit hard by plague in the 1300s. It's now a quiet hilltown with shuttered buildings, steep lanes, and a fine crop of small museums. Don't visit on a Monday, when most of the sights are closed. START: **Massa Marittima is 67km (41 miles) southwest of Siena, reached via the S73 and S441. Trip length: Half a-day.**

❶ ★ **Duomo.** Massa's Old (lower) Town clusters around triangular **Piazza Garibaldi,** with Massa's cathedral, a harmonious mixture in travertine of Pisan-Romanesque and Gothic styling. Above the main door lintel is a relief celebrating the life of Massa's patron saint and one-time bishop, 9th-century African immigrant Cerbonius, to whom the building is dedicated—spot the scene for which he's most famous,

when he took a flock of geese to see the Pope. ⏱ 25 min. Piazza Garibaldi. No phone. Free admission. Daily 8am–noon & 3–6pm.

Climb steep Via Moncini, heading through the Porta alla Silici and into the New (upper) Town.

❷ **Torre del Candeliere.** A flying arch, made as a viaduct for Sienese garrisons, connects the fortress ramparts to this 1228 tower. It has served as a clock tower since 1443 and is still impressive at two-thirds of its original 60m (197 ft.) height. ⏱ *20 min. Piazza Matteotti. www.coopcollinemetallifere.it.* ☎ *0566-902289. Admission 3€. Apr–Oct Tues–Sun 10:30am–1:30pm & 3–6pm; Nov–Mar Tues–Sun 11am–1pm & 2:30–4:30pm.*

❸ ★ **Museo degli Organi Meccanici**. This is a unique collection of organs rescued from churches across Italy and restored to working order. Some of the instruments date back to 1600; there's also an early *ghironda* (hurdy-gurdy) and a line of fortepianos dating from 1700s Vienna to the early 20th century. ⏱ *20 min. Corso Diaz 28. www.museodegli organi.it.* ☎ *0566-940282. Admission 5€. Mar–May & Oct to mid-Jan 10:30am–12:30pm & 3–6pm; June–Sept 10:30am–1pm & 3–7pm.*

❹ ★ **Museo d'Arte Sacra.** Massa's art highlight showcases Ambrogio Lorenzetti's glorious *Maestà*, painted in the 1330s. Considered "crude" by baroque tastes, it was lost and wasn't rediscovered until 1867, by which point it had been divided, nailed together, and was serving as a bin. Elsewhere in the small collection is a fine stained-glass *Crucifixion* by Ambrogio's brother, Pietro. ⏱ *40 min. Corso Diaz 36. www.museiartesacra.net.* ☎ *0566-901954. Admission 5€. Apr–Oct*

Tues–Sun 10am–1pm & 3–6pm; Nov–Mar Tues–Sun 11am–1pm & 3–5pm.

❺ **Museo della Miniera.** To learn more about the town's mining heritage—the first mining code in European history was drawn up here in the 14th century—don your hard-hat and head underground. The guided visit covers 700m (2,300 ft.) of reconstructed 1940s mineshaft. ⏱ *45 min. Via Corridoni. www.coopcollinemetallifere.it.* ☎ *0566-902289. Admission 5€. Tours approximately hourly Apr–Oct Tues–Sun 10am–1pm & 3–5:45pm; Nov–Mar Tues–Sun 10am–noon & 3–4:30pm.*

Eating & Staying in Massa

It may be small (just 4 tables), but country-styled **La Tana del Brillo Parlante,** Vicolo Ciambellano 4 (☎ 0566-901274; closed Wed), is one of our favorite places to dine in all Tuscany. The seasonal menu hosts familiar regional flavors, but dishes are prepared with verve and originality. Entrees range from 14€ to 17€, reservations are essential, and the restaurant accepts cash only. The standout lodgings in town are at **La Fenice Park Hotel,** Corso Diaz 63 (www.lafeniceparkhotel.it; ☎ 0566-903941), a handsome shuttered palazzo in the Città Nuova with 17 traditional Tuscan rooms. Doubles range from 115€ to 150€.

Massa Marittima.

Montepulciano

- ① Palazzo Comunale
- ② Cattedrale di Santa Maria
- ③ Palazzo Nobili-Tarugi
- ④ Museo Civico
- ⑤ Contucci
- ⑥ Gattavecchi
- ⑦ Santa Maria dei Servi
- ⑧ Frassineti
- ⑨ Mazzetti Albo Mosaics
- ⑩ Caffè Poliziano
- ⑪ Tempio di San Biagio

Where to Stay

Duomo **13**
Il Riccio **16**
Vicolo dell'Oste **17**

Where to Dine

Acquacheta **15**
La Bottega del Nobile **18**
La Grotta **12**
Osteria del Conte **14**

The garnet-colored Vino Nobile, beloved by epicures, first put the handsome town of Montepulciano on the map in the Etruscan era. At an altitude of 605m (1,985 ft.), Montepulciano is also Tuscany's loftiest hilltown, with remarkable views over the vineyards from up on its volcanic crag. A climb along the steeply graded, serpentine main street is the highlight of a visit—the name changes many times along the length, but locals call the street simply "Il Corso." Piazza Grande is at the summit, with its plain, never-finished Duomo, but take heart—from here the rest of your explorations are all downhill. START: **Montepulciano is on the S146, reached from Florence via the A1 (111km/69 miles) and Siena via the S2 (67km/40 miles). Trip length: 1 day.**

① ★ **Palazzo Comunale.** The highest point in town is **Piazza Grande,** enveloped by Renaissance *palazzi* and this Gothic town hall. The crenellated clock tower was added by Michelozzo (1396–1472), inspired by the Palazzo Vecchio (built in the 1200s), in Florence. A

climb up the tower gives you a chance to get your Montepulciano geography straight—and take in expansive views over the Valdichiana below. ⏱ *30 min. Piazza Grande.* ☎ *0578-7121. Admission 2€. Mon–Fri 10am–6pm, Sat 10am–1pm.*

Piazza Grande.

❷ ★ Cattedrale di Santa Maria Assunta. To the world, this uncompleted Duomo presents a blank facade, but the sparse interior is not without its treasures. We visit just to gaze at Taddeo di Bartolo's 1401 triptych, *Assumption of the Virgin*, above the high altar. It glows, with the artist's use of subtle pinks, blood orange, eggplant purple, and plenty of gold leaf. ⏱ *20 min. Piazza Grande. No phone. Free admission. Daily 9am–12:30pm & 3:15–7pm.*

❸ ★★ Palazzo Nobili-Tarugi. Facing the Duomo across Piazza Grande, this *palazzo*—with its half-moon arches, Ionic columns, and great portico—is attributed to Antonio da Sangallo the Elder. The much-photographed 1520 fountain out front incorporates two Etruscan columns, topped by two griffins and two lions bearing the Medici coat of arms. The interior is closed to the public. ⏱ *15 min. Piazza Grande.*

❹ Museo Civico. The Sienese-Gothic Palazzo Neri-Orselli houses most of Montepulciano's art treasures. Its collection of some 200 Tuscan paintings features works from the 13th to 17th centuries. Other gems include 15th-century illuminated choir books, enameled

terracottas by Andrea della Robbia (1435–1525), and Etruscan funerary urns. ⏱ *30 min. Via Ricci 10. www.museocivicomontepulciano.it.* ☎ *0578-717300. Admission 5€. Tues–Sun 10am–1pm & 3–6pm (until 7pm June–July, 10am–7pm in Aug, Fri–Sun only Nov–Feb).*

❺ Vino Nobile. Montepulciano's vintners have organized a consortium-cum-showroom, the Consorzio del Vino Nobile di Montepulciano (www.consorziovinonobile.it; ☎ 0578-757812). The public can visit, at the Palazzo del Capitano del Popolo on Piazza Grande, and sample members' wines. *Three tasting glasses 5€–10€. Easter–Oct Mon–Sat 1–5pm.* Montepulciano is littered with enoteche and cantine (wine cellars) where you can sample (usually free) and purchase Vino Nobile and other local products.

❻ ★ Contucci. In Montepulciano's main square, this renowned winery occupies the cellars of the 13th-century Palazzo Contucci, home to popes and Grand Dukes over the years. Contucci was one of the first makers of Vino Nobile, still a proud tradition today. *Palazzo Contucci, Piazza Grande. www.contucci.it.* ☎ *0578-757006.*

The "noble wine" of Montepulciano is the local specialty.

⑦ ★★ Gattavecchi. Labels such as its outstanding Riserva dei Padri Serviti and 100% sangiovese Parceto have been well-received worldwide. Ask to see the cellars: They have been in continuous use since before 1200, originally by the friars of the church next door. *Via di Collazzi 74. www.gattavecchi.it.* ☎ *0578-757110.*

⑧ Santa Maria dei Servi. The little parish church next to Gattavecchi is notable for a curious little *Madonna and Child* inserted smack in the middle of another painting, to the left of the altar. The *Madonna* has been attributed to the 13th-century Sienese workshop of Duccio di Buoninsegna. ⏱ *10 min. Piazza di Santa Maria. No phone. Free admission. Irregular hours.*

⑨ ★ Frassineti. Intricate intarsia art handcrafted from wood sourced around the globe. Landscapes of the rural Val d'Orcia are a specialty, costing around 200€ a piece. *Via*

dell'Opio nel Corso. www.arnaldo frassineti.com. ☎ *0578-717295. No credit cards.*

⑩ ★ Mazzetti Albo Mosaics. Large framed mosaics, of scenes from Montepulciano and around, are handmade by Albo in his workshop. Prices from 350€. *Via dell'Opio nel Corso 14. www.laboratorio mosaici.com.* ☎ *0578-757272.*

⑪ ★★ Caffè Poliziano. This cafe-wine bar, which opened in 1868, quietly recalls the days when Pirandello and Fellini quaffed here. *Via Voltaia nel Corso 27. www.caffe poliziano.it.* ☎ *0578-758615. $–$$$.*

⑫ ★★ Tempio di San Biagio. This masterpiece of High Renaissance architecture was the greatest achievement of architect Antonio da Sangallo, who finished it in 1529. By training and practice a designer of fortresses, he was obviously inspired by Bramante's design for St. Peter's in Rome. Built on a Greek cross plan, it was fashioned to house a statue of the Madonna. Crowned by its dome, the church has two campaniles—one left unfinished. When shadows start to lengthen, the yellow travertine masonry glows like gold. ⏱ *20 min. Via di San Biagio (10-min. downhill walk from Porta di Grassi). No phone. Free admission. Daily 9am–12:30pm & 3:30–7:30pm.*

Tempio di San Biagio.

Where to **Stay & Dine**

★★ Acquacheta CENTRO STORICO *TUSCAN/GRILL* The menu's short at this informal little *osteria* inside a converted wine *cantina:* pasta five ways, flame-grilled meat, salads, plus a lengthy pecorino list. Their *fiorentina alla brace* is the best steak in town. *Via del Teatro 22. www.acquacheta.eu.* ☎ *0578-717086. Entrees 7€–18€. Lunch, dinner Wed–Mon. Closed mid-Jan to mid-Mar.*

★ Duomo CENTRO STORICO Small to midsize rooms at this family-run favorite, named for the cathedral opposite, are decorated in Tuscan *arte povera* style. *Via San Donato 14. www.albergoduomo montepulciano.it.* ☎ *0578-757473. 13 units. Doubles 75€–95€, w/breakfast.*

★★ Il Riccio CENTRO STORICO Rooms vary from rather palatial (a coveted few with private, view-filled terraces) to modest, but wherever you settle, the friendly welcome, a unique setting above a 13th-century cloister in Montepulciano's oldest street, and the best roof terrace in town ensure a memorable stay. *Via di Talosa 21.* ☎ *0578-757713. www.ilriccio.net. 10 units. Doubles 100€–110€, w/breakfast.*

★ La Bottega del Nobile CENTRO STORICO *TUSCAN* In snug, brick-walled cellars below a tasting room an affable young staff serves thick Tuscan steaks and hearty ragouts, and eagerly pairs just the right wine with the course being served. *Corso 95. www. labottegadelnobile.com.* ☎ *0578-757016. Entrees 8€–16€. Lunch, dinner daily.*

★ Vicolo dell'Oste CENTRO STORICO Tuscan chic prevails in this house on a narrow lane off the Corso, where wood-beamed ceilings set off streamlined modern furnishings. Deluxe touches such as large Jacuzzis are tucked into the corners of some rooms, and practical amenities include simple kitchens in several rooms. *Via delle Oste. www.vicolodelloste.it.* ☎ *0578/758393. 5 units. Doubles 95€–110€, w/breakfast.*

★ La Grotta SAN BIAGIO *ITALIAN* This old-fashioned brick-vaulted dining room opposite the Tempio di San Biagio serves upscale Italian classics, most of it harvested from the local countryside. *Via San Biagio 2.* ☎ *0578-757607. Entrees 16€–21€. Lunch, dinner Thurs–Tues. Closed Jan –Mar.*

★ Osteria del Conte CENTRO STORICO *TUSCAN* A trek to the top of town is well rewarded with a delicious meal in this simple room overseen by a mother-and-son team who are devoted to home cooking and warm hospitality. *Via di San Donato 19. www.osteriadelconte. it.* ☎ *0578/756062. Entrees 9€–14€. Thurs–Tues 12:30–2:30pm & 7:30–9:30pm.*

Grilled steak at Acquacheta.

Pienza

To Siena

Via della Madonnina

To Montepulciano, A1 Autostrada

Piazza Dante Alighieri

Via Enzo Mangiavacchi

Via delle Mura

Largo Roma

Corso Il Rossellino

Via Elisa

Via Gozzante

❼

❻

❾

❿ Piazza Spagna

Via Pia

Via Dogale

Via Case Nuove

Palazzo Comunale

Piazza Pio II

❹

Chiesa di S. Francesco

Palazzo Piccolomini

❶ ❸

❷ *i*

❺

Palazzo Borgia

Corso Il Rossellino

❽ Via del Casello

❶❶ ❶❷

❶❸ →

❶❹ →

Via Gozzante

Via di Circonvallazione

Duomo

0 — 100 m
0 — 300 ft

Ⓟ **Parking**

ⓘ **Tourist Information**

❶ Piazza Pio II	**Where to Stay**
❷ Duomo	Giardino Segreto **9**
❸ Museo Diocesano	La Bandita Townhouse **12**
❹ Palazzo Piccolomini	La Casa di Adelina **13**
❺ Nannetti e Bernardini	**Where to Dine**
❻ Pummarò	La Porta **14**
❼ Enoteca di Ghino	Latte di Luna **11**
❽ Bar Il Casello	Trattoria di Fiorella **10**

This model Renaissance town was the creation of Pope Pius II, who wanted to transform the village of his birth, Corsignano, into a place that would glorify his name. He was born here as Silvio Piccolomini, in an impoverished branch of a noble Sienese family; he later added "Aeneas" as a first name out of love of the tales of Virgil, and after years as a humanist scholar, gout sufferer, and itinerant diplomat, served as pope from 1458 to 1464. His envisioned city never grew beyond a few blocks, but it remains a masterpiece. Zeffirelli recognized it for the stage setting it is, deserting Verona to film "Romeo and Juliet" here in 1968. START: **Pienza is 55km (33 miles) southwest of Siena, reached via the S2 and S146. Trip length: Half a-day.**

❶ ★★ **Piazza Pio II.** Begin in the center of the tiny town: Virtually all the sights are on this set-piece piazza or nearby. The square is enclosed by the Duomo, Palazzo Piccolomini, and Palazzo Vescovile (Bishop's Palace).

The fourth side features the distinctly non-Renaissance **Palazzo Comunale,** home to the town hall and municipal offices. The bell tower, added later, was built lower than the Duomo's to emphasize the power of the Church over civil authority. ⏱ *15 min.*

Piazza Pio II.

2 ★★ Duomo. The classicized Renaissance facade complete with Roman arches and pediment conceals a Gothic interior influenced by the Austrian "hall churches" Pius admired on his travels. The Piccolomini family is honored with a coat-of-arms (cross and five upturned crescents) in the rose window and all over the church. Pius commissioned four leading Sienese artists to paint devotional altarpieces, and

Pienza's Duomo.

they're all still here: counterclockwise from the right aisle, works by Giovanni di Paolo, Matteo di Giovanni, Vecchietta, and Sano di Pietro. Alas, the whole thing is built on clay and sandstone and may one day collapse: Check out the slope to the altar and ceiling cracks. ① *30 min. Piazza Pio II.* ☎ *0578-748548. Free admission. Daily 7am–1pm & 2:30–7pm.*

3 ★ Museo Diocesano. This neat little collection housed inside the Bishop's Palace looted local churches for its array of 14th- and 15th-century Sienese paintings, including a *Madonna and Child with Saints* by Vecchietta (1410–80). More surreal is a life-size carved *San Regolo* holding his own severed head. ① *30 min. Corso Rossellino 30.* ☎ *0578-749905. Admission 4.10€. Mid-Mar to Oct Wed–Mon 10am–1pm & 3–6pm; off season Sat–Sun 10am–1pm & 3–5pm.*

4 ★ Palazzo Piccolomini. The papal home of Pius II is architect Bernardo Rossellino's masterpiece, although it's obviously influenced by L. B. Alberti's Palazzo Rucellai in Florence (p 46, **8**). In Tuscan Renaissance architecture, it's usually the harmonious facade that's the star attraction. That's not the case

Pienza gets quiet after day-trippers leave.

here, nor are the stuffy salons and living quarters going to instill excitement. But at the rear is a three-story loggia overlooking a hanging garden with a drop-dead view over the Val d'Orcia. Descendants of Pius lived here until 1968. ○ *30 min. Piazza Pio II. www.palazzopiccolominipienza.it.* ☎ *0577-286300. Admission 7€. Set audio tours only. May to Oct Tues– Sun 10am–6:30pm; closes 4:30pm Nov to Mar, at 5pm in Apr. Closed 2nd half of Nov & Jan 7–Feb 14.*

❺ Nannetti e Bernardini. Italy's most famous pecorino, a sheep's-milk cheese, is sold in shops along Corso Rossellino, among which this rustic, artisan deli is our favorite. Fancier varieties are soaked in wine or dusted with truffles. For a lunchtime bite on the move, try the *porchetta* (salty herbed pork) *panino. Corso Rossellino 81. www.nannettie bernardinipienza.com.* ☎ *0578-748627. No credit cards.*

❻ ★ Pummaro. You'll find yet another reason to love Pienza when you stop for a slice or a quick meal at the town's favorite pizzeria, where toppings include local ham, salami, and pecorino cheese. *Via del Giglio 4.* ☎ *0578-748568. $.*

❼ ★★ Enoteca di Ghino. Outstanding vintages of the very best wines from Tuscany and beyond. Bottles from 10€ to 10 times that. *Via del Leone 16. www.enoteca dighino.it.* ☎ *0578-748057.*

❽ Bar Il Casello. This sleek, air-conditioned bar and cafe is the social center of town, with snacks during the day, Tuscan reds and whites by the glass, and devastating views over the Val d'Orcia. In season, it's open Tuesday through Sunday until 1am, shockingly late by local standards. *Via del Casello 3.* ☎ *0578-749105. $.*

Where to **Stay & Dine**

★ **Giardino Segreto** CENTRO STORICO A haven of tranquility just a few paces off the Corso, these simple rooms are arranged around a peaceful herb garden. Mini-apartments are a great choice for budget family travel. *Via Condotti 13. www. ilgiardinosegretopienza.it.* ☎ *0578-748539. 6 units. Doubles 50€–70€; apts. (sleeping 4–5) 105€–125€, w/ breakfast. Closed Jan 15–Feb 15.*

★★ **La Bandita Townhouse** Huge, loftlike guest quarters seem better suited to New York or Berlin than to a small Tuscan town (and it's telling that the elevator is the only one for miles around), but they certainly prove that contemporary chic can be comfy. Timeless pleasures include honey-colored stone walls and the view into the large garden and over the surrounding countryside. *Corso il Rossellino. www. la-bandita.com.* ☎ *0578-749005. 12 units. Double 250€–395€, w/ breakfast.*

★★★ **La Casa di Adelina** Montichiello, a walled village 10km (6 miles) east of Pienza, is an enchanting warren of piazzas and stone towers. Adding to the charm are these three rooms and three apartments, (some in a grand old house on a central square, one in a nearby house, and another in a medieval tower). All are full of antiques and tasteful vintage modern and contemporary pieces. Breakfast is served in a beamed lounge by affable host Francesco. *Piazza San Martina 3, Montichiello.*

Local cheeses in Pienza.

www.lacasadiadelina.eu. ☎ *0578-755167. 6 units. Double 100€–140€, w/ breakfast. Closed 2 wks. in Feb.*

★ **La Porta** MONTICCHIELLO TUSCAN For a special treat, drive 10km (6 miles) southeast to the medieval village of Montichiello to this renowned *osteria* right at the village gate. Regional fare includes *tagliata di manzo al Vino Nobile* (Valdichiana beef in red wine) and *faraona al vinsanto con patate arrosto* (guinea hen in sweet wine sauce with roast potato). Book ahead for terrace dining in fair weather. *Via del Piano 1, Monticchiello. www.osterialaporta.it.* ☎ *0578-755163. Entrees 12€–20€. Lunch, dinner Fri–Wed. Closed last week in June & mid-Jan 10–early Feb.*

★ **Latte di Luna** CENTRO STORICO TUSCAN This laid-back trattoria near the eastern town gate draws a diverse regular crowd—from foreign exchange students to local *carabinieri*. Don't miss the homemade *semifreddi* (similar to ice cream) for dessert. *Via San Carlo 2–4.* ☎ *0578-748606. Entrees 7€–16€. Lunch, dinner Wed–Mon. Closed Feb to mid-Mar.*

★★ **Trattoria da Fiorella** CENTRO STORICO TUSCAN An old stable is now an inviting dining room, with just eight or so tables on the main floor and a few more on a balcony above. The town's famous pecorino gets the star treatment in *crespelle al forno ripiene con zucchini e pecorino fresco,* baked crêpes filled with zucchini and young pecorino cheese), while several hearty homemade pastas, some with rich sauces of *cinghiale* (wild boar), and grilled steak and pork also show off the local bounty. *Via Condotti 11. www.trattoriada fiorella.it.* ☎ *0578-749045. Entrees 8€–15€. Lunch, dinner Thurs–Tues.*

Pisa

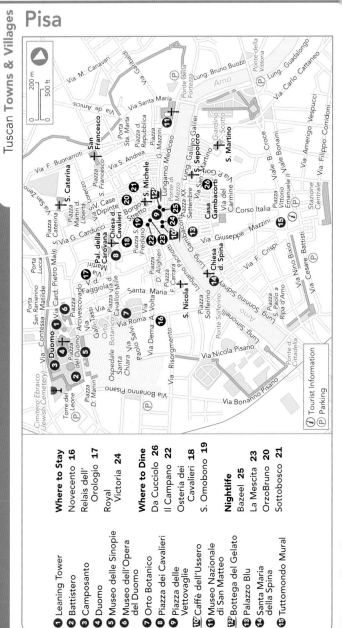

Where to Stay

Novecento **16**

Relais dell' Orologio **17**

Royal Victoria **24**

Where to Dine

Da Cucciolo **26**

Il Campano **22**

Osteria dei Cavalieri **18**

S. Omobono **19**

Nightlife

Bazeel **25**

La Mescita **23**

OrzoBruno **20**

Sottobosco **21**

❶ Leaning Tower
❷ Battistero
❸ Camposanto
❹ Duomo
❺ Museo delle Sinopie
❻ Museo dell'Opera del Duomo
❼ Orto Botanico
❽ Piazza dei Cavalieri
❾ Piazza delle Vettovaglie
❿ Caffè dell'Ussero
⓫ Museo Nazionale di San Matteo
⓬ Bottega del Gelato
⓭ Palazzo Blu
⓮ Santa Maria della Spina
⓯ Tuttomondo Mural

When Pisans discuss the good old days, they're talking about the 12th century. Buildings such as the Duomo and Leaning Tower were created in those heady days of Pisan power. Pisa enjoyed great maritime influence because of its harbor at the mouth of the Arno River, and the Pisan-Romanesque architecture that developed through the rich years of the city's prominence is the reason so many outsiders pass through today. Pisa began to decline following its defeat at sea by the Genoese in 1285 and the silting up of its vital harbor, and the city eventually succumbed to Florence. If you spend a little extra time here, you'll get to know the lively center beyond the Campo dei Miracoli. START: **Pisa is 88km (55 miles) from Florence, taking the FI-PI-LI highway along the Valdarno. Trip length: 2 days to see the city properly.**

❶ ★★★ **Leaning Tower** (Torre Pendente). The freestanding *campanile*, or bell tower, of the cathedral, the most famous building in Italy, was begun in 1173. It was intended to be vertical but started to lurch almost immediately: You just can't stack that much marble on sinking subsoil. However, construction continued, with two long interruptions, until 1360, and in December 2001 it was righted to lean a mere 4m (14 ft.)—but you'll still notice the disorienting effects as you climb spiral steps to the top. It was supposedly from here that Galileo dropped balls of different masses, disproving Aristotle's

theories about the acceleration of falling bodies. ⏱ *30 min. Piazza del Duomo. www.opapisa.it. ☎ 050-835011. Admission 18€ (17€ with reservation). Apr–Sept daily 8am–8pm; Oct daily 9am–7pm; Nov–Feb daily 10am–5pm; Mar daily 9am–6pm. Minimum age 8.*

❷ ★★ **Battistero.** This stunning example of the Pisan-Romanesque style (with its own distinct lean) was begun in 1152 by Diotisalvi and finally crowned with a Gothic dome in the 14th century. The hexagonal pulpit (1260) by Nicola Pisano is carved with five scenes from the *Life of Christ* and supported by pillars resting on the backs of three

The Leaning Tower of Pisa, the Cattedrale, and the Baptistery.

The grounds by the Duomo and the Leaning Tower.

marble lions. ⏱ *30 min. Piazza del Duomo. www.opapisa.it.* ☎ *050-835011. Apr–Sept daily 8am–8pm; Oct daily 9am–7pm; Nov–Feb daily 10am–5pm; Mar daily 9am–6pm.*

❸ ★★ **Camposanto.** In 1278, Giovanni di Simone designed this cemetery, allegedly over dirt from the Holy Land shipped to Pisa by the Crusaders. Some 600 members of medieval Pisan nobility are interred here. The entire building was once decorated with frescoes by Benozzo Gozzoli, Andrea di Bonaiuto, and others, many of which were destroyed when the Camposanto was hit by a U.S. incendiary bomb in 1944. The best of what remains is Buffalmacco's sobering *Triumph of Death,* painted in the late 1330s. ⏱ *45 min. Piazza del Duomo. www.opapisa.it.* ☎ *050-835011. Apr–Sept daily 8am–8pm; Oct daily 9am–7pm; Nov–Feb daily 10am–5pm; Mar daily 9am–6pm.*

Note: **Admission charges** for the monuments and museums of the Campo are tied together. The Cattedrale is free (you can enter at any time with a ticket to any other site, but will be assigned a fixed time if only visiting the cathedral). Any other single sight is 5€, any two sites cost 7€, and three cost 8€. Admission to the Leaning Tower is separate (see below). For more information, visit **www.opapisa.it**.

❹ ★★ **Cattedrale.** This cathedral, started by Buschetto in 1063 using a mix of classical and Arab styles, became the most influential Romanesque building in Tuscany. The facade was erected by Rainaldo in the 1200s, with arches that diminish in size as they ascend. The pulpit by Giovanni Pisano (1302–11)

Saints on Pisa's Battisterro.

even outshines the one by his dad in the baptistery. ⏱ *40 min. Piazza del Duomo. www.opapisa.it.* ☎ *050-835011. Admission free. Apr–Sept daily 8am–8pm; Oct daily 9am–7pm; Nov–Feb daily 10am–5pm; Mar daily 9am–6pm.*

❺ ★ Museo delle Sinopie. The sketches (or *sinopie*) displayed here survived beneath the Camposanto's ruined frescoes after the 1944 bombardment. (Fresco artists drew in red-brown pigment before applying their paint.) Compare the different drawing styles of such painters as Benozzo Gozzoli, Taddeo Gaddi, and Andrea di Bonaiuto. ⏱ *45 min. Piazza del Duomo. www.opapisa.it.* ☎ *050-835011. Apr–Sept daily 8am–8pm; Oct daily 9am–7pm; Nov–Feb daily 10am–5pm; Mar daily 9am–6pm.*

❻ ★ Museo dell'Opera del Duomo. Mostly Romanesque and Gothic art removed for safekeeping from the monuments of Piazza del Duomo is showcased here, including Bonnano Pisano's extraordinary 12th-century San Ranieri door (that originally hung on the Duomo right opposite the Tower) and plenty of *famiglia* Pisano sculpture. The courtyard has a unique view of the Campo dei Miracoli. ⏱ *45 min. Piazza Arcivescovado 6. www. opapisa.it.* ☎ *050-835011. Apr–Sept daily 8am–8pm; Oct daily 9am–7pm; Nov–Feb daily 10am–5pm; Mar daily 9am–6pm.*

❼ ★ Orto Botanico. Europe's oldest botanical garden, founded in 1543, is the perfect spot to breathe deep and wander unbothered after the chaos of the Campo. ⏱ *45 min. Via Ghini 5.* ☎ *050-2211313. Admission 4€. June–mid-Sept, 9am–7pm; mid-Sept–May, Mon–Sat 9am–6pm, Sun 9am–1pm. Closed 1 week around Aug 15.*

❽ ★★ Piazza dei Cavalieri. The Palazzo del Popolo commands the square that was the seat of government when Pisa was one of the world's most powerful maritime republics. Meanwhile, the statue of Cosimo I Medici is a reminder that Florence conquered Pisa in the early 1500s and the city never regained its might or glory. ⏱ *10 min.*

❾ ★ Piazza delle Vettovaglie. The bustling heart of the medieval and Renaissance city is a fish and vegetable market that fills a 16th-century loggia every morning except Sunday. ⏱ *15 min.*

❿ Caffè dell'Ussero. One of Italy's oldest literary cafe-bars was installed in 1775 on the ground floor of riverside Palazzo Agostini. Young men of the Risorgimento drank and plotted here as students. The coffee and pastries are delicious. *Lungarno Pacinotti 27.* ☎ *050-581100. Closed Sat and Aug. $.*

⓫ ★★ Museo Nazionale di San Matteo. An old convent that was once a prison today houses

Pisa's Piazza dei Cavalieri and statue of Cosimo I Medici.

Pisa After Dark

Away from the Campo, central Pisa has a lively nighttime scene, kept buzzing by the city's large student population. Stone-clad **Bazeel,** Lungarno Pacinotti 1 (www.bazeel.it; ☎ 340-2881113), always seems to be the bar of the minute, attracting Pisa's fashionable set for *aperitivo*, live music, DJs, or big-screen sports. For beer lovers, **OrzoBruno,** Via Case Dipinte 6 (www.orzobruno.it; ☎ 050-578802), has a selection of light and dark microbrews. Bookstore-cum-cafe **Sottobosco,** Piazza San Paolo all'Orto 3 (☎ 050-9912364), comes alive at night with live acoustic music, cocktails, and a beautiful clientele. Once dinner service is over, **La Mescita,** Via Cavalca 2 (www.osterialamescitapisa.it; ☎ 050-957019), transforms itself into an atmospheric late-night enoteca with a respectable wine list.

sacred art and sculpture gathered from Pisa's holy places. It's memorable largely for many lesser-known works by some major artists, like Masaccio's *St. Paul* (1426), the only piece of his much-studied *Pisa Altarpiece* still in Pisa. Look out too for Simone Martini's outstanding polyptych of the *Virgin and Child with Saints*. ⏱ *75 min. Piazzetta San Matteo 1.* ☎ *050-541865. Admission 5€. Tues–Sat 8:30am–7pm, Sun 9am–1:30pm.*

12 ★ **Bottega del Gelato.** Pisa's best ice cream. Enough said. Slurp in the shade as you stroll under the arcades of adjacent Borgo Stretto, Pisa's main shopping street. *Piazza Garibaldi 11.* ☎ *050-575467. $.*

13 **Palazzo Blu.** It's easy to see why this handsome, Liberty-style riverside *palazzo* got its name. These days it's an intriguing space used to showcase the works of lesser-known historical painters who worked in Pisa, as well as

contemporary shows. ⏱ *45 min. Lungarno Gambacorti 9. www. palazzoblu.org.* ☎ *050-916950. Free admission. Tues–Fri 10am–7pm, Sat–Sun 10am–8pm.*

14 ★★ **Santa Maria della Spina.** All the truly ancient churches of Pisa face the sea, the original source of the maritime city's protection and wealth. Among them is this extravagant Gothic masterpiece, nestled next to the river and wrought by Giovanni Pisano and Pisa's other leading Gothic sculptors. There's little point going inside. ⏱ *10 min. Lungarno Gambacorti (at Via Sant'Antonio).* ☎ *050-21441. Admission 2€. Hours vary, but typically Tues–Sun 11am–12:45pm & 3–5:45pm.*

15 ★ **Tuttomondo Mural.** A few months before his death in 1990, New York street artist Keith Haring completed this giant mural on the theme of "peace and harmony." The dazzling and complex painting interweaves 30 of his trademark Pop Art figures. ⏱ *10 min. Via Zandonai.*

Where to Stay

Where to Dine

★ **Novecento** CENTRO STORICO This immaculately converted Liberty villa set around a courtyard garden is Pisa's best boutique offering. Rooms are small but ooze style, and represent a good value so close to the Campo. *Via Roma 37. www.hotelnovecento.pisa. it.* ☎ *050-500323. 14 units. Doubles 70€–150€, w/breakfast.*

★★ **Relais dell'Orologio** CENTRO STORICO A former private home of a noble family is the most intimate hotel in town, with a sophisticated yet welcoming ambience. The same owners run a B&B, the nearby **Relais dei Fiori,** for tighter budgets. *Via della Faggiola 12. www.hotelrelaisorologio.com.* ☎ *050-830361. 21 units. Doubles 120€–180€, w/breakfast.*

★ **Royal Victoria** CENTRO STORICO In business since 1839, this traditional hotel blends harmoniously with Pisa's Renaissance-style riverfront. Request a room overlooking the Arno. *Lungarno Pacinotti 12. www.royalvictoria.it.* ☎ *050-940111. 48 units. Doubles 65€–150€, w/breakfast.*

Dining Tip

Choose a restaurant that's well away from the Campo, to ensure you eat better food at better prices.

★★ **Da Cucciolo** SOUTH BANK PISAN This enchantingly old-fashioned back-street trattoria is frequented by locals who know good eating at a good price. It's the place to try simple Pisan classics like *seppie e bietole* (a stew of cuttlefish and chard). *Vicolo Rosselmini 9.* ☎ *050-26086. Entrees 8€–14€. Lunch daily, dinner Mon–Sat.*

★★ **Il Campano** CENTRO STORICO *PISAN* A meal in the brick-and-stone rooms of an 18th-century tower house focuses on hearty Tuscan fare: *pappardelle alla lepre* (homemade pasta with hare sauce), *tagliata di scamerita di maiale* (grilled pork chops), and Florentine steaks. *Via Cavalca 19. www.ilcampano.com.* ☎ *050-580585. Entrees 10€–24€. Lunch Fri–Tues, dinner Thurs–Tues.*

★ **Osteria dei Cavalieri** CENTRO STORICO *TUSCAN* The best food within a few minutes of the Campo is traditional, but skilled chefs lighten and modernize many of the region's robust classics. *Via San Frediano 16. www.osteria cavalieri.pisa.it.* ☎ *050-580858. Entrees 11€–16€. Lunch Mon–Fri, dinner Mon–Sat. Closed Aug.*

★ **S. Omobono** CENTRO STORICO *PISAN* Dine among locals right on Pisa's market. The daily menu sticks to local classics such as *baccalà alla livornese* (salt cod stewed with tomatoes). *Piazza S. Omobono 6.* ☎ *050-540847. Entrees 8€–10€. Lunch, dinner Mon–Sat. Closed 2 wks. in Aug.*

Pistoia

① Cappella del Tau
② San Giovanni Fuorcivitas
③ Battistero
④ Cattedrale di San Zeno
⑤ Galleria Vittorio Emanuele
⑥ Armando
⑦ Sant'Andrea
⑧ Ospedale del Ceppo
⑨ Pistoia Sotterranea
⑩ Bruno Corsini

Where to Stay

Patria **14**

Piccolo Ritz **15**

Where to Dine

Cacio Divino **11**

Gargantuà **13**

La BotteGaia **12**

Midway between rivals Pisa and Florence, the ancient Roman city of Pistoia inherited Romanesque architecture and Gothic sculpture from the former and the best of the Renaissance through proximity to the latter. It was once known for firearms—and lays questionable claim to be the birthplace of the pistol (or *pisto-lese*)—but these days is better known for nurturing life, in both the plant nurseries that ring the city and the thriving produce market surrounded by excellent informal restaurants right at its heart.
START: **Pistoia is 35km (22 miles) northwest of Florence, just off the A11. Trip length: 1 day.**

① ★★ **Cappella del Tau.** This remarkable little chapel was completely frescoed in 1372 by Niccolò di Tommaso with scenes that covered every inch of the walls and ceiling. Now seriously damaged, what remains illustrates the *Life of St. Anthony Abbot* (lower register); *Stories from the New Testament* (middle register); and *Stories from* the *Old Testament* (upper register and vaults). The wall facing the door is covered by a huge *Last Judgment:* The space is now shared, somewhat incongruously, with giant bronzes by Pistoiese sculptor Marino Marini (1901–80). ⏱ *20 min. Corso Fedi 28.* ☎ *0573-32204. Free admission. Mon–Sat 8:30am–1:30pm.*

The Cattedrale di San Zeno.

❷ ★ San Giovanni Fuorcivitas.

The side facade of this small, supremely Romanesque church is an orderly festival of blind arcades, inlaid diamond lozenges, and stripes to put a zebra to shame. Inside the main attraction is the pulpit (1270) by Fra' Guglielmo da Pisa, a student of Nicola Pisano. ⏱ *15 min. Via Cavour.* ☎ *0573-24784. Free admission. Daily 8am–noon & 4–6:30pm.*

❸ Battistero.

Anchoring one corner of Pistoia's set-piece piazza, the city baptistery was built in characteristic bands of dark green and white by Cellino di Nese from 1337 to 1359, based on a design by Andrea Pisano. The Gothic pulpit was added in 1399, and the *Madonna* above the door is the work of Tommaso and Nino Pisano. ⏱ *10 min. Piazza del Duomo. No phone. Free admission. Fri–Sun 10am–1pm & 3–6pm.*

❹ ★ Cattedrale di San Zeno.

The current incarnation of Pistoia's Duomo dates from 1220, soon after which an old defensive tower close by, bristling with Ghibelline swallowtail crenellations, was given Romanesque striped arches and converted to serve as its bell tower. The glazed terracotta decorations

of the entrance barrel vault and the lunette above the main door are Andrea della Robbia creations. Inside the **Cappella di San Jacopo** is the Duomo's greatest treasure, the silver-gilded Altare di San Jacopo. In the crypt are the remains of the 5th-century church and marvelously medieval bits of a Guido da Como pulpit (1199), dismembered in the 17th century. ⏱ *20 min. Piazza del Duomo.* ☎ *0573-25095. Free admission. Mon–Sat 9:30am–6pm, Sun 10:30–6pm.*

❺ ★ Galleria Vittorio Emanuele.

Skip forward 8 centuries from the Romanesque to Art Nouveau: This early-20th-century shopping mall (now rather tired) sports exuberant external decoration crafted by the town's Michelucci ironworks. ⏱ *10 min. Via degli Orafi (at Via della Nave).*

❻ Armando.

This lively place is both a favorite local coffee stop and a purveyor of sublime cream and fruit pastries. *Via Curtatone e Montanara 38.* ☎ *0573-23128. $.*

❼ ★★★ Sant'Andrea.

Pistoia's undisputed artistic heavyweight is Giovanni Pisano's pulpit (1298–1301) inside this 12th-century

Baptistery of Pistoia.

church. The third of the four great Pisano pulpits (the others are in Pisa and Siena) and the first carved by Giovanni without the help of his dad, Nicola, this is the work with which the Pisan sculptor brought his art to absolute Gothic perfection, relying on a trademark narrative density and emotive power. Bring a .50€ coin for the light box. ⏱ *20 min. Piazzetta Sant'Andrea.* ☎ *0573-21912. Free admission. Daily 8am–12:30pm & 3–6:30pm.*

⑧ ★★ Ospedale del Ceppo. Pistoia's star outdoor attraction is the facade of this still-operational hospital: a Giovanni della Robbia frieze (1514–25) of glazed terracotta panels to surmount a Michelozzo-designed loggia. The six panels, plus a decaying one added later by

Filippo Paladini, represent the seven acts of mercy, divided by the cardinal and theological virtues. ⏱ *10 min. Piazza Giovanni XXIII.*

⑨ ★ Pistoia Sotterranea. This fascinating guided underground visit follows the path of a diverted stream, under a couple of intact bridges now below the Ospedale del Ceppo. Over the centuries the stream has served as a power source for an olive press, a public laundry, a refuse dump, and a source of drinking water—often simultaneously. The fascinating tour takes in the history of the hospital above (founded in 1277 and still going strong) and ends at the tiny, frescoed teaching and autopsy theater built in the 1700s. ⏱ *1 hr. Piazza Giovanni XXIII 13. www.irsapt. it.* ☎ *0573-368023. Tours (some in English) 9€. Daily at 10:30am, 11:30am, 12:30pm, 2pm, 3pm, 4pm, 5pm (Apr–Sept also 6pm).*

⑩ ★ Bruno Corsini. A famous purveyor of the city's famous confetti di Pistoia—little candies that are mainstays at weddings and other celebrations throughout Italy—also sells delicious chocolates and other sweets. *Piazza San Francesco 42. www.brunocorsini. com.* ☎ *0573-20138.*

Giovanni della Robbia's frieze on the Ospedale del Ceppo.

Where to Stay   Where to Dine

You'll probably visit Pistoia on a day trip from Florence or Lucca, but should you decide to stay over, you'll have some good choices.

★★ Patria CENTRO STORICO The most stylish perch in central Pistoia has midsize, contemporary-yet-warm rooms that sport parquet flooring and chic furnishings with a contemporary slant. *Via Crispi 8–12. www.patriahotel.com.* ☎ *0573-358800. 27 units. Doubles 110€–250€, w/breakfast.*

★★ Picolo Ritz CENTRO STORICO   An old-fashioned station hotel well-located at the edge of the historic center is pleasantly Tuscan, with such handsome touches as tiled floors, beamed ceilings, and iron bedsteads. *Via Atto Vannucci 67. www.hotelpiccolo ritzpistoia.com.* ☎ *0573 977474. 25 units. Doubles 65€–85€, w/breakfast.*

★★ Cacio Divino CENTRO STORICO *MODERN TUSCAN* Surprisingly daring Tuscan flavor combinations and contemporary presentation at fair prices. Expect the likes of *pici alla lepre sul cacao amaro* (hand-rolled pasta with hare sauce on bitter chocolate) served with a smile. *Via del Lastrone 13. www.cacio-divino.it.* ☎ *0573-1941058. Entrees 9€–11€. Lunch, dinner daily (mid-June to mid-Sept closed Sun lunch).*

★ Gargantuà CENTRO STORICO *MODERN TUSCAN*   This lively enoteca-restaurant tucked into a tiny piazza sports bright, Catalan-style decor and a menu of pasta, *bruschette,* and simple Tuscan mains. There's a well-chosen list of wines by the glass, too, and you're welcome to just drink and snack if you're not that hungry. *Piazza dell'Ortaggio 12. www.taverna gargantua.com.* ☎ *0573-23330. Entrees 9€–15€. Lunch, dinner daily.*

★ La BotteGaia CENTRO STORICO *MODERN TUSCAN* This much recommended place serves classic Tuscan cuisine, elevated a notch above the norm, alongside more daring delicacies such as slow-cooked, milk-fed veal. Grab a table out back for views across to the Duomo and Baptistery. *Via del Lastrone 17 (also an entrance behind the Baptistery). www.labottegaia.it.* ☎ *0573-365602. Entrees 10€–14€. Lunch Tues–Sat, dinner Tues–Sun. Closed 2 weeks in Aug.*

San Gimignano

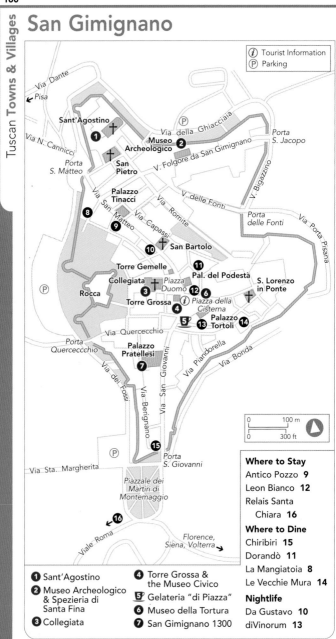

(i) Tourist Information
(P) Parking

Via Dante
← Pisa

Sant'Agostino ❶

Via N. Cannicci

Porta S. Matteo

Museo Archeologico ❷

Via della Ghiacciaia

V. Folgore da San Gimignano

Porta S. Jacopo

San Pietro

V. Bigazzino

Palazzo Tinacci

Via delle Fonti

Via Romite

Via San Matteo

Via Capassi

Porta delle Fonti

Via Porta Pisana

❽

❾

San Bartolo ❿

Torre Gemelle

Pal. del Podestà ⓫

S. Lorenzo in Ponte

Collegiata ❸

Piazza Duomo

⓬ ❻

Piazza della Cisterna

Rocca

(P)

Torre Grossa ❹

(i)

Palazzo Tortoli ⓭ ⓮

Via Quercecchio

5️⃣

Porta Quercecccchio

Palazzo Pratellesi ❼

Via dei Fossi

Via Bergnano

Via San Giovanni

Via Piandorella

Via Bonda

Via Sta. Margherita

(P)

⓯

Porta S. Giovanni

0   100 m
0   300 ft

Piazzale dei Martiri di Montemaggio

⓰

Viale Roma

Florence, Siena, Volterra →

Where to Stay
Antico Pozzo **9**
Leon Bianco **12**
Relais Santa
   Chiara **16**

Where to Dine
Chiribiri **15**
Dorandò **11**
La Mangiatoia **8**
Le Vecchie Mura **14**

Nightlife
Da Gustavo **10**
diVinorum **13**

❶ Sant'Agostino
❷ Museo Archeologico & Spezieria di Santa Fina
❸ Collegiata
❹ Torre Grossa & the Museo Civico
5️⃣ Gelateria "di Piazza"
❻ Museo della Tortura
❼ San Gimignano 1300

Tuscany's best-preserved medieval town once had more than 70 towers, symbols of local clan rivalry and one-upmanship, and a visible sign of the town's wealth in the years running up to the Black Death of 1348. The painter Benozzo Gozzoli was born here, and novelists and film directors have used it as a stage (E. M. Forster in *Where Angels Fear to Tread* and Franco Zeffirelli in *Tea with Mussolini*). Try to stay overnight: The place can feel like a theme park during the day, but San Gimignano at dusk is one of Tuscany's special places. START: **San Gimignano is off the Florence-Siena raccordo, 40km (24 miles) northwest of Siena and 52km (32 miles) southwest of Florence. Trip length: 1 day.**

1 ★★ **Sant'Agostino.** In 1464, a plague swept San Gimignano, and the citizens prayed to St. Sebastian to end it. When the sickness passed, they dutifully hired native son Benozzo Gozzoli to paint a thankful scene on the nave's left wall showing this patron saint of plagues and his cloak of angels breaking the plague arrows being thrown down by a vengeful God. The town liked the results, so they commissioned Gozzoli to spend the next 2 years frescoing the apse of their Romanesque-Gothic church with *Scenes from the Life of St. Augustine*. Right in front, Piero del Pollaiuolo's 1483 *Coronation of the Virgin* resides on Benedetto di Maiano's sculpted 1494 marble altar. ⏱ *20 min. Piazza*

Sant'Agostino. ☎ *0577-907012. Free admission. Daily 7am–noon & 3–7pm (Nov–Apr closes 6pm); Jan–Apr closed Mon morning.*

2 **Museo Archeologico & Spezieria di Santa Fina.** San Gimignano's modest Etruscan collection proves the town's roots run much deeper than the Middle Ages. The museum is installed in the 1253 Spezieria, the pharmacy branch of the medieval Santa Fina hospital. Upstairs is the town's surprisingly large and sporadically interesting **Galleria di Arte Moderna e Contemporanea,** usually deserted. ⏱ *30 min. Via Folgore 3.* ☎ *0577-940348. Admission 3.50€. Apr–Oct daily 9:30am–6:30pm, Nov–Feb daily 11am–5pm, Mar daily 10am–5pm.*

The streets of San Gimignano.

San Gimignano is a picturesque place to shop.

❸ ★★★ Collegiata. The city's principal church dates from the 11th century, but its present look is mostly from the 1400s. Inside, scenes from the Old and New Testaments painted by Bartolo di Fredi and (probably) Lippo Memmi face each other across the nave. The left wall is frescoed with 26 scenes from the Old Testament (look for the panel showing the Pharaoh and his army being swallowed by the Red Sea) and the right wall with 22 scenes from the New Testament (a very shifty-looking Judas receives

his 30 pieces of silver for betraying Christ). At the end of the nave on the right is one of our favorite spots in all Tuscany: Guiliano da Maiano's Renaissance Chapel of Santa Fina, frescoed in 1475 by Domenico Ghirlandaio with two scenes from the life of the local saint, a young girl named Fina who was so devout that when she fell ill with paralysis she refused a bed and lay instead on a board, never complaining even when worms and rats fed off her decaying flesh. Look for the towers of 15th-century San Gimignano in the background of her funeral, on the left. ⏱ *45 min. Piazza del Duomo.* ☎ *0577-940316. Admission 4€. Apr–Oct Mon–Fri 10am–7:30pm, Sat 10am–5:30pm & Sun 12:30–7:30pm; Nov–Mar Mon–Sat 10am–5pm & Sun 12:30–5pm.*

Travel Tip

For 7.50€, you can buy a discount ticket that covers the Torre Grossa and Museo Civico (❹); the tiny Museo Archeologico (❷); and the strange little Museo Ornitologico (☎ 0577-941-388), a few glass cases containing stuffed birds in the confines of a dimly-lit, deconsecrated church.

The facade of the church of Collegiata.

The medieval skyscrapers of San Gimignano.

❹ ★★ Museo Civico & Torre Grossa. Climb 54m (175 ft.) up the highest tower in town for one of Tuscany's best panoramas, over the bucolic hills around San Gimignano and across the whole Val d'Elsa. (Though if you climb the hill to the right of the Collegiata, you'll get almost the same view for free from San Gimignano's ruined fortress.) The same ticket includes the art at the 13th-century **Palazzo del Popolo.** Lippo Memmi's impressive *Maestà* (from 1317) dominates the Council Chamber. Slightly racier are frescoes by his father, Memmi di Filippuccio, showing scenes from a medieval wedding night. The remainder of the collection is strong on pre-Renaissance painting. ⏱ *45 min. Piazza del Duomo 1.* ☎ *0577-990312. Admission 6€. Nov–Feb daily 11am–5pm; Mar daily 10am–5pm; Apr–Oct daily 9:30am–6:30pm.*

❺ ★★ Gelateria "di Piazza." The queues out the door tell their own story: This place has been named Gelato World Champion more than once with good reason. Our top choices are Vernaccia wine flavor and Crema di Santa Fina, made with saffron. (But not on the same cone.) *Piazza della Cisterna 4. www.gelateriadipiazza.com.* ☎ *0577-942244. $.*

Market Days on Beautiful Squares

Two of Tuscany's loveliest squares, Piazza del Duomo and **Piazza della Cisterna,** stand side by side in the heart of town. On Thursday and Saturday mornings, vendors hawk their wares in Piazza del Duomo, in the long shadows of Gothic palaces and seven towers. Piazza della Cisterna, named for its 1237 well, is lined with 13th- and 14th-century buildings and hosts a fine hotel or two as well as the best gelato in town (❺, above).

San Gimignano After Dark

Unsurprisingly, San Gim is a sleepy town after dark. However, it is blessed with a handful of excellent wine bars that serve the region's famed reds alongside Vernaccia di San Gimignano, the only DOCG white wine made in Tuscany. **Enoteca Gustavo,** Via San Matteo 29 (☎ 0577-940057), draws a mixed crowd of visitors and locals. Vernaccias and Chiantis (from 3€) are usually good, often sold by the glass, and served alongside snacks such as *crostini* or *bruschetta* or Panforte for the sweet-toothed. Our favorite spot to sip a glass or two is one of the handful of panoramic tables at **diVinorum,** Via degli Innocenti 5 (www.divinorumwinebar.com; ☎ 0577-907-192). It has more than 20 wines by the glass, and accompanying *bruschettoni* (large bruschettas) cost around 8€.

❻ ★ **Museo della Tortura.**
Though certainly not for young or easily frightened children, San Gimignano's original torture museum provides a fascinating, and reasonably scientific, presentation of some grim subject matter. The setting, in the Torre del Diavolo (Devil's Tower), and implements like the "Iron Maiden of Nuremberg" and "Heretic's Fork," might just give you nightmares. Commentary in English completes the grisly experience. 🕐 30 min. Via San Giovanni 125. www.torturemuseum.it. ☎ 0577-940526. Admission 10€. Apr–Oct daily

10am–7pm; Nov–Mar Sat–Sun 10am–6pm (sometimes shorter hours).

❼ ★ **San Gimignano 1300.** It took a team of five skilled craftsmen (two named Michelangelo and Raffaello, believe it or not) 3 years and a ton of clay to build the 800 structures that make up this enchanting 1:100 scale model of San Gimignano around 1300, with its 72 towers intact. 🕐 20 min. Via Berignano 23. www.sangimignano1300.com. ☎ 327-439-5165. Admission 5€. Daily 10am–6pm (closes 5pm Jan–Feb).

Wine buffs will find San Gimignano well-stocked with enoteche.

Where to Stay & Dine

★★ **Antico Pozzo** CENTRO STORICO   Dante slept in this 15th-century *palazzo*, now the ancient center's best hotel. Rooms vary in size, and superior units have frescoes. *Via San Matteo 87. www.anticopozzo.com.* ☎ *0577-942014. 18 units. Doubles 90€–170€, w/breakfast. Closed 3 weeks in Jan–Feb.*

★ **Chiribiri** CENTRO STORICO *ITALIAN*   The little basement eatery knocks out Italian and regional meat and pasta classics with gusto. A bonus: It's open 11am to 11pm nonstop, so if you or yours have odd meal times, they can feed you, but you'll need to pay in cash. *Piazzetta della Madonna 1.* ☎ *0577-941948. Entrees 8€–12€. Lunch, dinner daily.*

★★ **Dorandò** CENTRO STORICO *MODERN TUSCAN*   The city's most refined restaurant, with stone walls and a vaulted roof, serves creative seasonal dishes based on medieval recipes. All with a slow-food ethos. *Vicolo dell'Oro 2. www. ristorantedorando.it.* ☎ *0577-941862. Entrees 20€–25€. Lunch, dinner daily (Oct–Easter closed Mon). Closed Dec 10–Jan 31.*

★ **La Mangiatoia** CENTRO STORICO *TUSCAN*   Many dishes at this intimate old-town restaurant—like *cinghiale di Remigio* (boar stewed in white wine)—derive from ancient Sangimignanese recipes. *Via Mainardi 5.* ☎ *0577-941528. Entrees 13€–16€. Lunch, dinner daily. Closed Nov–Jan.*

★ **Leon Bianco** CENTRO STORICO   This 11th-century townhouse has many original features, views of the Val d'Elsa, and a location right on San Gim's principal piazza. Most of the medium to large rooms come with beamed ceilings. *Piazza della Cisterna 8. www.leonbianco.com.* ☎ *0577-941294. 26 units. Doubles 85€–140€, w/breakfast.*

★★ **Le Vecchie Mura** CENTRO STORICO *TUSCAN*   Seasonal, quintessentially Tuscan dishes—*ribollita*, wild boar in Vernaccia wine—are served in a stylish vaulted interior or on the knock-out panoramic terrace. *Via Piandornella 15. www.vecchiemura. it.* ☎ *0577-940270. Entrees 10€–18€. Dinner Wed–Mon. Closed Nov–Feb.*

★ **Relais Santa Chiara** OUTSIDE WALLS   For a swimming pool, a summertime blessing, this modern hotel away from the chaos of the center (but still walkable into town) is your best bet. Midsize rooms come with terracotta floors, marble mosaics, and terraces. *Via Matteotti 15. www.rsc.it.* ☎ *0577-940701. 41 units. Doubles 120€–220€, w/breakfast. AE, DC, MC, V.*

One of the rooms at Antico Pozzo.

Siena

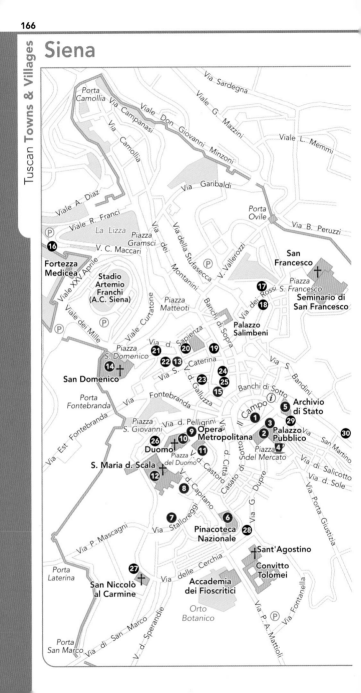

1 Piazza del Campo
2 Palazzo Pubblico
3 Torre del Mangia
4 Gino Cacino
5 Archivio di Stato
6 Pinacoteca Nazionale
7 Via Stalloreggi
8 Martini Marisa
9 Battistero
10 Duomo
11 Museo dell'Opera Metropolitana
12 Santa Maria della Scala
13 Casa di Santa Caterina
14 San Domenico
15 Vitra

Where to Stay
Antica Residenza Cicogna **19**
Campo Regio Relais **20**
Frances' Lodge Relais **33**
Hotel Alta Domus **21**
Palazzo Bulgarini **30**
Palazzo Ravizza **27**
Santa Caterina **32**

Where to Dine
Da Divo **26**
Grotta Santa Caterina da Bagoga **23**
La Chiacchera **22**
La Sosta di Violante **31**
Le Logge **29**
L'Osteria **17**
Ristorante Guido **25**
Taverna San Giuseppe **28**

Nightlife
Enoteca Italiana **16**
Enoteca i Terzi **24**
Kopakabana **18**

ⓘ Tourist Information
Ⓟ Parking

If you have time for only one stop besides Florence, make it Siena. Dominating the medieval trade routes between France and Rome, the city in its day had Italy's richest banks and finest Gothic architecture, a quasi-democratic government under "the Nine," and its own constitution. Once Florence's rival in might and artistic patronage, Siena never fully recovered from the Black Death of 1348–49, which mowed down the population from 100,000 to 30,000. Now, the medieval character of its center appears frozen in time—the city is a living museum for art, architecture, and history buffs, with a vibrant civic culture. START: **Siena is 70km (43 miles) south of Florence along the Firenze–Siena raccordo. Trip length: 2 days to see the city properly.**

❶ ★★★ Piazza del Campo.

The most dramatic piazza in Italy was laid out in the early 12th century on the site of the Roman forum and is shaped like a sloping scallop shell or fan. By 1340, the city's leaders had paved the square in brick and divided it into nine sections in honor of the Council of Nine (the *Nove*), who ruled Siena during its golden age. Today it's the setting for the **Palio** (see below).

At the upper end of the square stands the **Fonte Gaia,** created from 1408 to 1419 by Jacopo della Quercia. What you see today is an inferior copy from 1868 (the badly damaged original is in **Santa Maria della Scala, ⓬**). ⏲ *15 min.*

Siena's Piazza del Campo.

❷ ★★★ Palazzo Pubblico.

This Gothic *palazzo* was constructed in a crenellated style from 1297 to 1310 to house the city's government. Siena's faithful added the loggia chapel by the entrance, the **Cappella della Piazza,** to thank God for delivering them from the Black Death.

Inside is one of Europe's outstanding civic museums, two rooms in particular marking the pinnacle of artistic achievement in Siena. In the **Sala del Mappamondo** is Simone Martini's 1315 *Maestà,* showing the city's protector under a huge canopy. It's not just a religious work: Christ's scroll reads: *Love Justice, ye who judge the Earth.*

Bareback Anarchy: the Palio

Twice a year, on July 2 (the Provenzano) and August 16 (the Assunta), Europe's most daring horse race takes place on Siena's Campo. Jockeys representing 10 of the city's 17 *contrade* (districts) fly around the dirt-filled square three times with one aim: winning the banner, **il Palio.** Forget sportsmanship. The single rule is that no jockey can grab another horse's reins. But you can drug an opponent the morning of the race, kidnap him the night before, or "whip him with a leather belt made from the skin of the bull's penis," explains a marshal. The jockey, after all, is irrelevant: The horse wins whether there's a rider on it or not.

All this has taken place in tribute to the Virgin Mary since at least 1310. In the weeks after a race, you'll often find the winning *contrada* out en masse, marching the streets banging drums and singing traditional songs.

Next door in the **Sala del Pace** (where "the Nine" sat), the walls are covered by Ambrogio Lorenzetti's *Allegories of Good and Bad Government* (1338). This work of medieval civic art is without parallel, commissioned to remind rulers of the qualities of good government and a prosperous city: Justice, Wisdom, and Peace all appear. Alas, in the wake of the Black Death (that also killed Lorenzetti), *Bad Government* on the opposite wall came to pass: Fear, Treason, and War stalked Siena for decades.
🕐 *90 min. Piazza del Campo.*
☎ *0577-292226. Admission 9€ without reservation; 8€ with reservation; cumulative ticket with Torre del Mangia & Santa Maria della Scala 20€ or 13€ with Santa Maria della Scala only. Mid-Mar to Oct daily 10am–7pm, Nov to mid-Mar daily 10am–6pm.*

❸ ★ **Torre del Mangia.** The 14th-century tower of the Palazzo Pubblico was named after a gluttonous bell-ringer, Giovanni di Duccio, nicknamed "Mangiaguadagni" or "eater of profits." At 102m (336

ft.), it is the tallest secular monument from the Middle Ages standing in Tuscany, so if you're expecting a great view you won't be disappointed. Don't attempt the climb if you're claustrophobic.
🕐 *30 min. Piazza del Campo.*
☎ *0577-292226. Admission 10€; 20€ with Palazzo Pubblico & Santa Maria della Scala. Mar to mid-Oct daily 10am–7pm, otherwise 10am–4pm.*

Torre del Mangia.

Artwork at the Pinacoteca Nazionale.

4 ★ **Gino Cacino.** This venerable deli, suppliers to some of Siena's notable restaurants, will load you a sandwich from whatever's behind the counter. *Piazza del Mercato 31.* ☎ *0577-223076. $.*

5 ★ **Archivio di Stato.** Housed inside Bernardo Rossellino's Renaissance Palazzo Piccolomini, the State Archive preserves a remarkable set of wooden covers dating back to 1258 and made for the city's account books, called the *Tavolette di Biccherna.* They were painted from the 13th to 17th centuries with religious scenes, daily working life in the civic offices, and important events in Siena's history—Sano di Pietro, Vecchietta, and Ambrogio Lorenzetti even did a few. ⏱ *45 min. Via Banchi di Sotto 52.* ☎ *0577-241-745. Free admission. Mon–Sat hourly at 9:30, 10:30 & 11:30am.*

6 ★ **Pinacoteca Nazionale.** Although more famous works by Sienese masters are found elsewhere,

this remains an impressive and representative showcase of the city's great artists. Look out for some Duccio, the charming narrative detail of Simone Martini's *Beato Agostino Novello* altarpiece, and Giovanni di Paolo's *Presentation at the Temple:* Despite two attempts at a composition stolen straight from Ambrogio Lorenzetti (in the Uffizi), he still couldn't get the perspective right. Downstairs are the cartoons by Sienese Mannerist Domenico Beccafumi (1486–1551), from which some of the marble panels on the Duomo pavement were created. ⏱ *1 hr. Via San Pietro 29. www.pinacoteca nazionale.siena.it.* ☎ *0577-286143. Admission 4€. Sun–Mon 9am–1pm, Tues–Sat 8:15am–7:15pm.*

7 ★ **Via Stalloreggi.** The little street where Duccio di Buoninsegna once had his studio still houses some of the last remaining artisan workshops within the walls. **Sator Print,** Via Stalloreggi 70 (www.sator print.com; ☎ 0577-247478), sells hand-decorated prints and calligraphy based on historic Sienese designs. Nothing inside is cheap, but you'll find an affordable, authentic gift or souvenir with little

Siena's Duomo.

Inside Siena's Duomo.

trouble—or just stop by to see the maestro at work. At the **Bottega d'Arte,** Via Stalloreggi 47 (www.arteinsiena.it; ☎ 339-2700280), buy original art in the style (and using the techniques) of the old Sienese masters. ⓘ *40 min.*

❽ Martini Marisa. This fine purveyor of hand-painted Sienese majolica ceramics uses designs based on the traditional black, white, and burnt-sienna motif, based on floor panels in the Duomo. *Via del Capitano 5–11. www.anticasiena.it.* ☎ *0577-288177.*

❾ ★ Battistero. The 14th-century Baptistery stands on its own little square on top of a steep flight of steps, hiding behind a Gothic facade. Its prize possession is a baptismal font embellished with some of the finest sculpture of the Quattrocento (1400s). The hexagonal marble font (1411–30) is by Jacopo della Quercia in the Gothic–Renaissance style. Two of the bronze statues around the basin, *Faith* and *Hope,* are by Donatello. Reliefs on the font include Ghiberti's *Baptism of Christ* and *John before Herod* (similar in style to his "Gates of Paradise" in Florence) as well as *Herod's Feast* by Donatello, all from 1427. Vecchietta frescoed the ceiling and lunettes around 1450. ⓘ *30 min. Piazza San Giovanni (behind Duomo).*

☎ *0577-283048. Admission 4€ or OPA Pass. Mid-June to mid-Sept daily 9:30am–8pm; mid-Sept to Oct & Mar to mid-June daily 9:30am–7pm; Nov–Feb daily 10am–5pm.*

❿ ★★★ Duomo. The architectural highlight of Siena's golden age is the Cattedrale di Santa Maria Assunta (its formal name). Beginning in the 12th century, architects set out to create a dramatic facade with colored bands of marble mixing the Romanesque and Italian Gothic styles. Inside, between 1369 and 1547, over 40 Sienese artists, including Francesco di Giorgio and Domenico Beccafumi, created the 56 Biblical and allegorical marble intarsia designs on the floor (only on view mid-Aug to Nov). The artistic highlight is the **Libreria Piccolominea,** added in 1485 by Cardinal Francesco Piccolomini (later Pope Pius III) to house the library of his more famous uncle, Pope Pius II. Frescoes by Umbrian painter Pinturicchio tell the story of Pius II's life, starting in the back right as you walk in. The nearby 13th-century pulpit is by Nicola Pisano (Giovanni's father). ⓘ *45 min. Piazza del Duomo.* ☎ *0577-283048. Admission 4€, 7€ when floor on display, or OPA Pass. Mar–Oct Mon–Sat 10:30am–7:30pm, Sun 1:30–6pm; Nov–Feb Mon–Sat 10:30am–5:30pm, Sun 1:30–6pm.*

Siena After Dark

Besides enjoying the spectacle of an evening lounging in the Campo, stop in at **Kopakabana**, Via de' Rossi 52 (☎ 0577-223744), for the best homemade gelato in town—the panpepato flavor is up there with the best we've ever tasted. **Enoteca Italiana**, Fortezza Medicea (www.enoteca-italiana.it; ☎ 0577-228834), is the only state-sponsored wine bar in Italy, in vaults that were built for Cosimo I de' Medici in 1560. Drink by the glass, or buy one of 1,600 bottles on sale. **Enoteca i Terzi**, Via dei Termini 7 (www.enotecaiterzi.it; ☎ 0577-44329), is under the vaulted ceiling of a 12th-century tower, with wines by the glass and fin e food if you're hungry. For something younger, livelier, and more local, head down Via Pantaneto toward the university buildings. Names change, but the bars always go on here till late.

⓫ ★★ Museo dell'Opera Metropolitana. Anyone with a serious interest in Sienese art should make for here: Duccio di Buoninsegna's 1311 *Maestà* is where it all began. Not only did Duccio invent a genre, he influenced the generation that included Simone Martini and the Lorenzettis. The Sienese were so pleased with his giant two-sided altarpiece it was paraded through the streets on its way to the Duomo. In the same room is Pietro Lorenzetti's 1342 *Birth of the Virgin*, which, fortunately for us, he managed to finish before the plague finished him. Downstairs are Giovanni Pisano's original sculptures for the Duomo.

The art is housed in a building originally intended to be the right aisle of a massive new cathedral, until the Black Death called a halt to Siena's golden age. A climb to its **Facciatone (Big Façade),** from inside the museum, rewards you with dizzying views down into the Campo. 🕐 1 hr. Piazza del Duomo. ☎ 0577-534571. Admission 7€ or OPA Pass. Mar–Oct Mon–Sat 10:30am–7pm, Sun 1:30–6pm; Nov–Feb Mon–Sat 10:30am–5:30pm, Sun 1:30–5:30pm.

Travel Tip

The best value way to see Siena's ecclesiastical sights is with the OPA Si Pass. Valid for 3 days, and costing 15€ from March through October and 10€ the rest of the year, it gets you into the Duomo, Battistero, Museo dell'Opera, and modest Oratorio di San Bernardino. It also allows access to the recently discovered Cripta, an atmospheric trip through the frescoed (pre-Duccio) chambers of the ancient cathedral under the Duomo. See www.operaduomo.siena.it.

⓬ ★★ Santa Maria della Scala. This 14th-century hospital, one of Europe's oldest, has gradually been turned into a museum and cultural complex displaying art and archaeological treasures. Most intriguing is the **Pellegrinaio**, the old Pilgrims' Ward, frescoed with scenes from everyday life in the hospital in the 1440s. Elsewhere seek out a disturbing *Massacre of the Innocents* by Matteo di Giovanni, in the **Cappella della Madonna;** the tiny oratory where

St. Catherine used to pray all night; the restored **Sagrestia Vecchia** with a damaged and complex fresco cycle completed by Vecchietta in 1449; **Bambimus,** Siena's Museum of Children's Art, where paintings are hung at tot-friendly heights; and the labyrinthine basement—a great spot to get lost. ⏱ *90 min. Piazza del Duomo. www.santamariadellascala.com.* ☎ *0577-534571. Admission 9€ or cumulative ticket with Museo Civico & Torre del Mangia 20€ or 13€ with Museo Civico only. Mon–Wed 10:30am–4:30pm, Thurs–Sun 10:30am–6:30pm; Oct 16–Mar 16 daily 10:30am–4:30pm.*

⓭ ★ Casa di Santa Caterina. Caterina Benincasa (1347–80), 24th child of a Sienese dyer, grew up to become one of the patron saints of Italy. She took the veil at the age of 16, and experienced what she called a "mystical marriage" to Christ 3 years later. The house where she lived as a Dominican nun still stands today, except it now has a Renaissance loggia and two baroque oratories, the **Oratorio della Cucina** being the most lavishly appointed, with a 16th-century majolica floor.

⏱ *20 min. Costa di San Antonio 6 (at Via dei Pittori).* ☎ *0577-280801. Free admission. Daily 9:30am–7pm.*

⓮ ★ San Domenico. This severe-looking church in the monastic Gothic style was founded in 1125 and since the 1300s has been closely linked with St. Catherine, who is said to have had visions here. Inside you can see a small frescoed portrait by her contemporary, Andrea Vanni (1332–1414), the only known picture by someone who knew her. Slightly grislier, her head is preserved and venerated inside the **Cappella di Santa Caterina.** It's surrounded by Sodoma's frescoed scenes from her life, including her controversial appearance at the *Execution of Niccolò di Toldo.* ⏱ *20 min. Piazza San Domenico. No phone. Free admission. Mar–Oct daily 7am–6:30pm, Nov–Feb daily 9am–6pm.*

⓯ ★ Vitra. Admire modern designs in all shapes and sizes at this funky artisan glassware store. Everything is handmade in Siena. Closed all day Sunday and on Monday morning. *Via dei Termini 2 (at Piazza Independenza).* ☎ *0577-51208.*

Museo dell'Opera Metropolitana del Duomo.

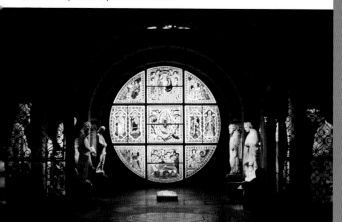

Where to Stay

★★ Antica Residenza Cicogna

CENTRO STORICO   In this friendly, family-run B&B, rooms are compact but dripping with character. All are thoughtfully furnished and come with carefully matched fabrics. *Via dei Termini 67. www.anticaresiden-zacicogna.it.* ☎ *0577-285613. 7 units. Doubles 90€–120€, w/breakfast.*

★★★ Campo Regio Relais

CENTRO STORICO   This chic little townhouse hideaway whisks you from the bustle of the central streets. Rooms are decorated with traditional and luxurious elegance, and a knock-out breakfast terrace faces the Duomo. *Via della Sapienza 25. www.camporegio.com.* ☎ *0577-222073. 6 units. Doubles 150€–450€, w/break-fast. Usually closed Jan to mid-Mar.*

★★★ Frances' Lodge Relais

DUE PONTI   With the towers of Siena beckoning in the near dis-tance, a pool glimmering in the gar-den, and quiet corners nestled on a hillside planted with olive trees, this beautiful estate seems like a slice of heaven. Richly colored rooms and suites are charmingly decorated to be warm, comfortable, and rather exotic. *Strada di Valdipugna 2. www.franceslodge.it.* ☎ *0577-42379. 6 units. From 240€ double, w/breakfast. Closed mid-Nov to late Mar.*

★ Hotel Alta Domus CENTRO

STORICO   A modern redo of the former drying rooms of a medieval woolworks provides homey and spot-less lodgings with a slightly contem-porary flair. The place has the quiet air of a retreat—along with city-view balconies in the more expensive rooms. *Via Camporegio 37. www.hotelalmadomus.it.* ☎ *0577-44177. 28 units. 85€–120€ double, w/breakfast.*

★★ Palazzo Bulgarini CENTRO

STORICO   The converted *piano*

Palazzo Ravizza.

nobile salons of an old palace aren't as opulent as they once were, but enough of the grandeur remains to elicit a gasp as you enter one of the enormous guest rooms embellished with marble fireplaces, ceiling fres-coes, and parquet floors. Unchanged are the views from the rear rooms over the Val d'Orcia. *Via Pantaneto. www.bbpalazzobulgarini. com.* ☎ *391-3968571. 6 units. 75€– 110€ double, w/breakfast.*

★★ Palazzo Ravizza PORTA

SAN MARCO   Siena's coziest *pen-sione* since the 1920s, this Renais-sance *palazzo* has antiques, frescoes, big, high-ceilinged rooms, and a huge, view-filled garden. A friendly, homelike atmosphere is part of the package. *Pian dei Mantel-lini 34. www.palazzoravizza.it.* ☎ *0577-280462. 35 units. Doubles 90€–150€, w/breakfast.*

★★ Santa Caterina PORTA

ROMANA   A hospitable, 18th-cen-tury villa with midsize rooms and chunky antique furniture is backed by a terraced garden overlooking the Val d'Orcia. *Via E. S. Piccolomini 7. www.hscsiena.it.* ☎ *0577-221105. 22 units. Doubles 105€–180€, w/breakfast.*

Where to **Dine**

★★ **Da Divo** CENTRO STORICO *MODERN TUSCAN* Innovative dishes rooted in Sienese tradition are served in an Etruscan cave with a classy candlelit atmosphere. *Via Franciosa 25–29. www.osteriadadivo. it.* ☎ *0577-284381. Entrees 20€– 24€. Lunch, dinner Wed–Mon. Closed 2 weeks in Jan–Feb.*

★ **Grotta Santa Caterina da Bagoga** CENTRO STORICO *SIENESE* This tiny, brick-vaulted kitchen run by former Palio-winning jockey "Bagoga" is especially strong on stews, such as *coniglio alla Senese* (rabbit on the bone with capers, tomatoes, and herbs). *Via della Galluzza 26. www.ristorante bagoga.it.* ☎ *0577-282208. Entrees 7€–15€. Lunch, dinner Tues–Sat.*

★★ **La Chiacchera** CENTRO STORICO *SIENESE* This tiny, rustic hole-in-the-wall serves large portions of *ribollita* (hearty vegetable soup), *salsicce e fagioli* (sausage and white beans), or *tegamata di maiale* (a Sienese pork casserole). *Costa di Sant'Antonio 4 (near San Domenico). www.osterialachiacchera. it.* ☎ *0577-280631. Entrees 7€–9€. Lunch, dinner daily.*

Dining alfresco in Piazza del Campo.

★★ **La Sosta di Violante** PORTA ROMANA *MODERN ITALIAN* This place offers fresh, modern cooking away from the Campo scrum. *Mozzarelline fritte* (fried mozzarella) with onion jam is a delight. *Via Pantaneto 115. www.lasostadiviolante.it.* ☎ *0577-43774. Entrees 10€–16€. Lunch, dinner Mon–Sat. Closed 1 week in Jan.*

★ **Le Logge** CENTRO STORICO *TUSCAN* The best seasonal cuisine is highlighted in a refined and old-fashioned atmosphere just off the Campo. The veal is the tastiest in town, and the delicate black truffle is used liberally in season. *Via del Porrione 33.* ☎ *0577-48013. Entrees 16€–26€. Lunch, dinner Mon–Sat.*

★★ **L'Osteria** CENTRO STORICO *TUSCAN* This *osteria* is as local as it comes in the old center. The grill is the star: beef all ways, veal, and Cinta Senese, the finest breed of pig. *Via de' Rossi 79–81.* ☎ *0577-287592. Entrees 8.50€–15€. Lunch, dinner Mon–Sat.*

★★ **Ristorante Guido** CENTRO STORICO *SIENESE* Generations of diners have enjoyed this wonderfully old-world place. *Pici fatti al cacio e pepe* (with cheese and pepper) is a house classic, as is grilled Tuscan beef. *Vicolo Beato Pier Pettinaio 7. www.ristoranteguido.com.* ☎ *0577-280042. Entrees12€–22€. Lunch, dinner Thurs–Tues.*

★★ **Taverna San Giuseppe** CENTRO STORICO *SIENESE/ TUSCAN* A vaulted room from the 12th century is the setting for meals many long remember as among the best they've had in Italy. *Pici* with a ragù of *cinghiale* (wild boar) is surprisingly delicate, while ricotta-filled *gnudi* almost floats off the plate. *Via G. Dupré 132. www.tavernasan giuseppe.it.* ☎ *0577-42286. Entrees 10€–21€. Lunch, dinner Mon–Sat.*

Volterra

1 Porta all'Arco
2 L'Incontro
3 Palazzo dei Priori
4 Duomo
5 San Francesco
6 Pinacoteca e
  Museo Civico
7 Ecomuseo
  dell'Alabastro
8 Camillo Rossi
9 Teatro Romano
10 Fabula Etrusca
11 Museo Etrusco
  Guarnacci
12 alab'Arte

Where to Stay
Foresteria
  Volterra 21
La Locanda 15
Podere
  Marcampo 13
San Lino 14

Where to Dine
Enoteca del Duca 17
Osteria La Pace 20
Vecchia Osteria dei Poeti 16

Nightlife
Enoteca Scali 18
La Vena di Vino 19

Volterra rises like a fortress, 540m (1,800 ft.) above the rolling agricultural plains of the Valdicecina. The Etruscans who settled here in the 9th century B.C. made their living trading and working what's under your feet: alabaster (for sculpting) and alum (for dyes). The town has many Etruscan remains and a medieval appearance, with foreboding *palazzi*, cobblestone streets and alleyways, and shops hawking masterful craftwares. Come for the artisan shopping, the *Twilight* connections as the hometown of the Volturi vampire coven, and a major Etruscan museum. START: **Volterra is 72km (45 miles) from Florence, on the S68 30km (19 miles) west of where it branches off the Florence–Siena raccordo. Trip length: 1 day.**

1 ★ **Porta all'Arco.** Volterra's remaining ancient gate, all that's left of what were once 7.5km (4½ miles) of Etruscan city walls, marks the start of a steep ascent into the *centro storico*. So important is the

gate to the town that Partisans defending Volterra in 1944 risked their lives bricking it up in case it became the target of a Nazi assault. ⏱ *10 min.*

Crumbling Etruria

Northwest of the city center (3.5km/2 miles), Le Balze is one of Tuscany's more quietly frightening scenes—a bowl-shaped ravine where fast-paced erosion is devouring the edges of Volterra. Aided by periodic earthquakes, it has already exposed and then destroyed much of the Etruscan necropolis at this end of town. Now it threatens the medieval Badia church, abandoned after an 1846 quake brought the precipice to its doorstep. The best spot to appreciate the scale of the erosion is from the minor road out of town towards Montecatini Valdicecina.

2 **L'Incontro.** Our favorite cafe in the historic center sells artisan chocolates, homemade pastries, and crazy gelato flavors like biscuit or mojito. Later on, you can also enjoy Tuscan vintages by the glass. *Via Matteotti 18.* ☎ *0588-80500. $.*

3 ★ **Palazzo dei Priori.** Built between 1208 and 1257, this is the oldest Gothic town hall in Tuscany; Florence's Palazzo Vecchio was modeled after it. The council hall and antechamber are open to the public. On view is a damaged *Annunciation with Four Saints* by Jacopo di Cione (or perhaps Orcagna) from 1383. Opposite, across Piazza dei Priori, is the

Palazzo Pretorio, with its **Torre del Porcellino,** a tower named for the stone piglet that protrudes near the top. ⏱ *20 min. Piazza dei Priori.* ☎ *0588-86050. Admission 5€ or with Volterra Card. Mid-Mar to Oct daily 10:30am–5:30pm; Nov to mid-Mar Sat–Sun 10am–4:30pm.*

4 ★ **Duomo.** A simple 12th-century facade hides a lush interior with a coffered Renaissance ceiling. Immediately left of the entrance is the **Cappella dell'Addolorata,** with a charming terracotta *Nativity* embellished with frescoes by Benozzo Gozzoli. More moving still is the wooden *Deposition* in the right transept, carved by an anonymous Pisan in 1228.

Streets of Volterra.

Alabaster, or *Pietra Candida*

Volterra is often nicknamed "the town of alabaster." Since the era of the Etruscans, locals have shaped objects both practical and artistic from these calcium sulphate deposits. Revived in the late 19th century, the local artisan industry has been going strong since, turning out ghostly-white lampshades, sculptures, jewel boxes, and even elegant sinks. To learn more, visit the town's alabaster museum, the **Ecomuseo dell'Alabastro,** Piazzetta Minucci (☎ 0588-87580). Admission costs 8€, or as part of the 14€ Volterra Card, and daily hours are 9:30am to 7pm in summer; in winter it's open daily 10:30am to 4:30pm.

The octagonal **Baptistery** across the little piazza, from 1283, has an inlaid marble font (1502) by Andrea Sansovino. ⏱ *30 min. Piazza San Giovanni. No phone. Free admission. Mon–Thurs, Sat–Sun 8am–noon & 3–6pm; Fri 8am–noon & 4–6pm (closes 5pm daily in winter).*

Travel Tip

The Volterra Card (www.volterratur.it) lets you do the rounds of Volterra sites for 14€. The card, available at the tourist office and participating sites, is good for 3 days for admission to the Ecomuseo dell'Alabastro, the Etruscan museum, the Palazzo dei Priori, the Pinacoteca, and the Teatro Romano.

⑤ ★ San Francesco. Dating to just a few years after St. Francis's death, this former convent at the western edge of the medieval town rewards a 5-minute downhill trek. The highlight is the **Cappella Croce del Giorno,** frescoed in 1410 by Cenni di Francesco. His subject matter, like Piero della Francesca 40 years later in Arezzo (p 79, **⑧**), is the *Legend of the True Cross.* ⏱ *15 min. Piazza San Francesco 3. No phone. Free admission. Daily 9am–6pm. Hours erratic, especially off-season.*

⑥ ★★ Pinacoteca e Museo Civico. This combined picture gallery and museum of artifacts is acclaimed for its religious paintings—mostly the work of Tuscan artists from the 14th to the 17th centuries. Taddeo di Bartolo's *Enthroned Madonna* altarpiece from 1411 is a glory in gold. Room 12 houses the real treasures, including an astoundingly modern, angst-ridden *Deposition* painted by a young Rosso Fiorentino in 1521, and two large 1491 Luca Signorelli panels, notably an intricate, fantastical *Annunciation.* ⏱ *45 min. Via dei Sarti 1. ☎ 0588-87580. Admission 8€ or with Volterra Card. Mid-Mar to Oct daily 9am–7pm; Dec daily 9am–6pm; Nov & Jan to mid-Mar daily 10am–4:30pm.*

⑦ ★ Camillo Rossi. This workshop, founded in 1912, is one of Volterra's best outlets for alabaster *objets. Piazza Pescheria 1. www.rossialabastri.com. ☎ 0588-86133.*

⑧ ★ Teatro Romano. From Volterra's medieval ramparts you can look down on the remains of a 1st-century Roman theater, and later spa baths, among the best preserved in central Italy (the view from above may suffice and save you the admission fee). ⏱ *10 min. Viale*

Baptistery of Volterra's Duomo.

Francesco Ferrucci (at Porta Fioren-tina). ☎ *0588-86050. Admission 4€ or with Volterra Card. Mid-Mar to Oct & Dec daily 10:30am–5:30pm; other-wise Sat–Sun 10am–4:30pm.*

⑨ ★ **Fabula Etrusca.** Intricate handmade jewelry cast using ancient goldsmith techniques and modeled after original Etruscan designs. Prepare your credit card before entering. *Via Lungo le Mura del Mandorlo 10. www.fabulaetrusca. it.* ☎ *0588-87401.*

⑩ ★★ **Museo Etrusco Guar-nacci.** This place has one of the best (yet rather poorly displayed) Etruscan collections in Italy. The 600 cinerary urns, dating from the 6th to the 1st century B.C., are made variously of alabaster, tufa, and terra cotta. The most celebrated piece is in Room XV: an elongated bronze known as the *Ombra della*

Sera, an early-3rd-century-B.C. votive figure of a young boy—look at it side-on to spot some anatomi-cal "innovations" added by the unknown creator. Other highlights include the *Urna degli Sposi,* depicting a grumpy-looking pair of newlyweds, and a series of reliefs of Homer's *Odyssey.* ⏱ *45 min. Via Minzoni 15.* ☎ *0588-86347. Admis-sion 8€ or with Volterra Card. Mid-Mar to Oct daily 9am–7pm; Dec daily 9am–6pm; Nov & Jan to mid-Mar daily 10am–4:30pm.*

⑪ **alab'Arte.** To see alabaster in various stages of completion, have a poke around Volterra's last open sculptural workshop. You're free to buy anything that strikes your fancy. *Via Orti S. Agostino 28. www.alab arte.com.* ☎ *0588-87968.*

Volterra After Dark

Nightlife here is on the quiet side. Grottolike **La Vena di Vino,** Via Don Minzoni 30 (www.lavenadivino. com; ☎ 0588-81491), is a reliable wine bar with a good range of reds, plus cheese platters to accompany them. **Enoteca Scali,** Via Guamacci 3 (www.enotecascali.com; ☎ 0588-81170), is a nice spot for a plate of salami and cheese and some fine Tuscan vintages.

Piazza in Volterra.

Where to Stay

★ **Foresteria Volterra** OUTSIDE WALLS   Just outside the city gates and an excellent choice for budget travelers. Rooms are slightly institutional but spotless, cheery, and well-equipped—and come in all configurations, from single up to quad. *Borgo San Lazzero. www.foresteriavolterra.it.* ☎ *0588-80050. 35 units. Doubles 65€–85€, w/breakfast.*

La Locanda CENTRO STORICO Rooms in this converted convent are color-schemed by floor. In the heart of the old town, all are a good size, clean, and comfortable. A couple of doubles have hydro-massage baths. *Via Guarnacci 24–28. www.hotel-lalocanda.com.* ☎ *0588-81547. 18 units. Doubles 70€–110€, w/breakfast.*

★★ **Podere Marcampo** OUTSIDE WALLS   In addition to 360° views of Volterra and Le Balze, plus a swimming pool, this place has retained its traditional farmhouse feel, with terracotta flooring, exposed beams, and dark-wood fittings that keep the large, fully-equipped apartments and hotel-style doubles rooted in their Tuscan heritage *Signposted by road, 1.5km (1 mile) northwest of Volterra. www.agriturismo-marcampo.com.* ☎ *0588-85393. 6 units. Doubles 80€–120€, w/breakfast; apts. sleeping 4–5 105€–160€.*

★ **San Lino** CENTRO STORICO The only lodging inside the medieval walls with a pool, this place was originally built as a convent in 1480. Superior rooms on the second floor cost a little extra but have more space, more character, and the choice of a view over the rear garden and small pool. *Via S. Lino 26. www.hotelsanlino.com.* ☎ *0588-85250. 44 units. Doubles 90€–110€, w/breakfast.*

Where to Dine

★ **Enoteca del Duca** CENTRO STORICO *MODERN TUSCAN* The town's most refined dining is installed in a 16th-century building with high ceilings and terracotta floors. Try the *lavagnette* (homemade egg pasta) with celery and pecorino pesto, or the pigeon breast. *Via di Castello 2. www.enoteca-delduca-ristorante.it.* ☎ *0588-81510. Entrees 15€–25€. Lunch, dinner Wed–Mon (also Tues dinner in summer).*

★★ **Osteria La Pace** CENTRO STORICO *VOLTERRAN/TUSCAN* No restaurant in Volterra can boast such a long provenance, serving since 1600 and in the hands of the same family since 1939. The old brick walls and vaults look just as they must have 400 years ago, and the kitchen follows suit with perfectly prepared versions of such Volterra classics as *tagliatelle* with chestnuts and mushrooms and a hearty stew of wild boar. *Via Don Giovanni Minzoni 29. www.osteriala pace.com.* ☎ *0588-86511. Main courses 7€–11€. Wed–Mon noon–11pm.*

★ **Vecchia Osteria dei Poeti** CENTRO STORICO *TUSCAN*   For Tuscan staples like pappardelle with hare or Volterran cooking, try this traditional dining room right on the main drag. The lengthy Tuscan wine list has options from 10€ to over 100€ a bottle. *Via Matteotti 54.* ☎ *0588-86029. Entrees 9€–22€. Lunch, dinner Fri–Wed.* ●

The **Savvy Traveler**

Before You Go

Government Tourist Offices

In the U.S.: 686 Park Ave., 3rd Floor, New York, NY 10065, ☎ 212/245-5618; 3800 Division St., Chicago, IL 60165, ☎ 312/644-0996; and 10850 Wilshire Blvd., Suite 575, Los Angeles, CA 90024, ☎ 310/820-1898.

In Canada: 69 Yonge St., Suite 1404, Toronto, ONT, M5E 1K3; ☎ 416/925-4882; www.italiantourism.com.

In the U.K. & Ireland: 1 Princes St., London, W1B 2AY; ☎ 020/7408-1254; www.italia.it/en.

In Australia & New Zealand: Level 2, 140 William St., East Sydney, NSW 2011; ☎ 02/9357-2561; www.visititaly.com.au.

Entry Requirements

U.S., Canadian, U.K., Irish, Australian, and New Zealand citizens with a valid passport don't need a visa to enter Italy if they don't expect to stay more than 90 days and don't expect to work there. If after entering Italy you find you want to stay more than 90 days, you can apply for a permit for an extra 90 days, which as a rule is granted immediately. Go to the nearest *questura* (police headquarters) or your home country's consulate.

For passport information and applications in the **U.S.,** call ☎ 877/487-2778 or check http://travel.state.gov; in **Canada,** call ☎ 800/567-6868 or check www.passportcanada.gc.ca; in the **U.K.,** call ☎ 0300/222-0000 or visit www.ips.gov.uk; in **Ireland,** call ☎ 01/671-1633 or check www.dfa.ie; in **Australia,** call ☎ 131-232 or visit www.passports.gov.au;

A Vespa ride through Tuscany.

and in **New Zealand,** call ☎ 0800/225050 or check www.passports.govt.nz. Allow plenty of time before your trip to apply for a passport; processing usually takes a few weeks but can take longer during busy periods (especially spring). When traveling, safeguard your passport and keep a copy of the critical pages with your passport number in a separate place. If you lose your passport, visit the nearest consulate of your native country as soon as possible for a replacement.

The Best Times to Go

April to June and late September to October are the best months to visit Tuscany. However, they are also the most expensive: Hotels are generally on high-season rates, for May, June, and September at least.

From late June through mid-September, when the summer rush is full blown, Siena and the Tuscan hilltowns can teem with visitors. August is the worst summer month weather-wise, as it's usually uncomfortably hot and muggy; but it's sometimes a good month to bag a deal on a room in Florence. (When you get there, expect theaters, many upscale restaurants, and most nightclubs to be closed, however.) Through the middle weeks of August, the entire region goes on vacation, and many family-run restaurants and shops are closed (except at the spas, beaches, rural areas, and islands—where the Italians head en masse).

From late October to Easter, many attractions go on shorter winter hours, or occasionally close for renovation. Some rural hotels and restaurants take a month or two off between November and February, spa and beach destinations such as Viareggio become padlocked ghost towns, and it can get much colder than you'd expect; it might even snow in the hills.

Festivals & Special Events

SPRING. Easter is always a big event in Tuscany, especially in Florence at the **Scoppio del Carro** (Explosion of the Cart), with its Renaissance pyrotechnics on Easter Sunday. An 18th-century cart, pulled by two snowy white oxen loaded with fireworks, arrives at the Piazza del Duomo, where it's ignited.

More cultural, Florence's **Maggio Musicale Fiorentino** (Musical May; www.maggiofiorentino.com) features a month's worth of opera, classical, and dance in concert halls around the city; these days it runs into June.

The **Festa del Grillo** (Cricket Festival) takes place in May, on the Sunday after Ascension Day. In Florence's Cascine Park, vendors used to sell live crickets in decorated cages. After a parade along the Arno, children would release them into the grass. These days, the crickets are battery-powered.

In late May or June, Cortona hosts the **Giostra dell'Archidado** (www.giostraarchidado.com), a crossbow competition in 14th-century costume.

One Sunday early in June, the **Regatta of the Ancient Maritime Republics** takes place—a rowing competition among the four medieval maritime republics of Venice, Amalfi, Genoa, and Pisa. Its location rotates annually between the four. Pisa hosts again in 2021.

Also in Pisa, the **Luminara di San Ranieri** celebrates the city's patron saint by lining the Arno with flickering torches, from dusk on June 16.

SUMMER. Pisa's liveliest month ends on the final Sunday, with the **Gioco del Ponte** (Game of the Bridge; www.giocodelpontedipisa.it)—teams in Renaissance costumes on opposite banks of the river have a tug-of-war over the Ponte di Mezzo with a 7-ton cart.

St. John the Baptist's Day, June 24, sees the first in the weeklong series of **Calcio Storico Fiorentino** (www.calciostoricofiorentino.it). Florence's Piazza Santa Croce is transformed into a pitch for ancient, and rough, "football" matches.

From mid-June to late August, Fiesole hosts the **Estate Fiesolana** (www.estatefiesolana.it), a summer festival of music, ballet, film, and theater. Several performances take place in the ruined Roman amphitheater, which seats 3,000 spectators.

The biggest event of the Tuscan calendar is the **Palio delle Contrade,** the twice-annual bareback horse race between the 17 districts of Siena. The race occurs around the dirt-packed main square, with parades and partying before and afterwards. The first (the Palio di Provenzano) is on July 2; the second (the Palio dell'Assunta) on August 16.

The **Giostra dell'Orso** (Joust of the Bear; www.giostradellorso-pistoia.it) takes place in Pistoia on July 25. The match pits mounted knights in medieval garb against targets shaped like bears.

San Gimignano Estate is a festival of concerts, opera, and film staged outdoors in Piazza del Duomo. For 2 weeks in either July or August, Siena's Accademia Musicale Chigiana presents its **International Festival** (www.chigiana.it), one of Tuscany's best classical concert programs.

Montepulciano's major festival happens on the last Sunday in August. The town's districts race wine barrels up the length of the steep Corso, in the **Bravio delle Botti** (www.braviodellebotti.com).

Tuscany Bookmarks

www.firenzeturismo.it: Logistics, museums, art, history, itineraries, events, even weather forecasts—the official city catch-all.

www.ioamofirenze.it: Florence food, wine, nightlife, and events blog, written (in Italian) by a savvy local.

www.ilpalio.org: The all-things Palio site has history, race trivia, video of recent Palios, and a list of winners since 1644.

www.pisa-airport.com: Information about Pisa's Galileo Galilei International Airport, Tuscany's international gateway.

www.theflorentine.net: The website of Florence's major English-language magazine.

www.turismo.intoscana.it: This official resource is useful for an overview of Tuscany as a whole.

www.trenitalia.com: The state railway website is an essential planning tool for train travel across Tuscany.

www.arttrav.com: News, views, and reviews from Florence and Tuscany, written by an expat art historian.

www.wga.hu: Online art museum with a comprehensive Renaissance collection.

www.summerinitaly.com/traveltips/transport-strikes-in-italy: Information on pending strikes throughout Italy.

In both June and September in Arezzo, the **Giostra del Saracino** (Saracen's Joust; www.giostradel saracinoarezzo.it) takes place—a tournament between mounted knights in 13th-century armor and the effigy of a Saracen warrior.

AUTUMN. All Lucca is festooned with candles on the evening of September 13, for the **Luminara di Santa Croce.** A holy procession also starts from the cathedral.

The second week of September sees the **Expo del Chianti Classico** (www.expochianticlassico.com), a 4-day wine harvest festival in and around Greve.

In Montalcino, on the last weekend of October, residents celebrate the **Sagra del Tordo,** or "Feast of the Thrush." Locals in medieval costume stage an archery tournament and parades; expect plenty of hearty gastronomy.

WINTER. On December 25, the year's final **Display of the Virgin's Girdle** (the Sacro Cingolo) takes place in Prato. The belt that the Virgin handed to "Doubting" Thomas on her Assumption is revealed from the Duomo balcony, with Renaissance-styled drummers in attendance. The solemn ceremony is repeated on Easter Day, May 1, August 15 (the Feast of the Assumption), and most important, September 8, the Virgin's Birthday.

Italy's second-largest **Carnevale** (http://viareggio.ilcarnevale.com) is hosted by Viareggio. Events and parades take place throughout February.

Cellphones (Mobiles)

Italy (like most of the world) is on the GSM (Global System for Mobiles) cellphone system. GSM phones function with a removable

SIM card, encoded with your phone number and account information. U.S. world phones are compatible.

If necessary, U.S. visitors can rent a GSM phone before leaving home from **InTouch USA** (☎ 800/872-7626; www.intouchusa.us) or **Cellhire** (☎ 877/244-7242; www.cellhire.com). Alternatively, you can buy a local handset for under 10€. A basic Android smartphone costs less than 50€.

U.K. and Irish mobiles all work in Italy; call your service provider before departing to check call and (especially) data charges, which can be high. Remember that you are also charged for calls you *receive* on a U.K. mobile used abroad. All travelers should keep in mind that some smartphone apps work in the background and will consume data if you don't switch data functions off.

The cheapest option, for everyone with an unlocked handset, is to buy a SIM card when you get to Tuscany. The major Italian networks are **Vodafone, Wind, TIM,** and **3.** A local rechargeable SIM costs about 5€ and gives you far cheaper local calls (around .12€/min.) and data (10€/month for 4GB is standard). You must show photo I.D. when buying. They will likely ask for a *codice fiscale* (tax number), but it's not compulsory to have one.

Money

Italy falls somewhere in the middle of pricing in Europe—not as expensive as, say, Paris or Scandinavia, but not as cheap as Spain or Greece. Tuscany comes just behind Venice and Rome in terms of the costliest bit of Italy to travel, but the advice in this book should guide you to the best options to fit any budget.

It's a good idea to exchange at least some money—just enough to cover airport incidentals and transportation to your hotel—before you leave home, so you can avoid lines at airport ATMs.

Currency
Almost 20 years ago, Italy retired the lira and joined most of Western Europe in switching to the **euro.** Coins are issued in denominations of .01€, .02€, .05€, .10€, .20€, and .50€, as well as 1€ and 2€; bills come in denominations of 5€, 10€, 20€, 50€, 100€, 200€, and 500€.

Exchange rates are listed in most international newspapers and constantly updated at **XE.com.** To get a transaction as close to this rate as possible, pay with your credit card (although check foreign transaction fees with your card provider before leaving home).

Traveler's checks, while still the safest way to carry paper money, are going the way of the dinosaur. The evolution of international computerized banking and consolidated ATM networks has led to the triumph of plastic throughout the Italian peninsula—even if cold cash is still the most trusted currency in family joints, where credit cards may not be accepted.

You'll get the best rate locally if you **exchange money** at a bank or use one of its ATMs. The rates at "Cambio/change/wechsel" exchange booths are invariably less favorable but still a good deal better than what you'd get exchanging money at a hotel or shop (a last-resort tactic only).

ATMs

The ability to access your personal bank account through the **Cirrus** (www.mastercard.com) or **PLUS** (www.visa.com) network of ATMs (or "cashpoints")—or get a cash advance on an enabled Visa or MasterCard—is now standard throughout Italy. All you need to do is search out a machine that has your network's symbol displayed, pop in your card, and punch in your PIN (make sure it's four digits; six-digit PINs won't work). It'll spit out local currency drawn directly from your home account (and at a more favorable rate than converting cash). Keep in mind that many banks impose a fee every time a card is used at a foreign bank's ATM (up to $5 or more). Banks in Italy do not usually charge you a second fee to use their ATMs.

An ATM in Italian is *un Bancomat* (although Bancomat is a private company, its name has become the generic word for ATMs). Increased internationalism has been slowly doing away with the old worry that your card's PIN, be it on a bank card or credit card, need be specially enabled to work abroad, but it always pays to check with your issuing bank to be sure. Many banks also request pre-notification of foreign travel as an anti-fraud measure—and this is a wise precaution if you want to be sure your card won't be stopped. If at the ATM you get a message saying your card isn't valid for international transactions, it's possible the bank just can't make the phone connection to check it (occasionally this can be a citywide epidemic); try another ATM or another town.

If your card is equipped with the "Chip and PIN" security technology, be prepared to enter your PIN when you use the card to make purchases. This is increasingly common across Tuscany, although for now, traditional "swipe" cards are still accepted in central Italy (even while they are being phased out everywhere in Europe).

Credit Cards

Visa and MasterCard are almost universally accepted at hotels, restaurants, and shops; some at the upper end also accept American Express. Diners Club is accepted only occasionally, generally in expensive establishments throughout the region. If you arrange with your card issuer to enable the card's cash advance option (and get a PIN as well), you can also use them at ATMs. To use "Chip and PIN" credit cards, you'll need to know your PIN number to make a purchase.

Wire Services

If you find yourself out of money, a wire service can help you tap willing friends and family for funds. Through **MoneyGram** (☎ **800/328-5678** in U.S.; ☎ **0800-026-0535** in U.K.; www.moneygram.com) you can get money sent around the world in less than 10 minutes. MoneyGram's fees can vary, but a good estimate from the U.S. is $15 for sums up to $500 and $25 for up to $1,000, with a sliding scale for larger amounts. From the U.K, sending £500 costs £36, with a sliding scale for larger sums. A similar service is offered by **Western Union** (☎ **800/325-6000** in U.S.; ☎ **0800-833833** in U.K.; www.westernunion.com).

For all wire transfer companies, a currency exchange rate also applies. Additionally, the sender's credit card company may charge a fee for the cash advance as well as a higher interest rate.

Getting **There** & Getting Around

By Plane

The logical air entry point to Tuscany is Pisa's **Galileo Galilei Airport** (☎ 050-849300; www. pisa-airport.com), 3km (2 miles) south of Pisa and 84km (52 miles) west of Florence. Major budget and regular airlines such as **Ryanair** (www.ryanair.com), **easyJet** (www. easyjet.com), and **British Airways** (www.ba.com) connect Pisa to several European cities, and **Delta** (www.delta.com) offers seasonal flights direct to **New York's JFK.** The automatic transit service known as **PisaMover** whizzes you from the airport to Pisa Centrale station every 5 to 8 minutes. From there you can connect to Florence (50–80 min.; 8.40€) on a direct train. An alternative for anyone heading straight to Florence is the airport shuttle bus operated by **Autostradale** (www.autostradale.it). The 70-minute journey runs 17 times a day and costs 10€. A taxi from Pisa airport to Pisa Centrale station costs 9€ to 12€.

Tuscany's other major airport is **Amerigo Vespucci** (www.aeroporto. firenze.it; ☎ 055-3061300), in the suburb of Peretola, 5km (3 miles) west of central Florence. It's partly a domestic airport—**Alitalia** (www. alitalia.it) connects daily with Rome and **Vueling** (www.vueling.com) with Sicily. **CityJet** (www.cityjet.com) flies 6 days a week to London City Airport. **Vueling** also flies direct from London's Gatwick Airport, Madrid, and Barcelona; **Lufthansa** (www. lufthansa.com) connects daily to Frankfurt. To reach the center, take the half-hourly "Vola in bus" service (6€) operated by **BusItalia** (www. fsbusitalia.it; ☎ 800-373760). It terminates next to Santa Maria Novella. A **taxi** (www.socota.it; ☎ 055-4242) from the air terminal to anywhere in the center (or vice versa) costs 22€ during the day, 24€ on Sundays and holidays, and 25€ at night.

Italy's major intercontinental gateways are Milan's **Malpensa Airport** (www.milanomalpensa-airport. com; ☎ 02-232323), and Rome's **Fiumicino Airport** (www.adr.it/ fiumicino). Both are connected by major airlines to hubs across North America. **Alitalia** (www.alitalia.it) can connect you on to Florence from Rome, but if you're spending time touring locally before heading to Tuscany, the train is the best bet. By rail, Florence is within 2 hours of Milan, Venice, or Rome (www.trenitalia.com; ☎ 892021). See "By Train," below.

By Train

Every day, around 15 **Eurostar** trains (www.eurostar.com; ☎ 03432-186186 in U.K.; ☎ 646/934-6454 in North America) zip from London St. Pancras to Paris's Gare du Nord via the Channel Tunnel, in 2½ hours. In Paris, you can transfer to Gare de Lyon station for one of three daily direct TGV trains to Milan (7¼ hr.), from where you can connect to Pisa (3¼–4 hr.) or Florence (1¾ hr.). You can also reserve a daily night train direct from Paris to Milan with multi-person sleeping cars. The night train leaves Gare de Lyon in the evening and gets into Milano Centrale for breakfast. One-way tickets cost from 35€ to 110€ per person for a (cramped) six-berth couchette, to between 95€ and 190€ per person for a two-berth cabin.

Paris–Italy trains are operated by **Thello** (www.thello.com). All international trains need seat reservations in advance. The main Tuscan rail stations, receiving trains from most parts of Italy, are Florence and Pisa. Siena is an important provincial hub, although only served by slow *Regionale* services. Most arrivals in Florence are at the Modernist **Stazione Santa Maria Novella,** Piazza della Stazione (www.trenitalia.com or ☎ 892021 for nationwide rail information). Occasional trains halt at the less convenient **Stazione Rifredi** (connect for the short hop to Santa Maria Novella) or **Stazione Campo di Marte,** on the eastern fringe of the center; a bus service links these two terminals. High-speed trains arrive from Milan in around 100 minutes; and from Rome, in around 1½ hours. Both the **state railway** (www.trenitalia.com) and private operator **Italo** (www.italotreno.com) operate on the Milan–Florence–Rome line. Book 120 days ahead of departure for the cheapest high-speed fares.

In Pisa, trains arrive at **Stazione Pisa Centrale,** Piazza della Stazione, at the southern end of town. Of the major terminals in Tuscany, the best links are between Florence and Pisa, with trains departing every half-hour, at least. The trip between the two cities takes about an hour, costing 8.40€ for a one-way, second-class ticket.

Hourly trains also run directly between Rome and Pisa, taking 2½ to 4 hours and costing 23€ to 51€ for a one-way ticket, depending on the train.

Trains link Lucca and Pisa half-hourly, taking only 30 minutes and costing 3.30€ for a one-way ticket.

In Siena, trains arrive at **Stazione Siena,** Piazza Rosselli. The station is 15 minutes by frequent bus from the heart of Siena. The most useful link is the hourly service between Florence and Siena, taking 1½ hours and costing 9€ for a one-way ticket (although a bus between the two cities is more convenient— see "By Bus," below). Frequency and journey time between Siena and Chiusi, which lies just off the main Rome–Florence–Milan line, is about the same; a one-way ticket costs 8.40€. Journeys between Pisa and Siena (1¾ hr.) require a change in Empoli.

See p 98 for our recommended Tuscan rail & bus itinerary.

By Bus

A number of regional bus companies provide the best links between rail hubs like Florence, Siena, or Pisa, and the smaller towns of Tuscany. Among the most useful are: **CPT** (Pisa–Volterra link; www.pisa.cttnord.it; ☎ **050-884111**); **TIEMME** (Arezzo, Florence–Siena and around; www.tiemmespa.it; ☎ **0575-39881,** or 0577-204111); **ACV** (Florence–Chianti link; www.acvbus.it; ☎ **055-47821**); and **Vai-Bus** (Lucca and around; www.lucca.cttnord.it). Most have downloadable timetables online. Tickets are usually sold at newsstands, small general stores, and the bus travel office.

See p 98 for our recommended Tuscan rail and bus itinerary.

By Car

For motorists, the main link is the most traveled road in Italy—the **A1** autostrada (Italy's spinal expressway). This route comes in from the north and Milan, moving southeast toward Bologna before cutting abruptly south across the Apennines to Florence. If you're already in the south, you can travel the same road north between Rome and Florence.

Skirting the western coast of Italy, including the Versilia Riviera, the **A12** heads down from Genoa.

North of Pisa the A12 meets up with **A11,** which cuts east toward Florence. Florence and Siena are also linked by an expressway (the *raccordo*) with no route number; from Florence just follow the green signs for Siena.

For visitors heading to Arezzo and eastern Tuscany, follow the autostrada (A1) as though you're going to Rome, until you reach the exits for Arezzo to the immediate east of the road.

Autostrade are superhighways, denoted by green signs and a number prefaced with an A, like the A1 from Rome to Florence. A few aren't numbered and are simply called a *raccordo,* a connecting road between two cities (such as Florence–Siena and Florence–Pisa–Livorno, the "FI–PI–LI"). Autostrade are usually toll roads, although the fee is not too expensive. There's a toll calculator at www.autostrade.it: Florence to Lucca, for example, costs 4.80€; Florence to Rome is 18€.

Strade Statali are state roads, usually two lanes wide, indicated by blue signs. Their route numbers are prefaced with an SS or an S, as in the S222 from Florence to Siena. On signs, however, these official route numbers are used infrequently. Usually, you'll just see blue signs listing destinations by name with arrows pointing off in the appropriate directions. Even if it's just a few miles down the road, often the town you're looking for won't be mentioned on the sign at the appropriate turnoff. It's impossible to predict which of all the towns that lie along a road will be the ones chosen to list on any particular sign. Sometimes, the sign gives only the first minuscule village that lies past the turnoff; at other times it lists the first major town down that road, and some signs mention only the major city the

road eventually leads to, even if it's hundreds of miles away. It pays to study the map and fix in your mind the names of all the possibilities before coming to an intersection.

The **speed limit** on roads in built-up areas around towns and cities is 50kmph (31 mph). On the autostrada it's 130kmph (81 mph), except during wet conditions when it's 110kmph (68 mph). Italians have an astounding disregard for these limits—perhaps one reason why Italy, statistically speaking, has Western Europe's most dangerous roads. Nevertheless, police can ticket you and collect the fine on the spot. At 0.5 mg/l, Italy's official blood alcohol limit is stricter than in the U.S or U.K. The traffic police will throw you in jail if they pull you over and find you inebriated.

If you're from outside the E.U. but driving a private car in Tuscany, before leaving home apply for an **International Driver's Permit;** in the U.S, from your local American Automobile Association (AAA; www.aaa.com). In Canada, the permit is available from the Canadian Automobile Association (CAA; www.caa.ca). Technically, you need this permit and your home driver's license to drive in Italy, although in practice the license itself generally suffices. If you're driving a rented car, a valid driver's license from your home country is usually fine—but check with the rental company in advance.

If someone races up behind you and flashes their lights, that's the signal for you to slow down so they can pass you quickly and safely. Stay in the right lane on highways; the left is only for passing and for cars with large engines and the pedal to the metal. On a two-lane road, the idiot passing someone in the opposing traffic who has swerved into your lane expects you to veer obligingly over into the

Tuscan Tourist Offices

Arezzo: Palazzo Comunale, Piazza della Libertà (www.arezzointuscany.it; ☎ 0575-401945)

Chiusi: Via Porsenna 79 (www.prolocochiusi.it; ☎ 0578-227667)

Colle Val d'Elsa: Via del Castello 33 (www.prolococollevaldelsa.it; ☎ 0577-922791)

Cortona: Palazzo Casali, Piazza Signorelli 9 (☎ 0575-637221)

Elba: Viale Elba 4, Portoferraio (www.infoelba.it; ☎ 0565-914671)

Florence: Piazza della Stazione 4 (www.firenzeturismo.it; ☎ 055-212245); Via Cavour 1R (☎ 055-290832); Loggia di Bigallo, Piazza del Duomo (at Via dei Calzaiuoli)

Livorno: Via Pieroni 18 (www.comune.livorno.it/portaleturismo; ☎ 0586-820454)

Lucca: Piazzale Verdi (www.luccaturismo.it; ☎ 0583-583150)

Massa Marittima: Via Todini 3–5 (www.altamaremmaturismo.it; ☎ 0566-902756)

Montalcino: Costa del Municipio 1 (www.prolocomontalcino.com; ☎ 0577-849331)

Montecatini: Viale Verdi 66 (www.montecatiniturismo.it; ☎ 0572-772244)

Montepulciano: Piazza Don Minzoni 1 (www.prolocomontepulciano.it; ☎ 0578-757341)

Pienza: Palazzo Vescovile, Corso Il Rossellino 30 (☎ 0578-749905)

Pisa: Piazza Vittorio Emanuele II 16 (www.pisaunicaterra.it; ☎ 050-42291)

Pistoia: Via Roma 1 (at Piazza del Duomo; www.turismo.pistoia.it; ☎ 0573-21622)

Prato: Piazza Buonamici 7 (www.pratoturismo.it; ☎ 0574-24112)

San Gimignano: Piazza del Duomo 1 (www.sangimignano.com; ☎ 0577-940008)

Sansepolcro: Piazza Matteotti 1 (www.lavalledipiero.it; ☎ 0575-7321)

Siena: Santa Maria della Scala, Piazza del Duomo 1 (www.terresiena.it; ☎ 0577-280551)

Viareggio: Viale Carducci 10 (www.luccaturismo.it; ☎ 0584-962233)

Volterra: Piazza dei Priori 19–20 (www.volterratur.it; ☎ 0588-87257)

shoulder so three lanes of traffic can fit—he would do the same for you. Probably.

Benzina (gas or petrol) is even more expensive in Italy than elsewhere in Europe. Even a small rental car guzzles between 60€ and 80€ for a full tank.

There are many pull-in filling stations along major roads and on the outskirts of towns, as well as 24-hour rest stops along the autostrada. Almost all stations are closed for *riposo* and on Sundays, but many have a pump fitted with a machine that accepts bills so you can self-service your tank at 3am. Unleaded gas is *senza piombo.* Diesel (which is cheaper) is *gasolio.*

Car Rentals
In Tuscany, all roads lead to Florence, but you won't need a car once you get there: The Centro Storico is best explored on foot, and parking is expensive. Your best tactic is to tour Tuscany by car at the start or end of your trip, picking it up or returning it as you leave or arrive in Florence. You're usually allowed to park in front of your hotel long enough to unload your luggage. You'll then want to proceed to a garage. (Ask at your hotel; most have a deal with their nearest.)

You'll save money by booking a car before leaving home. The major global rental companies operating in Italy are **Avis** (www.avis.com), **Budget** (www.budget.com), and **Hertz** (www.hertz.com). U.S.–based agents offering European car rentals include **Auto Europe** (☎ 888/223-5555; www.autoeurope.com) and **Kemwel** (☎ 877/820-0668; www.kemwel.com). In some cases, members of the **American Automobile Association (AAA)** or AARP qualify for discounts.

From the U.K., we recommend **Holiday Autos** (www.holidayautos. co.uk; ☎ 020/3740-9859). Its prepaid vouchers include insurance, which is sky-high in Italy. A reliable local rental agency is **Europcar** (www.europcar.it; ☎ 199-307030). Meta-search sites like **Kayak.com, Rentalcars.com,** and **Skyscanner. net** are also worth checking to compare rates across various agents.

Both stick shift (manual) and automatic are commonly available at car-rental companies. The former is preferable for negotiating Tuscany's hilly terrain.

We'd also recommend you opt for the **Collision Damage Waiver (CDW),** even though it can be expensive and likely comes with a minimum contribution you are required to pay toward any claim. A bump in Italy isn't that uncommon. To protect against nasty excess charges, consider a Europe policy from **Insurance4CarHire.com** or a similar U.S. service.

Car-rental agencies also require you to purchase theft protection (it will probably be included in the price, however). Before buying added insurance, check your own personal auto insurance policy and credit card terms and conditions to see if they already provide coverage.

Fast **Facts**

AREA CODES Italy no longer uses separate city codes. Dial all numbers as written in this book, including the initial "0" when dialing from overseas.

BUSINESS HOURS General hours of operation for **stores, offices,** and **churches** are from 9:30am to noon or 1pm and again from 3 or 3:30pm to 6 or 7pm. That early afternoon shutdown is the *riposo,* the Italian *siesta.* Many stores close on Sunday or on Monday (morning only or all day). Some government services and business offices are open to the public only in the mornings. Traditionally, state museums are closed Mondays, but check entries

The Savvy Traveler

in the relevant chapters for exact hours. The biggest "sights" generally stay open all day, but many smaller ones close for *riposo* or open only in the morning (9am–2pm is common). Some churches open earlier than 9am, and the largest often stay open all day. **Bank hours** tend to be Monday through Friday from 8:30am to 1:30pm and 2:30 to 3:30pm or 3 to 4pm.

Use the *riposo* as the Italians do—take a long lunch, stroll through a park, travel to the next town, or return to your hotel to recoup your energy. The *riposo* is especially welcome in August.

CRIME See "Safety," below. Also note that it is illegal for you to knowingly buy **counterfeit goods** (and, yes, paying 10€ for a "Rolex" counts as *knowingly*). Tourists have left Florence with large fines among their vacation souvenirs.

DRUGSTORES You'll find **green neon crosses** above the entrances to most *farmacie* (pharmacies). You'll also find many *erboriste* (herbalist shops), which offer more traditional herbal remedies along with pharmaceuticals. Most keep everything behind the counter, so be prepared to point or mime. *Language tip:* Most minor ailments start with the phrase *mal di*, so you can just say "Mahl dee" and point to your head, stomach, throat, or whatever. Pharmacies rotate which will stay open all night and on Sundays, and each store has a poster outside showing the month's rotation.

ELECTRICITY Italy operates on a 220 volts AC (50 cycles) system. You'll need a simple adapter plug and for non-Europeans, a current converter for some appliances. Get whatever you need before leaving home—these items can be devilish to find in Italy.

EMBASSIES/CONSULATES The **U.S. Embassy** is in Rome at Via Vittorio Veneto 121 (http://italy.usembassy.gov; ☎ 06-46741). The **U.S. consulate** in Florence—for passport and consular services but not visas—is at Lungarno Vespucci 38 (http://florence.usconsulate.gov; ☎ 055-266951), open to emergency drop-ins Monday through Friday from 8:30am to 12:30pm. Afternoons and for non-emergencies, the consulate is open by appointment only; call ahead or book online.

The **U.K. Embassy** is in Rome at Via XX Settembre 80a (http://ukinitaly.fco.gov.uk; ☎ 06-4220-0001). It is not open to the public; call (24 hours) for consular assistance. There is no longer a **U.K. consulate** in Florence.

Of English-speaking countries, only the U.S. has a consulate in Florence. Citizens of other countries must go to Rome for help: The **Canadian Embassy** in Rome is at Via Zara 30 (☎ 06-85444-2911; www.italy.gc.ca). **Australia**'s Rome embassy is at Via Bosio 5 (www.italy.embassy.gov.au; ☎ 06-852721). The consular section is open by appointment only Monday through Friday from 9am to 2:30pm. **New Zealand**'s Rome representation is at Via Clitunno 44 (www.nzembassy.com/italy; ☎ 06-853-7501). The embassy for **Ireland** is at Villa Spada, Via Giacomo Medici 1, Rome (www.ambasciata-irlanda.it; ☎ 06-585-2381), open weekdays 9:15am to 1pm and 2:15 to 5:30pm.

EMERGENCIES Dial ☎ 113 for a police emergency. You can also call ☎ 112 for the *carabinieri* (gendarmerie-style police), ☎ 118 for an ambulance, or ☎ 115 for the fire department. If your car breaks down, dial ☎ 116 for roadside aid from the Automotive Club of Italy.

HOLIDAYS Businesses, banks, and shops are closed on the following national holidays: January 1; January 6 (Epiphany); Easter Sunday (*Pasqua*); Easter Monday (*Pasquetta*); April 25 (Liberation Day); May 1 (Labor Day); August 15 (*Ferragosto*); November 1 (All Saints' Day); December 8 (Immaculate Conception); December 25 (Christmas Day); December 26 (*Santo Stefano*). Towns and cities also largely shut on their patron saint's day (for example, June 24, St. John the Baptist, for Florence).

HOSPITALS The emergency ambulance number is ☎ 118. Hospitals in Italy are partially socialized, and the care is efficient, personalized, and of a high quality. The most central hospital in Florence is **Santa Maria Nuova,** a block northeast of the Duomo on Piazza Santa Maria Nuova (☎ 055-69381), open 24 hours. Pharmacy staff tend also to be competent health-care providers, so for less serious problems their advice will do fine. For significant but non-life-threatening ailments, you can walk into most hospitals and get speedy care—with no questions about insurance policies, no forms to fill out, and no fees to pay. **Obviously it's still crucial to carry an appropriate travel health insurance policy.** E.U. citizens should take an **EHIC** card to be certain of free reciprocal health care; until the U.K. fully completes its departure from the E.U., forms are available from post offices or at **www.ehic.org.uk**. Most hospitals will be able to find someone who speaks English. You'll find a comprehensive guide to medical services, including specialist and emergency care, on the official Florence city website. See the "Services & Utilities" section at **www.firenzeturismo.it/en**.

INTERNET ACCESS Internet cafes and Wi-Fi points are common in cities. Antiterror laws in Italy mean that all Internet point users must present their passports. In smaller towns you may have a bit of trouble, but almost all hotels now offer Wi-Fi throughout (or at the very least in the lobby, and usually for free). In a pinch, hostels, local libraries, cafes, and some bars have Wi-Fi. Don't always expect to find a connection in a rural *agriturismo* (digital detox is often part of the appeal). High-speed trains often have free Wi-Fi (but throttle Skype, video streaming, file sharing, and other data-hungry services).

LANGUAGE Although Italian is the local language around these parts, English is common, especially among under-40s. Anyone in the tourism industry will know the English they need to facilitate transactions. Most Italians are delighted to help you learn a bit of their lingo as you go, and they will certainly appreciate your attempts to converse with them in their native tongue. To help, we've compiled a list of key phrases and menu terms later in this chapter; see p 204.

LIQUOR LAWS Driving drunk is illegal, and unwise on Italy's twisty, narrow roads (or anywhere, for that matter). The legal drinking age in Italy is 16. Public drunkenness (aside from people getting noisily tipsy at big dinners) is unusual.

LOST & FOUND Be sure to tell all your credit card companies the minute you discover your wallet has been lost or stolen and file a report at the nearest police precinct (*questura*). Your credit card issuer and insurer may require a police report number or record of the loss. Most credit card companies have an emergency toll-free number to call if your card is lost or stolen; they may be able to wire you a cash advance or deliver an emergency credit card in a day or two.

To report a lost or stolen card, call the following Italian toll-free numbers: **Visa** at ☎ 800-819-014, **MasterCard** at ☎ 800-870-866, or **American Express** at ☎ 800-874-333, or for U.S. cardholders call at ☎ 715-343-7977 collect call from anywhere in the world. As a backup, write down the emergency number that appears on the back of each of your cards (*not* the toll-free or freephone number—you can't dial those from abroad; if one doesn't appear, call the card issuer and ask).

Identity theft and fraud are potential complications of losing your wallet, especially if you've lost your driver's license along with cash and credit cards. Placing a fraud alert on your credit records may protect you, and you can do so online with the three major U.S. credit-reporting agencies, **Equifax** (www.equifax.com), **Experian** (www.experian.com), and **TransUnion** (www.transunion.com; ☎ 800-680-7289). Finally, if you've lost all forms of photo I.D., call your airline and explain the situation; it might allow you to board the plane if you have a copy of your passport or birth certificate and a copy of the police report you've filed.

MAIL The Italian mail system is notoriously slow, and friends back home may not receive your postcards before they see you again in person. Postcards, aerograms, and letters, weighing up to 20g (.7 oz.), cost 1€ to send within Europe, 2.20€ to the U.S. Buy stamps from postal offices or wherever you see the black-and-white "T" (*tabacchi*) sign. Ask for *"un francobollo per gli Stati Uniti / per Gran Bretagna,"* and so on.

NEWSPAPERS & MAGAZINES Visitors will see plenty of familiar mastheads. The *New York Times International Edition, Wall Street Journal Europe,* and *USA Today* are available at many newsstands, even in small (tourist) towns. U.K. daily and Sunday newspapers are available (a day or two behind) at all good-sized newsstands. Florence's biweekly the *Florentine* is the major English-language publication; Lucca's monthly *Grapevine* serves English speakers living in or visiting the town. For comprehensive Florence listings, pick up *Firenze Spettacolo.* Italian-speakers should go for *La Nazione,* a national daily published in Florence; or *Il Tirreno,* more widespread closer to the coast.

POLICE For police emergencies, call ☎ 113. Italy has several different police forces, but you'll most likely only ever deal with two. The first is the urban *polizia,* whose city headquarters is called the *questura.* They can help with lost and stolen property. More useful for serious crimes is the *carabinieri* (☎ 112).

RESTROOMS Public toilets are going out of fashion, but most bars will let you use their bathrooms without a scowl or forcing you to buy anything. (It's polite to buy a *caffè* anyhow.) Ask *"Posso usare il bagno?"* (*poh*-soh oo-*zar*-eh eel ban-yo). *Donne/signore* are women and *uomini/signori* men. Don't expect anything luxurious, or even well-kept. Train stations usually have a bathroom, for a fee. In many of the public toilets that remain, the little old lady with a basket has been replaced by a coin-op turnstile.

SAFETY Other than the inevitable pickpockets, especially in Florence, random violent crime is practically unheard of in Tuscany. However, the area around Florence's Santa Maria Novella, and the Cascine Park, are best avoided at night; ditto the alleys around Santo Spirito and Santa Croce in the small hours.

In general, just be smart, especially in crowded spots. Keep your passport, credit and ATM cards, and photocopies of important documents under your clothes in a money belt or neck pouch. Use the hotel safe, if there is one. *For women:* Beware of drive-by purse snatchings, by young thieves on mopeds, particularly in Florence. Keep your purse on the wall side of the sidewalk and sling the strap across your chest. If your purse has a flap, keep the clasp facing your body. *For men:* Keep your wallet in a front pocket and perhaps loop a rubber band around it. (The rubber catches on the fabric of your pocket and makes it harder for a thief to slip the wallet out.)

SMOKING Italy banned smoking inside all bars, restaurants, and offices in 2005. Note, however, that smoking on outdoor terraces (including in restaurants) is allowed.

TAXES No sales tax is added to the price tag of your purchases, but a **value-added tax** (in Italy, IVA) is automatically included in just about everything. For major purchases, you can get this refunded (see p 62). Florence also levies an additional **accommodation tax.** You will be charged 1€ to 1.50€ per person per night per government-star rating of the hotel, up to a maximum of 10 nights. Children 12 and under are exempt. This tax is not usually included in any published room rate. Other towns including Siena have followed suit.

TELEPHONES & FAX Most remaining public payphones in Italy now take only **phone cards** (*carta* or *scheda telefonica*). You can buy prepaid phone cards at any *tabacchi* (tobacconists), many newsstands, and some bars in several denominations. Break off the corner before inserting it; a display tracks how much money is left as you talk.

Don't forget to take the card with you when you leave! Some public phones also take credit cards.

For **operator-assisted international calls** (in English), dial toll-free ☎ 170. Note, however, that you'll get better rates by calling a home operator for collect calls, as detailed here: To make calling card calls, insert a phone card or coin—it'll be refunded at the end of your call—and dial the local number for your service. For **Americans:** AT&T is at ☎ 800-172-44 and MCI at ☎ 800-90-5825. These numbers will connect a U.S. operator for you.

To **dial direct internationally** from Italy, dial ☎ 00, then the country code, the area code, and the number. Country codes are as follows: the United States and Canada 1; United Kingdom 44; Ireland 353; Australia 61; New Zealand 64. Make calls from a public phone if possible because hotels charge inflated rates, but take along plenty of *schede* to feed the phone. Better still, call over Wi-Fi: Some Internet points are equipped with headsets for **VoIP** (Voice over Internet Protocol) calling using services like Skype. Cellphones (see "Before You Go," above) often offer affordable international calling tariffs. Ask at a phone shop.

To access free **national telephone information** (in Italian) check **Paginegialle.it** (for business numbers) and **Paginebianche.it** (for personal numbers).

Your hotel will most likely be able to send or receive **faxes** for you, sometimes at inflated prices, sometimes at cost. Otherwise, some *cartolerie* (stationery stores), *copista* or *fotocopie* (photocopy shops), Internet cafes, and *tabacchi* (tobacconists) offer fax services.

TIME ZONE Italy is 6 hours ahead of Eastern Standard Time in the United States, 1 hour ahead of GMT or BST in the U.K. and Ireland.

TIPPING In **hotels,** a service charge is usually included in your bill. In family-run operations, additional tips are unnecessary and sometimes considered rude. In fancier places with a hired staff, however, you may want to leave a .50€ daily tip for the maid, pay the bellhop or porter 1€ per bag, and tip a helpful concierge 2€ for his or her troubles. In **restaurants,** 10% to 15% is often included in the bill, alongside a fixed charge for *"pane e coperto"* (bread and cover)—to be sure, ask *"è incluso il servizio?"* You may want to leave an additional gratuity up to 5% for good service, but don't feel obliged. Locals rarely leave anything. At **bars and cafes,** leave your change up to the next euro on the counter for the barman; if you sit at a table, you're being charged extra anyway, so there's no need to feel a duty to leave more than for a barman. **Taxi** drivers appreciate a euro or two.

WATER Although most Italians take mineral water with their meals, tap water is safe everywhere, as are any public drinking fountains you run across. Unsafe sources will be marked *"acqua non potabile."* If tap water comes out cloudy, it's only calcium or other minerals inherent in a water supply that often comes untreated from fresh springs.

A Brief **History**

1100–700 B.C. Villanovan culture thrives in what we now call Tuscany.

800–300 B.C. The Etruscans are the major power in central Italy.

600–510 B.C. The Etruscan Tarquin dynasty rules as kings of Rome.

508 B.C. Lars Porsena, Etruscan king of Clusium (now Chiusi), attacks the young Roman Republic and wins.

295–265 B.C. Rome conquers Etruria and allies with Umbria. The Roman Empire spreads throughout central Italy and Latinizes local culture.

59 B.C. Julius Caesar founds Florentia, and Florence is born.

56 B.C. The First Triumvirate (Caesar, Pompey, and Crassus) meets in Lucca.

A.D. 250 Florence's first Christian martyr, St. Minias, is beheaded in the city.

313 Roman Emperor Constantine the Great, a convert himself, declares religious freedom for Christians.

476 After a long decline, the Roman Empire falls.

570–774 The Lombard duchies rule over much of Tuscany and neighboring Umbria.

774–800S Charlemagne and the Carolingian dynasty picks up where the Lombards left off.

1115 Florence is granted independent status within the Holy Roman Empire (a territory that covered modern-day central Europe).

1125 Florence razes neighbor Fiesole to the ground. Florentine expansion begins.

1155 Frederick I Barbarossa is crowned Holy Roman Emperor and attempts to take control of part of Italy.

1173 Pisa begins its bell tower. Eleven years later, someone notices the tilt.

1215 Florentine families form factions reflecting the conflict between emperor and pope. Those favoring the pope are known as Guelphs, pro-Imperial supporters as Ghibellines.

1250–1600 Intellectual pursuit of knowledge and study of the classical and Arab worlds begins to take precedence over Christian doctrine and superstition: the Humanist era.

1260 Ghibelline Siena defeats Guelph Florence at the Battle of Montaperti. Siena dedicates itself to the Virgin Mary in thanks.

1284 Genoa trounces Pisa's fleet in the naval Battle of Meloria. A long Pisan decline begins.

1300 The Guelph triumph in Florence is secure, but they immediately split into the White and the Black factions.

1302 Dante is exiled from Florence on trumped-up charges. He never returns, and is buried in Ravenna in 1321.

1303–77 The pope moves from Rome to Avignon. St. Catherine of Siena is instrumental in returning the papacy to Italy.

1304–10 Florentine Giotto frescoes the Scrovegni Chapel, in Padua. Western painting would never be the same.

1308–21 Dante writes the *Divine Comedy,* which sets the Tuscan dialect as the precursor of modern Italian.

1310 Siena runs its first Palio on record.

1348 The Black Death rips through Italy, killing more than half the population. Siena loses more than two-thirds of its citizens.

1355 Siena's government of the Nine (the *"Nove"*) falls, ending almost a century of stability.

1361 Florence conquers Volterra.

1378–1417 The Western Schism: Avignon, Rome, *and* Pisa each appoint a pope, and the competing pontiffs get busy excommunicating one another.

1384 Florence conquers Arezzo.

1401 Lorenzo Ghiberti wins the competition to cast the Baptistery doors in Florence. May the Renaissance begin!

1406 Florence conquers Pisa.

1434–64 Cosimo "il Vecchio" consolidates Medici power over Florence.

1435 Leon Battista Alberti publishes *De Pictura,* the seminal work of Renaissance art theory, largely on optics and perspective.

1439 The Council of Florence: Eastern and Western churches briefly reconcile their ancient differences.

1458 The coronation, in Rome, of Sienese Pope Pius II is re-created outside the Palazzo Pubblico for the benefit of citizens of Siena.

1469–92 The rule of Lorenzo de' Medici "the Magnificent" in Florence, under whose patronage the arts flourish.

1475 Michelangelo Buonarotti is born in Caprese, near Arezzo.

1494 Puritanical Dominican Fra' Girolamo Savonarola helps drive the Medici from Florence and takes control of the city.

1495 The "Bonfire of the Vanities": At Savonarola's urging, Florentines carry material goods seen as decadent—including paintings by Botticelli, Lorenzo di Credi, and others—to Piazza della Signoria and burn them.

1498 At the pope's urging, Florentines carry Savonarola to Piazza della Signoria and set *him* on fire.

1498–1512 The Florentine Republic is free from the Medici.

1501–04 Michelangelo carves *David, "Il Gigante."*

1505 For a few months, Leonardo da Vinci, Michelangelo, and Raphael all live and work in Florence at the same time.

1527 Emperor Charles V sacks Rome. Medici Pope Clement VII escapes to Orvieto, where by papal bull he refuses to annul Henry VIII's marriage to Catherine of Aragon and helps give rise to the Anglican Church.

1530 The Medici firmly take back power in Florence.

1550 Vasari publishes his *Lives of the Artists,* effectively the first art history book.

1555–57 Florence conquers Siena. The Sienese Republic makes a last stand at Montalcino.

1569 Cosimo I de' Medici is the first Grand Duke of Tuscany.

1581 Part of the Uffizi opens as a painting gallery.

1633 Despite being championed by the Medici, Galileo is forced by the Church to recant his idea that Earth revolves around the sun.

1737 Gian Gastone, last of the Medici Grand Dukes, dies.

1796–1806 Napoléon sweeps through Tuscany, eventually declaring himself king of Italy.

1805 Napoléon gives Lucca to his sister Elisa Baciocchi as a duchy.

1814–15 Napoléon is exiled on Elba, which he rules as governor.

1824 Lorraine Grand Duke Leopold II starts draining the marshes of the Maremma. The reclamation is complete in 1950 with the defeat of malaria.

1848–60 The *Risorgimento* movement struggles for a unified Italy.

1860 Tuscany joins the new Kingdom of Italy.

1865–70 Florence serves as Italy's capital.

1921 The Italian Communist Party is founded, in Livorno, and goes on to play a major part in postwar democratic politics.

1922 Mussolini becomes the Fascist dictator of Italy.

1940–45 World War II. Fascist Italy initially participates as an Axis power, before descending into civil war between Fascists and Partisans.

1944 Nazi troops withdraw from Florence, blowing up the Arno bridges. Supposedly on Hitler's direct order, the Ponte Vecchio is spared.

1946 Italy votes to become a republic.

1948 Italy's regions are created: Tuscany and Umbria finally get an official dividing line between them.

1966 The Arno flood in Florence. Up to 6m (20 ft.) of water and mud destroys or damages countless works of art. More than 100 people die.

1985 Italy's worst winter on record; the frost hits grapevines heavily and comes close to destroying all the olive trees in Tuscany.

1988 Pedestrian zones go into effect in major cities, making historic centers traffic-free (almost).

1993 On May 27, a car bomb rips through the west wing of the Uffizi, killing five people and damaging many paintings.

1997 In Assisi, in neighboring Umbria, a series of earthquakes hit, and part of the basilica's ceiling collapses, destroying frescoes and damaging Giotto's *Life of St. Francis*.

1999 Tuscany rejoices when local filmmaker Roberto Benigni, after victory at Cannes, gathers three Oscars for his Holocaust fable *La Vita è Bella* (*Life Is Beautiful*).

2001 The first cases of BSE (mad cow disease) in Italy are confirmed. Beef consumption plummets 70%, and the government considers banning such culinary institutions as the *bistecca alla fiorentina*. The year ends on a high note when the Leaning Tower of Pisa reopens to the public, after more than a decade of desperate measures to keep it from collapsing. (Don't worry— it still leans.)

2002 Florence's football team, Fiorentina, known as *I Viola*, goes out of business. But her return to the highest echelons of European competition will take just 6 years.

2008 The city of Florence makes the first moves toward issuing a formal pardon for Dante, exiled 700 years previously. For the third time since the Millennium, Bruco wins Siena's Palio.

2009 Young center-left candidate Matteo Renzi is elected Mayor of Florence, and immediately sets about making the city more friendly to pedestrians (and less friendly toward car traffic).

2016 Having become Italy's youngest prime minister in 2014, Matteo Renzi resigns after losing a referendum on electoral reform.

Art & Architecture

Architecture

Ambulatory Continuation of the side aisles to make a walkway around the chancel space behind the main altar of a church.

Apse The semicircular or polygonal space behind the main altar of a church.

Arcade A series of arches supported by columns, piers, or pilasters.

Architrave The long vertical element lying directly across the tops of a series of columns (the lowest part of an entablature); or, the molding around a door or window.

Badia Abbey.

Baldacchino A stone canopy over a church altar.

Basilica A form of architecture first used for public halls and law courts in ancient Roman cities. Early Christians adopted the form—a long rectangular room, divided into a central nave with side aisles but no transept—to build their first large churches. A "basilica" is now sometimes used to denote an important church without a bishop's seat.

Bay   The space between two columns or piers.

Bifore   Divided vertically into two sections.

Blind Arcade   An arcade of pilasters (the arches are all filled in), a defining architectural feature of the Romanesque style.

Caldarium   The hot tub or steam room of a Roman bath.

Campanile   A bell tower, usually of a church but also of public buildings; it's often detached or flush against the church rather than sprouting directly from it.

Cantoria   Small church singing gallery, usually set into the wall above the congregation's heads.

Capital   The top of a column. The classical "orders" (types) are Doric (plain), Ionic (with scrolls, called volutes, at the corners), and Corinthian (leafy). There's also Tuscan (even simpler than Doric; the column is never fluted or grooved, and usually has no base) and Composite (Corinthian superimposed with Ionic). In many Paleochristian and Romanesque churches, the capital is carved with primitive animal and human heads or simple biblical scenes.

Cappella   Italian for chapel.

Caryatid   A column carved to resemble a woman (see also *telamon*).

Cattedrale   Cathedral (also Duomo).

Cavea   The semicircle of seats in a classical theater.

Cella   The innermost, most sacred room of a Roman pagan temple.

Chancel   Space around the high altar of a church, generally reserved for the clergy and the choir.

Chiesa   Italian for church.

Chiostro   Italian for cloister.

Ciborium   (1) Another word for *baldacchino* (above); (2) Box or tabernacle containing the Host (the symbolic body and blood of Christ taken during communion).

Cloister   A roofed walkway open on one side and supported by columns; usually used in the plural because often four of them faced one another to make interior open-air courtyards, centered around small gardens, found in monasteries and convents.

Collegiata   A collegiate church, having a chapter of canons and a dean or provost to rule over it but lacking the bishop's seat that would make it a cathedral.

Colonnaded   Lined with columns.

Cornice   Protruding section, usually along the very top of a wall, a facade, or an entablature; a pediment is usually framed by a lower cornice and two sloping ones.

Cortile   Italian for courtyard.

Crenellated   Topped by a regular series of toothlike protrusions and crevices; these battlements often ring medieval buildings or fortresses to aid in defense.

Crypt   An underground burial vault; in churches, usually found below the altar end and in Italy often the remnant of an older version of the church.

Cupola   Dome.

Cyclopian   Adjective describing an unmortared wall built of enormous stones by an unknown, central Italian, pre-Etruscan people. The sheer size led the ancients to think they were built by the Cyclopes.

Duomo   Cathedral (from *domus*, "house of God"), often used to refer to the main church in town even if it doesn't have a *cathedra*, or bishop's seat—the prerequisite for a cathedral.

Entablature   Section riding above a colonnade, made up of the architrave (bottom), frieze (middle), and cornice (top).

Forum   The main square in a Roman town; a public space used for assemblies, courts, and speeches, and on which important temples and civic buildings were located.

Frieze A decorative horizontal band or series of panels, usually carved in relief and at the center of an entablature.

Frigidarium Room for cold baths in a Roman bath.

Greek Cross Building ground plan in the shape of a cross whose arms are of equal length.

Latin Cross Building ground plan in the shape of a Crucifix-style cross, where one arm is longer than the other three (this is the nave).

Liberty Italian version of Art Nouveau or Art Deco, popular in the late 19th and early 20th centuries.

Loggia Roofed porch, balcony, or gallery.

Lozenge A decorative, regularly sided diamond (square on its corners), made of either marble inlay or a sunken depression, often centered in the arcs of a blind arcade on Romanesque architecture.

Lunette Semicircular wall space created by various ceiling vaultings or above a door or window; often it's decorated with a painting, mosaic, or relief.

Matroneum In some Paleochristian and early Romanesque churches, the gallery (often on the second floor) reserved for women, who were kept separate from the men during mass.

Narthex Interior vestibule of a church.

Nave The longest section of a church, usually leading from the front door to the altar, where the worshipers sit; often divided into aisles.

Palazzo Traditionally a palace or other important building; in contemporary Italian, it refers to any large structure, including office buildings (and has become the common way to refer to a city block, no matter how many separate structures form it).

Paleochristian Early Christian, used generally to describe the era from the 5th to the early 11th century.

Pediment A wide gable at the top of a facade or above a doorway.

Piano nobile The primary floor of a palace where the family would live, usually the second (American) but sometimes the third floor. It tends to have higher ceilings and larger rooms and be more lavishly decorated than the rest of the *palazzo*. The ground floor was usually for storage or shops and the attic for servants.

Pier A rectangular vertical support (like a column).

Pietra forte A dark gray, ocher-tinged limestone mined near Florence. Harder than its cousin *pietra serena* (below), it was used more sparingly in Florentine architecture.

Pietra serena A soft, light-gray limestone mined in the Florentine hills around Fiesole and one of the major building blocks of Florence's architecture—for both the ease with which it could be worked and its color, used to accent door jambs and window frames in houses and columns and chapels in churches.

Pieve A parish church; in the countryside, often primarily a baptismal site.

Pilaster Often called pilaster strip, it's a column, either rounded or squared off, set into a wall rather than separate from it.

Porta Italian for door or city gate.

Portico A porch.

Refectory The dining room of a convent or monastery—which, from the Renaissance on, was often painted with a *Last Supper* to aid religious contemplation at the dinner table.

Sacristy The room in a church that houses (or housed) the sacred vestments and vessels.

Sanctuary Technically the holiest part of a church, the term is used to refer to the area just around and behind the high altar.

Spandrel Triangular wall space created when two arches in an arcade curve away from each other (or from the end wall).

Spoglio Architectural recycling; the practice of using pieces of an older building to help raise a new one. (Roman temples were popular mines for both marble and columns to build early churches.)

Sporti Overhanging second story of a medieval or Renaissance building supported by wooden or stone brackets.

Stele A headstone.

Stemma Coat of arms.

Stucco Plaster composed of sand, powdered marble, water, and lime; often molded into decorative relief, formed into statuary, or applied in a thin layer to the exterior of a building.

Telamon A column sculpted to look like a man (also see *caryatid*).

Tepidarium The room for a warm bath in a Roman bath.

Terme Roman baths, usually divided into the calidarium, tepidarium, and frigidarium (see above).

Torre Italian for tower.

Transept The lateral cross-arm of a cruciform church, perpendicular to the nave.

Travertine A whitish or honey-colored form of porous volcanic tufa mined near Tivoli. The stone from which much of ancient Rome (and Montepulciano) was built.

Tribune The raised platform from which an orator speaks; used to describe the raised section of some churches around and behind the altar from which Mass is performed.

Two-light Of a window, divided vertically into two sections (see also *bifore*). A three-light window is divided vertically into three sections.

Tympanum The triangular or semi-circular space between the cornices of a pediment or between the lintel above a door and the arch above it.

Painting, Sculpture & Ceramics

Aerial perspective The tendency of objects to blur toward the background color as they approach the horizon, a phenomenon mastered by Tuscan painters by the mid-1400s.

Altarpiece A painting placed on or hung above the altar, often made from poplar wood and consisting of two or more panels. After 1310, all churches were required to have one.

Ambone Italian for pulpit.

Amphora A two-handled jar with a tapered neck used by the ancients to keep wine, oil, and other liquids.

Arriccio The first, rough layer of plaster laid down when applying fresco to a wall. On this layer, the artist makes the *sinopia* sketches.

Bottega The workshop of an artist. (On museum signs, the word means the work was created or carried out by apprentices or assistants in the stated master's workshop.)

Bozzetto A small model for a larger sculpture (or sketch for a painting); in the later Renaissance and Baroque eras, it also came to mean the tiny statuettes turned out for their own sake to satisfy the growing demand among the rich for table art.

Bucchero Etruscan black earthenware pottery.

Canopic vase Etruscan funerary vase housing the entrails of the deceased.

Cartoon In Italian *cartone*, literally "big paper," the full-size preparatory sketch made for a fresco or mosaic.

Chiaroscuro Using patches of light and dark colors in painting to model figures and create the illusion of three dimensions. (Caravaggio was a master at also using the technique to create mood and tension.)

Cinerary urn   Vase or other vessel containing the ashes of the deceased; Etruscan ones were often carved with a relief on the front and, on the lid, a half-reclining figure representing the deceased at a banquet.

Contrapposto   A twisted pose in a figure, first used by the ancients and revived by Michelangelo; a hallmark of the Mannerist school.

Diptych   A painting with two sections or panels.

Ex voto   A small plaque, statue, painting, or other memento left by a supplicant, signifying either his or her gratitude to a saint or the Madonna, or imploring the saint's help in some matter.

Fresco   The multistep art of creating a painting on fresh plaster (*fresco* means "fresh").

Gesso   Calcium sulphate, or gypsum, applied in up to 7 layers to treat a wooden panel before painting.

Graffiti   Incised decorative designs, made by painting the surface in two thin layers (one light, the other dark), then scratching away the top layer to leave the designs in contrast. Called *"sgraffito"* in Italian.

Grotesques   Carved or painted faces, animals, and designs, often deliberately exaggerated or ugly; used to decorate surfaces and composite sculptures (such as fountains) and to illuminate manuscripts.

Illuminated   Describing a manuscript or book, usually a choir book or bible, that has been decorated with colorful designs, miniatures, figures, scenes, and fancy letters, often produced by anonymous monks.

Intarsia   Inlaid wood, marble, precious stones, or metal.

International Gothic   Highly decorative style of painting with its roots in the art of Simone Martini. Leading Florentine exponents were Fra' Angelico and Gentile da Fabriano.

Majolica   Tin-glazed earthenware pottery usually elaborately painted; a process pioneered and mastered in Italy in the 14th to 17th century.

Pala   Altarpiece.

Pietra dura   The art of inlaying semi-precious stones to form patterns and pictures; often called "Florentine mosaic" and increasingly popular from the late 15th century.

Pinacoteca   Painting gallery.

Polyptych   A panel painting having more than one section that's hinged so it can be folded up. Two-paneled ones are called diptychs (see above); three-paneled ones are triptychs (see below). Any more panels use the general term.

Porphyry   Any igneous rock with visible shards of crystals suspended in a matrix of fine particles.

Predella   Small panel or series of panels below the main part of an altarpiece, often used to tell a story of Christ's Passion or a saint's life comic-strip style.

Putti   Cherubs (sing. *putto*); chubby naked toddler boys sculpted or painted, often with wings.

Sacra conversazione   Type of painting in which saints are arranged with the Madonna in a unified space, rather than relegated to wings, as in a polyptych (see above).

Sarcophagus   A stone coffin or casket.

Schiacciato   Literally, "flattened." A sculpture form pioneered by Donatello; figures are carved in extremely low relief so that from straight on they give the illusion of three-dimensionality and great depth, but from the side are oddly squashed.

Sfumato   A painting technique, popularized by Leonardo da Vinci, as important as perspective in achieving the illusion of great depth. The artist cloaks objects (landscape features like hills, or facial features) in a filmy haziness; the farther away the object, the blurrier it appears, and the more realistic the distance seems.

Sinpoia Underpainting or sketch made in red-brown pigment, the first drawing made on a wall to be frescoed.

Stoup A holy-water basin.

Tempera Type of paint in which pigments are bound with egg yolk; used for almost all paintings before oil took over around 1500.

Tondo A round painting or sculpture.

Trecento The 14th century (in Italian, literally "300s"), often used to describe that era of art dominated by the styles of Giotto and the International Gothic.

Triptych A painting with three sections or panels.

Useful **Terms** & **Phrases**

Tuscan, being the local lingo of Dante, is considered the purest form of Italian. (In Siena they will tell you that, actually, it's Sienese dialect that's perfect.) Theoretically that means travel in Tuscany will help you learn the most word-perfect Italian there is. Here are some key words and phrases to get you started.

Molto Italiano: A Basic Italian Vocabulary

ENGLISH	ITALIAN	PRONUNCIATION
Thank you	Grazie	graht-tzee-yey
Please	Per favore	PEHR fah-VOHR-eh
Yes	Sì	see
No	No	noh
Good morning or Good day	Buongiorno	bwohn-DJOR-noh
Good evening	Buona sera	BWOHN-ah SAY-rah
Good night	Buona notte	BWOHN-ah NOHT-tay
How are you?	Come sta?	KOH-may STAH?
Very well	Molto bene	MOHL-toh BEHN-ney
Goodbye	Arrivederci	ahr-ree-vah-DEHR-chee
Excuse me (to get attention)	Scusi	SKOO-zee
Excuse me (to get past someone on the bus)	Permesso	pehr-MEHS-soh
Where is . . . ?	Dovè . . . ?	doh-VEH?
the station	la stazione	lah stat-tzee-OH-neh
a hotel	un albergo	oon ahl-BEHR-goh
a restaurant	un ristorante	oon reest-ohr-AHNT-eh
the bathroom	il bagno	eel BAHN-nyoh
To the right	A destra	ah DEHY-stra
To the left	A sinistra	ah see-NEES-tra
Straight ahead	Avanti (or sempre diritto)	ahv-vahn-tee (SEHM-pray dee-REET-toh)

ENGLISH	ITALIAN	PRONUNCIATION
I would like	Vorrei	voh-RAY
Some (of)	Un po' (di)	oon poh dee
This/that	Questo/quello	QWAY-sto/QWELL-oh
A glass of	Un bicchiere di	oon bee-key-AIR-ay dee
(mineral) water	acqua (minerale)	AH-kwah (min-air-AHL-lay)
carbonated	gassata (or con gas)	gahs-SAH-tah (kohn gahs)
uncarbonated	senza gas	SEN-zah gahs
red wine	vino rosso	VEE-no ROH-soh
white wine	vino bianco	VEE-no bee-AHN-koh
How much is it?	Quanto costa?	KWAN-toh COH-sta?
It's too much.	È troppo.	ay TRO-poh
The check, please.	Il conto, per favore.	eel kon-toh PEHR fah-VOHR-eh
Can I see . . . ?	Posso vedere . . . ?	POH-soh veh-DARE-eh?
the church	la chiesa	la key-AY-zah
the fresco	l'affresco	lahf-FRES-coh
When?	Quando?	KWAN-doh
Is it open?	È aperto?	ay ah-PAIR-toe
Is it closed?	È chiuso?	ay key-YOU-zoh
Yesterday	Ieri	ee-YEHR-ree
Today	Oggi	OH-jee
Tomorrow	Domani	doh-MAH-nee
Breakfast	Prima colazione	PREE-mah coh-laht-tzee-OHN-ay
Lunch	Pranzo	PRAHN-zoh
Dinner	Cena	CHAY-nah
What time is it?	Che ore sono?	kay OR-ay SOH-noh
Monday	Lunedì	loo-nay-DEE
Tuesday	Martedì	mart-ay-DEE
Wednesday	Mercoledì	mehr-cohl-ay-DEE
Thursday	Giovedì	joh-vay-DEE
Friday	Venerdì	ven-nehr-DEE
Saturday	Sabato	SAH-bah-toh
Sunday	Domenica	doh-MEHN-nee-kah

Numbers

ENGLISH	ITALIAN	PRONUNCIATION
1	uno	(OO-noh)
2	due	(DOO-ay)
3	tre	(tray)
4	quattro	(KWAH-troh)
5	cinque	(CHEEN-kway)
6	sei	(say)
7	sette	(SET-tay)
8	otto	(OH-toh)

ENGLISH	ITALIAN	PRONUNCIATION
9	nove	(NOH-vay)
10	dieci	(dee-AY-chee)
11	undici	(OON-dee-chee)
20	venti	(VEHN-tee)
21	ventuno	(vehn-TOON-oh)
22	venti due	(VEHN-tee DOO-ay)
30	trenta	(TRAYN-tah)
40	quaranta	(kwah-RAHN-tah)
50	cinquanta	(cheen-KWAN-tah)
60	sessanta	(sehs-SAHN-tah)
70	settanta	(seht-TAHN-tah)
80	ottanta	(oht-TAHN-tah)
90	novanta	(noh-VAHNT-tah)
100	cento	(CHEN-toh)
1,000	mille	(MEE-lay)
10,000	dieci mila	(dee-AY-chee MEE-lah)

Italian **Menu** & **Food Terms**

Acciughe or Alici Anchovies.

Acquacotta "Cooked water," a watery vegetable soup thickened with egg and poured over stale bread.

Affettato misto Mix of various salami, prosciutto, and other cured meats; served as an appetizer.

Agnello Lamb.

Agnolotti Semicircular ravioli (often stuffed with meat and/or cheese).

Anatra Duck.

Anguilla Eel.

Antipasti Appetizers.

Aragosta Lobster.

Arista di maiale Roast pork loin, usually served in slices, and sometimes flavored with rosemary, garlic, and cloves.

Baccalà (alla livornese) Dried salted codfish (cooked in olive oil, white wine, garlic, and tomatoes).

Bistecca alla fiorentina Florentine-style steak, made with Chianina beef, brushed with olive oil and sprinkled with pepper and salt, then grilled over wood coals and served rare.

Bocconcini Small veal chunks sautéed in white wine, butter, and herbs. (Also the word for ball-shaped portions of any food, especially mozzarella.)

Braciola Loin pork chop.

Branzino Sea bass.

Bresaola Air-dried, thinly sliced beef filet, dressed with olive oil, lemon, and pepper—usually an appetizer.

Bruschetta A slab of bread grilled and then rubbed with garlic, drizzled with olive oil, and sprinkled with salt; often served al pomodoro (with tomatoes).

Bucatini Fat, hollow spaghetti. Classically served all'amatriciana (with a spicy hot tomato sauce studded with pancetta [baconlike cured pork]).

Cacciucco Seafood soup/stew of Livorno in a spicy tomato base poured over stale bread.

Cacio or Caciotto Southern Tuscan (and Roman) name for pecorino (sheep's-milk) cheese.

Cannellini White beans, the Tuscan's primary vegetable.

Cannelloni Pasta tubes filled with meat and baked in a sauce (cream or tomato). The cheese version is usually called *manicotti* (although either name may be used for either stuffing).

Cantuccini Twice-baked hard almond cookies, vaguely crescent-shaped and best made in Prato (where they're known as *biscotti di Prato*).

Capocollo Aged sausage made mainly from pork necks.

Caprese A salad of sliced mozzarella and tomatoes lightly dressed with olive oil, salt, and pepper.

Capretto Kid goat.

Caprino Soft goat's-milk cheese.

Carciofi Artichokes.

Carpaccio Thin slices of raw cured beef, pounded flat and often served topped with arugula (rocket) and Parmesan cheese shavings.

Casalinga Home cooking.

Cavolo Cabbage.

Ceci Chickpeas (garbanzo beans).

Cervelli Brains, often served *fritti* (fried).

Cervo Venison.

Cibrèo Stew of chicken livers, cockscombs, and eggs.

Cinghiale Wild boar.

Cipolla Onion.

Coniglio Rabbit.

Cozze Mussels.

Crespelle alla fiorentina Thin pancakes wrapped around ricotta and spinach, covered with tomatoes and cheese, and baked in a casserole.

Crostini Small rounds of bread toasted and covered with various pâtés, most commonly a tasty liver paste.

Dentice Dentex; a fish, similar to perch.

Fagioli Beans, almost always white cannellini beans.

Faraona Guinea hen (guinea fowl).

Farro Emmer or spelt, a barley-like grain (often in soups).

Fave Broad (fava) beans.

Fegato Liver.

Focaccia Like pizza dough with nothing on it, this bready snack is laden with olive oil, baked in sheets, sprinkled with coarse salt, and eaten in slices plain or split to stuff as a sandwich. In Florence, a thinner version is popularly called *schiacciata*.

Formaggio Cheese.

Frittata Thick omelet stuffed with meats, cheese, and vegetables; sometimes eaten between slices of bread as a sandwich.

Fritto misto A deep-fried mix of meats, often paired with fried artichokes. By the coast, usually a mixed fry of seafood.

Frutte di mare A selection of shellfish, often boosted with a couple of shrimp and some squid.

Funghi Mushrooms.

Fusilli Spiral-shaped pasta; usually long like a telephone cord, not the short macaroni style.

Gamberi (gamberetti) Prawns (shrimp).

Gelato Dense version of ice cream (*produzione propria* means homemade).

Gnocchi Pasta dumplings usually made from potato.

Granchio Crab.

Granita Flavored ice; *limone* (lemon) is the classic.

Involtini Thinly sliced beef or veal rolled with veggies (often celery or artichokes) and simmered in its own juices.

Lampreda Lamprey (an eel-like fish).

Lenticchie Lentil beans; Italy's best come from Castellúccio, in Umbria.

Lepre Wild hare.

Lombatina di vitello Bone-in loin of veal.

Maiale Pork.

Manzo Beef.

Mascarpone Technically a cheese but more like heavy cream, already slightly sweet and sweetened more to use in desserts like tiramisù.

Melanzana   Eggplant (aubergine).

Merluzzo   Cod.

Minestrone   A little-bit-of-every-thing vegetable soup, sometimes flavored with chunks of cured ham.

Mortadella   A very thick, mild pork sausage; the original bologna (because the best came from Bologna).

Mozzarella   A nonfermented cheese, made from the fresh milk of a buffalo (but increasingly these days from a cow), boiled and then kneaded into a rounded ball; served as fresh as possible.

Oca   Goose.

Orata   Sea bream.

Orecchiette   Small, thick pasta disks (literally, "little ears").

Osso buco   Beef or veal knuckle braised in wine, butter, garlic, lemon, and rosemary; the marrow is a delicacy.

Ostriche   Oysters.

Paglio e fieno   Literally, "hay and straw," yellow (egg) and green (spinach) tagliatelle mixed and served with sauce.

Pancetta   Salt-cured pork belly, rolled into a cylinder and sliced— the Italian bacon.

Panforte   Any of several huge bar-like candies vaguely akin to fruit-cake; a dense, flat honey-sweetened mass of nuts, candied fruits, and spices.

Panino   A sandwich.

Panna   Cream (either whipped and sweetened for ice cream or pie; or heavy and unsweetened when included in pasta sauce).

Panzanella   A cold summer salad made of stale bread soaked in water and vinegar, mixed with cubed tomatoes, onion, fresh basil, and olive oil.

Pappa al pomodoro   A bready tomato-pap soup.

Pappardelle alle lepre   Wide, rough pasta tossed in hare sauce.

Parmigiano   Parmesan, a hard, salty cheese usually grated over pastas and soups but also eaten alone; also known as *grana*.

Pecorino   A rich sheep's-milk cheese; in Tuscany it's eaten fresh and soft, or *stagionato* (aged, sometimes with truffle or chilli).

Penne strascicate   Hollow pasta quills in a creamy ragù (meat-and-tomato sauce).

Peperonata   Stewed peppers and onions under oil; usually served cold.

Peperoncini   Hot chili peppers.

Peperoni   Green, yellow, or red sweet peppers.

Peposo   Spicy, slow-cooked beef stew with peppercorns.

Pesce al cartoccio   Fish baked in a parchment envelope.

Pesce spada   Swordfish.

Piccione   Pigeon.

Pici or Pinci   A homemade pasta made with just flour, water, and olive oil, rolled in the hands to pro-duce lumpy, thick, chewy spaghetti to which sauce clings. This local name is used around Siena and to its south.

Piselli   Peas.

Pizza   Comes in two varieties: *al taglio* (by the slice) and *al forno* in a pizzeria (large, round pizzas for dinner with a thin, crispy crust, or with doughy crusts if it's Neapoli-tan style). Specific varieties include *margherita* (plain pizza of toma-toes, mozzarella, and basil), *napo-letana* (tomatoes, oregano, mozzarella, and anchovies), *capric-ciosa* (a loaded combination of prosciutto, artichokes, olives, and sometimes egg or anchovies), and *quattro stagioni* (four seasons of fresh vegetables, sometimes also with ham).

Polenta   Cornmeal mush, ranging from soupy to a dense cakelike ver-sion similar to cornbread; often mixed with mushrooms and other seasonal fillings, served plain alongside game, with a stew, or sometimes sliced and fried.

Pollo Chicken; *alla cacciatora* is huntsman style, with tomatoes and mushrooms cooked in wine; *alla diavola* is spicy hot grilled chicken; *al mattone* is cooked under a hot brick.

Polpette Small veal meatballs.

Polpo Octopus.

Pomodoro Tomato (plural *pomodori*).

Porcini Large, wild bolete mushrooms, what the French call *cèpes*.

Porri Leeks.

Ribollita A thick stewlike vegetable soup made with black cabbage, olive oil, celery, carrots, and whatever else *Mamma* has left over, all poured over thick slabs of bread.

Ricotta A soft, fluffy, protein-rich cheese made from the watery whey (not curds, as most cheese) and often used to stuff pastas. *Ricotta salata* is a salted, hardened version for nibbling.

Risotto Rice, often arborio, served sticky and creamy.

Rombo Turbot fish.

Salsa verde Green sauce, made from capers, anchovies, lemon juice and/or vinegar, and parsley.

Salsicce Sausage.

Saltimbocca Veal scallop topped with a sage leaf and a slice of prosciutto and simmered in white wine.

Salvia Sage.

Sarde Sardines.

Scaloppine Thin slices of meat, usually veal.

Scamorza An air-dried (sometimes smoked) cheese similar to mozzarella; often sliced and grilled or melted over ham in a casserole, giving it a thin crust and gooey interior.

Schiacciata See "Focaccia."

Scottiglia Stew of veal, chicken, various game, and tomatoes cooked in white wine.

Semifreddo A cousin to *gelato* (ice cream), it's a way of taking nonfrozen desserts (tiramisù, zuppa inglese) and freezing and moussing them.

Seppia Cuttlefish (halfway between a squid and small octopus); its ink is used for flavoring and coloring in some pasta and risotto dishes.

Sogliola Sole.

Spezzatino Beef or veal stew, often with tomatoes.

Spiedino A shish kebab (skewered bits of meat, onions, and slices of tomato or peppers grilled).

Spigola A fish similar to sea bass or grouper.

Stracciatella Egg-drop soup topped with grated cheese; also a flavor of gelato (vanilla with chocolate ripple).

Stracotto Overcooked beef, wrapped in bacon and braised with onion and tomato for hours until it's so tender it dissolves in your mouth.

Strozzapreti Ricotta-and-spinach dumplings, usually served in tomato sauce; literally "priest chokers." Also called *strangolapreti*.

Stufato Pot roast, usually in wine, broth, and veggies.

Tagliatelle Flat pasta ribbons.

Tartufo (1) Truffles; (2) An ice cream ball made with a core of fudge, a layer of vanilla, a coating of chocolate, and a dusting of cocoa; order it *affogato* (drowning), and they'll pour brandy over it.

Tonno Tuna.

Torta A pie. *Alla nonna* is Grandma's style and usually is a creamy lemony pie; *alle mele* is an apple tart; *al limone* is lemon; *alle fragole* is strawberry; *ai frutti di bosco* is with berries.

Torta al testo A flat, unleavened bread baked on the hearthstone and often split to be filled with sausage, spinach, or other goodies.

Tortellini Rings or half-moons of pasta stuffed with ricotta and spinach or chopped meat (chicken and veal). Sometimes also called *tortelli* and *tortelloni*.

Trippa Tripe (cow's stomach lining). Served *alla fiorentina* means casseroled with tomatoes and onions, topped with grated parmesan cheese.

Trota Trout.

Vermicelli Very thin spaghetti.

Vitello Veal. A *vitellone* is an older calf about to enter cowhood. *Vitello tonnato* is thinly sliced veal served cold and spread with tuna mayonnaise.

Vongole Clams.

Zabaglione/zabaione A custard made of whipped egg yolks, sugar, and Marsala wine.

Zampone Pig's feet, usually stewed for hours.

Zuccotto A tall liqueur-soaked sponge cake, stuffed with whipped cream, ice cream, chocolate, and candied fruits.

Recommended Books & Films

Books

GENERAL & HISTORY *Florence, Biography of a City* (1993) is popular historian Christopher Hibbert's overview on the city of the Renaissance, written in accessible prose. Hibbert is also author of **House of Medici: Its Rise and Fall,** a group biography of Florence's most famous rulers.

Frances Stonor Saunders' **Hawkwood: Diabolical Englishman** is more than just the story of the English mercenary's brutal Tuscan campaigns; it's also the most comprehensive account of medieval life and power politics in pre-Renaissance Tuscany.

Stones of Florence contains Mary McCarthy's often scathing, but usually fond, views on contemporary Florence (written in the early 1950s). It's also an indispensable art- and architecture-historical companion.

The only favorable sequel to McCarthy's classic is **City of Florence** by Yale professor R. W. B. Lewis.

More recently, a few literary histories set in Florence have enjoyed wild success. Ross King's slim tome **Brunelleschi's Dome** tells the fascinating story behind the building of Florence's Duomo. Dava Sobel's **Galileo's Daughter** uses the scant documents available to re-create the relationship between the great Pisan scientist and one of his illegitimate daughters, and his fight against blasphemy charges, which nearly got him killed.

More recent history is covered by Iris Origo in **War in Val d'Orcia,** her personal diary of life on a Tuscan farm (and the front line) in 1943 and 1944.

ART & ARCHITECTURE The first major work of art history ever written was penned in 1550 (with a later, expanded edition published in 1568) by a Tuscan artist. Giorgio Vasari's **Lives of the Artists, Vols. I and II** is a collection of biographies of the great artists from Cimabue to Vasari's 16th-century contemporaries.

For a more modern art-history take, the indispensable but expensive tome/doorstop is Frederick Hartt's **History of Italian Renaissance Art.** An easier, more colorful introduction, complete with illustrations, is Michael Levey's **Early Renaissance** and his **High Renaissance.** There is no better book on Sienese art from Duccio to Francesco di Giorgio than the affordable **Sienese Painting,** by Tim Hyman.

Michelangelo, a Biography by George Bull is the classic scholarly take on the artist's life. For a livelier look, try Irving Stone's **Agony and the Ecstasy.** Written as a work of historical fiction, it takes some liberties with the established record, but it's a good read.

LITERATURE & FICTION No survey of Tuscan literature can start anywhere but with Dante Alighieri, the 14th-century poet whose *Divine Comedy,* also published separately as *Inferno, Purgatorio,* and *Paradiso,* was Italy's first great epic poem since antiquity and the first major work to be written in the local vernacular (in this case, Florentine) instead of Latin. Dan Brown's far-fetched *Inferno* was an homage to, and is largely set in, Florence.

The next generation of Tuscan writers produced Giovanni Boccaccio, whose *Decameron,* a story of 100 tales told by young nobles fleeing the Black Death, is Italy's *Canterbury Tales.*

Tuscany also came up with the third great medieval Italian writer, Francesco Petrarca (Petrarch), whose *Selections from the Canzoniere and Other Works,* in a brand-new translation, gives you a taste of his lyrical poetry.

Even more real-world practical was Niccolò Machiavelli, whose handbook for the successful Renaissance leader, *The Prince,* won him fame and infamy simultaneously.

If you don't have time to read all the above, pick up a secondhand copy of the *Italian Renaissance Reader,* edited by Julia Conaway Bondanella and Mark Musa, with selections from Boccaccio's *Decameron,* Petrarch's *Canzoniere,* Leonardo da Vinci's notebooks, Benvenuto Cellini's *Autobiography,* Machiavelli's *Prince,* Michelangelo's sonnets, and others.

E. M. Forster's *A Room with a View,* half of which takes place in Florence, and *Where Angels Fear to Tread,* set in San Gimignano, are perfect tales of uptight middle-class British Edwardian society and how it clashes with the brutal honesty and seductive magic of Italy.

W. Somerset Maugham's tense 1941 novella of expat society and sexual intrigue, *Up at the Villa,* is set mostly in Fiesole.

More recent, Mark Mills' part-1950s, part-Renaissance murder-mystery, *Savage Garden,* is an atmospheric and at times charming read. Michele Giuttari's hard-edged police thrillers, *A Florentine Death, Death under a Tuscan Sun,* and the *Black Rose of Florence* take a more sinister look at central Italy.

For kids, the Tuscan classic is *Pinocchio,* by Carlo Collodi.

TRAVELOGUE Wolfgang von Goethe was, by most reckonings, the world's first famous Grand Tourist, and he recorded his traipse through Italy in *Italian Journey.*

Mark Twain became internationally famous for his report on a tour of Europe and Palestine called *The Innocents Abroad,* a good quarter of which is about Italy. Henry James's *Italian Hours* pulls together travel essays written by the young author.

Celebrated novelist D. H. Lawrence recorded his 1927 archaeological travels around Etruria in *Etruscan Places. A Traveller in Italy* (Methuen, 2006) is the informed account H. V. Morton wrote of his trip through the peninsula in the 1930s, with gorgeous, insightful prose by one of the best travelogue writers of the last century.

Frances Mayes' *Under the Tuscan Sun,* and its sequel *Bella Tuscany,* chronicle her experience of buying and renovating a house outside Cortona (where the book remains controversial). It spawned a huge industry of "I bought a house in Tuscany/Umbria/Sicily/wherever and renovated it and here's the charming story of how I learned to fit into Italian society" books—or, rather, it breathed new life, and a more prominent placement on the bookshelves, into a largely ignored genre that had already been claimed (and done much better) by Tim Parks (in the Veneto) and the late Barbara Grizzuti Harrison (in Sicily).

Films

Tuscany's countryside and hilltowns have served as backdrops for everything from Kenneth Branagh's **Much Ado About Nothing** to 1999's **A Midsummer Night's Dream** and Zeffirelli's **Tea with Mussolini.** In **The English Patient,** Ralph Fiennes convalesces in the monastery at Sant'Anna in Camprena, south of Siena, and there are cameos from Montepulciano and Pienza. **Stealing Beauty,** starring Liv Tyler, was filmed on the Brolio estate, near Gaiole in Chianti.

The Taviani brothers' **Fiorile (Wild Flower)** is a story within a story, reviewing the last 100 years of Italian history as a father details the lineage of a family curse.

James Ivory's **A Room with a View** is based on the E. M. Forster novel (see above). Although only half the film is actually set in Florence, it's the sharpest glimpse into the 19th-century British infatuation with Tuscany. **Hannibal,** the further grisly adventures of Anthony

Hopkins' Oscar-winning character from *The Silence of the Lambs,* is set partly in Florence. Another recent blockbuster to come out of the region is **Twilight: New Moon,** the film adaptation of the second in Stephanie Meyer's *Twilight* trilogy of teen-vampire novels. Although Meyer sets the crucial scenes of her tale in Volterra, the Tuscany scenes were actually filmed in Montepulciano. Tom Hanks reprised his role as Prof. Robert Langdon in **Inferno,** based on Dan Brown's novel; Florence features heavily.

Perhaps the greatest native talent to come out of Tuscany in the past decade or so is actor, director, writer, and comedian Roberto Benigni, creator of several slapstick mistaken-identity romps *(Johnny Stecchino, Il Mostro).* Then, in 1998 this Tuscan native won three Oscars, including Best Foreign Film and Best Actor (only the second non-English-speaking actor to do so)—with **La Vita è Bella (Life Is Beautiful),** an unlikely tragicomic fable (set partly in Arezzo) of one Jewish father trying to protect his young son from the horrors of the Holocaust by pretending the concentration camp they've been sent to is part of a big game. ●

Index

See also Accommodations and Restaurant indexes, below.

Accommodations

Photo **Credits**